Daisy

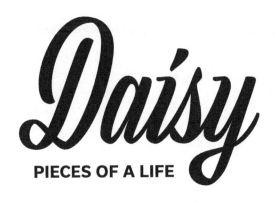

Daisy

PIECES OF A LIFE

Gathered and edited by
Timothy James Bazzett
from the letters and diaries of

DAISY WHALEN BAZZETT

RATHOLE BOOKS

Daisy

Published by Rathole Books
Reed City, Michigan
www.ratholebooks.com

ISBN 13: 978-0-9771119-6-1

Printed in the United States of America
10 9 8 7 6 5 4 3 2

Cover and interior design by Scott Bazzett
First Edition: October 2021
First Paperback Edition: Octobere 2021

For more information, visit us online at:
www.ratholebooks.com

Ellis Bazzett & Daisy Whalen
Oakley, 1934

"When I grow too old to dream,
I'll have you to remember.
And when I grow too old to dream,
Your love will live in my heart."

WHEN I GROW TOO OLD TO DREAM
©1934 Oscar Hammerstein II

Contents

Foreword

Daisy Whalen was my mother. Born on the family farm in Oakley in 1916, she was a curious, precocious, bright child. So much so that when she began school, she quickly read through the early Primers and readers and was put into the third grade at six years old. This pattern

Valedictorian! June 1932

of a voracious curiosity persisted throughout her school years. She was only fifteen when she graduated from Chesaning High School in 1932, the valedictorian of her class. Her father did not allow her to date in high school. So when she began college, on a scholarship, at Central State Teachers College (CSTC) in Mount Pleasant, at the age of sixteen, she was, by her own admission, "just about as green as they come" when it came to dating, and had a few stories of some disastrous, even humiliating experiences that first year at Central. But in the next summer she met my dad, Ellis Bazzett. He was six years older than her, and was managing the grain (and bean) elevator in her small hometown of Oakley, one of many owned by the Christian Breisch Company. She tells of her first awareness of my dad that summer – "I'd seen Ellis in church, sitting a few seats ahead of me. He had the most clean-looking back-of-the-head ever."

And Mom made it a point then to take walks past the elevator, "hoping to see (or be seen by) the young elevator manager. And I was, as I learned later." She says it "was a wonderful time, that summer of 1933." Later that year, after working at other Breisch Company mills in Carson City and Middleton, my dad took a new job as a salesman for General Mills, and had to relocate, first to Grand Rapids, and later to Kalamazoo and Detroit. He was on the road most of the time, selling products to local grocers. My mother was devastated at his leaving, but he promised to come see her on weekends as often as he could. And he did. And thus commenced a four-year long-distance courtship. The letters which follow attest to how their relationship grew and deepened. The same letters are also an informative – and intimate – look at college life during the years of the Great Depression.

In the interest of space-saving, I have compressed Mom's letters, eliminating paragraphing. But I have kept all of the idiosyncrasies of her "style." The word "night," for example, is nearly always rendered at "nite," and "though" becomes "tho." And it often seemed as if her favorite punctuation was a dash, sometimes used to create a run-on sentence that would go on and on. She knew better, of course. I can attest to that, as she always did her best to correct the grammar – and written work too – of me and all my siblings. She did become, after all, an English teacher, and – for all practical purposes – she remained one for the rest of her life, often underlining and correcting typos, spelling or grammar errors in articles – and even books – she happened to be reading.

It will also become obvious through the letters that Mom was indeed the "baby" of the family, and as such she was pampered and catered to. Even though the country was in the midst of a severe economic depression, and thousands of Americans were without jobs and often went hungry, Mom always seemed to have pocket money for snacks, or to go out to lunch or shopping, and went to the movies nearly every weekend. Her father also loved the movies, as I can remember, years later, our Grandpa Whalen often would take us to the "show" in nearby Owosso – sometimes the drive-in movies – whenever my brothers and I would visit Oakley. So Mom came by her passion for the movies honestly. Ironically, for most of my growing-up years, I hardly remember Mom and Dad ever going to the movies at all, so I guess she gave all that up once she became a "responsible" adult and parent.

And, while it is obvious from Mom's letters that she always had some part-time jobs while at school, typing, office work or working banquets or in the cafeteria – the source of some of the ready cash – she never seemed to work at all during her summer vacations, instead going on camping trips with her folks, or simply lazing around and going to the movies. Her dad's steady work as a U.S. mail carrier throughout the years of the Great Depression made their family seem almost 'wealthy' in comparison to others less fortunate. But it is notable that both of her brothers were struggling some during these years, moving from job to job wherever they could find work.

But enough, I suppose. I will let Mom's letters speak for themselves. So here they are, a personal look at college life and courtship in the 1930s.

Tim Bazzett
Reed City, MI – in the year 2021

The Letters

1933

1933 Chippewa

Sep 7, 1933   Oakley to Carson City

Dear Ellis — Sorry that we won't be able to come up Saturday night because Clarence is working at the canning factory in Owosso and works late at night. But we'd like to have you come here Saturday night if you can. If we're not here when you come, we'll be back soon because we'll just be gone to Owosso. We'll be looking for you Saturday, but if you can't get here then, be sure and come Sunday. You don't know what you'll be missing if you don't come to the picnic. Be sure and come. Yours in a hurry, Daisy

Clarence (b. 1914) was Mom's brother, two years older. The canning factory was probably a W.R. Roach & Company plant, which had facilities in several Michigan cities, canning a variety of fruits and vegetables. The Roach operation were in business from 1902 until 1944, when it was bought by Stokely Bros. & Co. And Mom had two brothers. Harold (b. 1910) was the older, a bit wilder and often at odds with their father, Will Whalen. Clarence, on the other hand, Mom always thought of as 'the good son.'

Sep 19, 1933   Oakley to Middleton

Dear Ellis – I'm exactly 3/17 of the way around the hem of a skirt, and had to stop to thread my needle, incidentally, to write you. I wonder if you could find a nice young man to bring with you Sunday night to accompany my roommate. Not too young, you understand, but grown-up. And if he's half as nice as you, I'm sure he'll do very well. Now don't you feel proud of the impression you've made on me? But if you can't get anyone, don't worry, but bring yourself and we'll get a Central man. I've got some grand news for you. I hope no one has told you yet. I'll tell you when I see you. (Domestic news) It rained cats and dogs here all morning & I baked three apple pies and three tarts – real tarts. We brought a new Philco down from Owosso yesterday & we've been having a lot of fun having two radios going at once. (End of domestic news) Now I must get back to my skirt – 14/17 to go. If you make any changes in your plans for Sunday nite, will you let me know? Thank you, Daisy

P.S. I'd thot of writing you a very sweet letter for a joke, but I was afraid you might take it seriously, so I'm just adding a little sugar to this one to make it sweet. Daisy

Mom's father was a U.S. mail carrier, so he was always employed through the darkest days of the Great Depression. So yeah, they could even afford two radios.

1934

1934 Chippewa

Sep 25, 1933   213 Ronan Hall (CSTC), Mt Pleasant to Carson City

Dear Ellis — 9:30 PM and all's well in the dorm. We did finally get rid of the freshmen for a while. They're all down in the rec room at a party. Gee, we've just about been pestered to death this evening. They're very fresh and very green and no more need be said. I really don't think that I was ever quite like they are. At least I hope I wasn't. A bunch of them have been in here off and on ever since evening meal & turned our room upside down. But they're nice kids all of them. Oh, we had a terrible electric storm last night, 1-5 AM it lasted, and gee, I wished I was home or anywhere else but here. But it is a lot of fun getting back and seeing so many kids that we know, although a lot of them aren't back. Tomorrow we register, but today we didn't have anything to do but wander around in the Ad Bldg & watch the freshmen, & we went downtown this PM & I'm so darn tired I don't know which way I'm going or what I'm saying half the time. You must have thought me rather poor company last nite but I didn't realize how tired I really was 'til I hit the hay - then I couldn't sleep. Gee, I wish you were only four miles away instead of forty - maybe you don't. But gee, I'm going to get awfully lonesome for you - I'm missing you already. It seems as if it's been ages & ages since last nite when I came. I'm getting a little sleepy. I saw Miss Ronan this morning & she didn't give me much encouragement as far as a job is concerned, but I'll know this week whether I'll get on steady. But if I don't I'll be subbing in the dining room & typing for Miss Trefethen probably. But I was so disappointed and discouraged. Oh well, I suppose I'll live through it. And I wanted to tell

*you that if you ever come through here on business or anything to be sure &
stop. And also, if you feel like coming up anytime to just drop me a line & I'll
surely be in. Ye gods! They're up again. The freshmen I mean, & sounds as if
they're trying to tear the bldg up. And we can stay out latest on Saturday &
Friday nights. Gee, this is a rather dippy letter, but I just happen to feel that
way tonite. If you don't get this letter, please let me know & I'll try to find out
your address. But you'll write anyway, won't you? Please. I miss you a lot.
Love, Daisy*

Miss Ronan – Bertha M. Ronan – had been a Phys Ed professor at
Central 1903-1923 and was Dean of Women until she retired in 1942.
The first Ronan Hall, where Mom lived, built in 1924, was named
for her. That building was demolished in 1970. Miss Lois Trefethen
was the dietitian, who had an apartment in Ronan Hall. The "Ad," or
Administration Building, later was renamed Warriner Hall, for E.C.
Warriner, who was the college President while Mom was there. It is still
in use, probably the oldest building on the CMU campus.

Ronan Hall   C.S.T.C

Sep 30, 1933   Central State Teachers College [letterhead stationery]

Dear Ellis — I must tell you that I'm not to be held accountable for anything that was in my last letter. For one reason, I don't remember a thing that was in it & surely do not recall the line you quoted. But I am wide awake today and in full possession of my faculties. It's just a glorious day & I got oodles of sleep last night - up at seven & went for a walk before breakfast and have our room all cleaned up & I wish you could see it now. We have our Indian blankets. Helen's is blue & red & green & tan; mine is red & blue & tan & black. Our rugs are maroon & yellow & green & blue & red & brown. Our waste baskets are red & black & green & silver. And other colorful articles too numerous to mention. In a nutshell, we have a color 'scream' very satisfying to us if not to anyone of an artistic nature. We spent a quiet evening at home last night & I read a very inspiring and educational book, "Grass." Thursday evening we were serenaded. One of our campus crooners was under our window & sang love songs to the accompaniment of a guitar. It was so romantic. I fell so hard that I'm all black & blue. I hope you don't mind my paragraphing. I seem to be all out of the habit. I'm getting settled to my routine now and it isn't half bad - or rather it wouldn't be if it weren't for the fact that according to our scheme we have mapped out, we have absolutely no time for studying. But that seems to be one of the necessary evils involved in going to college. If it weren't for that, we would enjoy ourselves completely. This is my schedule: 8: Rural Sociology - Dr Smith; 9: Psychology - Mr Marshall; 10: French - Miss Barnard; 11: English - Dr Beck; 2: Latin - Miss Barnard. I'd enjoy it if it were not for the French & Latin from dear old Barnard. That woman knows too much for her own good (& incidentally for ours). I have here on the desk a very sharp-pointed carpet tack. We have been discussing the advisability of depositing it in her chair some fine morning. (Have a visitor - continued later.)

12:30 PM - Have given two finger-waves, did my weekly ironing & ate my lunch since I discontinued this. Football game at 2:00 and must go downtown before the game. We're playing St Mary's College today & it looks like rain now. I'm enclosing our schedule for the year in case you might be interested in any of the games either here or there. It now behooves me to betake myself to the bathroom & polish my ivories. Am looking forward to going home next weekend. Until we meet again, Sincerely yours, Daisy

P.S. And as to that crack about my culinary ability - I'm thinking up an answer. The crowd is gathering for the game & a plane, red with silver wings, just landed in the field. Crowded for time. Daisy

Miss Anna M. Barnard was Head of the Foreign Languages Department at Central from 1899 until her retirement in 1944. Barnard Residence Hall, constructed in 1948, was named in her honor. My wife and I lived in an apartment in an old house directly across the street from Barnard Hall in 1967-68. The dorm was demolished in 1997.

Oct 16, 1933   CSTC

Dear Ellis – (1 PM) After all, I shouldn't be writing to you now. I wonder if you know what happened to the last letter I wrote you. I have an off-day in Latin today so no classes for me this afternoon. Maybe you think I'm sorry! It's such a dreary day – rainy & consequently rather damp. But wasn't yesterday marvelous? Except for church at 9 & a walk at 2, I spent the whole day typing – 10:15-1: & 3:15-7:30 straight. Two sets of card files for English. We had a test in English this morning, and after class when I looked up the answers, I didn't feel so good. I am learning many things in Psychology. Friday night there was an all-college dance in the rec room here at the dorm. The music was good & there was a good crowd & I had a fairly good time. (Good's rather working overtime.) Saturday night I served at a dinner for the Michigan Authors Association at the speakers' table. There were about 125 there. Thursday or Friday night I'm serving again at a dinner in the cafeteria. My roommate is going to be gone next weekend, so I'll be all alone. I wonder if you'd like to come up Sunday afternoon, Oct 22? You've never been here in the daytime and seen the campus, have you? And there are the most beautiful woods about a mile west of the Ad that I think you might enjoy visiting if the weather is nice. They're called the Cathedral Woods. So if you're not planning on anything else & would like to come, will you let me know? If you can or can't? Saturday nite, after the dinner held here in the dorm, we had the most delicious toasted ham sandwiches. I brought an electric plate back with me & we find it very useful. Four of our old pals are coming back for Homecoming the weekend of Oct 28 & we'll surely enjoy it then. If you let me know before Saturday, I'll forgive you for not answering the letter I wrote after Steph's wedding. Sincerely, Daisy

Mom owned her own typewriter, a portable Olivetti, which she used to make money, typing papers for friends, classmates, and sometimes faculty.

1934 Cafeteria workers at CTSC:
Doris Sheldon, Helen Critchell, Vonnie Wilcox & Daisy

Oct 19, 1933   CSTC to Middleton

Dear Ellis — (3:20) Was rather surprised to receive such a prompt reply. I hope your mother will let you come over to my house & play Sunday. How about 2:30? Or later, if that's too early to suit your convenience. I've been a very busy woman all week & expect to be the rest of the week too. I worked last night & am working again tonight – dorm 5:45-6:30, & Kiwanis banquet at cafeteria 6:15-8. First number on lecture course tonight at 8 – Dorothy Sands – she promises to be exceptional. Cliophiles last night at 8 & French Club at 7. Scotch Hop tomorrow 4-5:30. Finger wave scheduled for 4 today. Tea – 4-5:30. And Saturday I must study & do my washing & ironing & go downtown & get everything off my mind (?) so I won't have anything to do Sunday. It's raining today – as usual, but I'm sure the sun will shine for us Sunday. Yours in a great hurry, Daisy

Dorothy Sands (1893-1980) was a popular stage actress and lecturer. The Cliophiles were a history club, named for Clio, the Greek muse, patron of history.

1934 Cliophiles

Oct 24, 1933   CSTC

Dear Ellis — (JAB) Gee, I wish I had my sled & mittens. The ground is all white this morning & I've just had my breakfast but now I've gotta hurry off to class & can't even enjoy the first snow. Really & truly, cross my heart, "The Bowery" is Sunday nite. I said I'd tell you whether it was or not, but it really is, so if I don't hear from you I'll be looking for you Sunday nite about a quarter of seven, OK? Well, I hope you're enjoying the snow (if you have any) & don't sleep too much – and don't shoot too many pheasants. Yours, Daisy (JAB = Just After Breakfast)

P.S. Now don't go without your mittens & boots – you mustn't catch cold, you know. D.

"The Bowery" is probably a reference to the then-new Raoul Walsh film, starring Wallace Beery, George Raft and Jackie Cooper.

Oct 30, 1933   CSTC

Dear Ellis — (7 PM) It's just such a gorgeous night, so warm, and moonlight, with one very bright star that I made a wish on & I feel so good because I slept from 3-5 and took a shower & had apple pie for dinner & it's just so good to be alive in Indian summer & I have my good ol' faithful pen back from the repair shop & I just have to give vent to my feelings, so I'm writing you a letter. Good reasons as any, aren't they? But here's the real reason. I just remembered that I forgot to say good-bye to the little gray roadster that I might never see again. It was a grand little car & I had a lot of fun in it.

Will you tell it good-bye for me? And I hope we'll have as many good times in its successor. I hope you'll learn to like it better in Middleton & won't get too lonesome. Now I must study. Good-nite, Daisy

P.S. 7:15 AM Tues – I just had to stop and tell you that it's grand weather again this morning & the fire engine woke me up – fire down at the refinery I guess – 5 explosions & I thought it was someone out shooting pheasants. It's just like spring & I've got all my lessons prepared for today. It's a little bit foggy – not much. I hope you'll feel as happy & peppy when you get this as I do when I'm sending it. Good morning, Daisy

---

Nov 1, 1933   CSTC to Middleton

Dear Ellis — Well, well, children must play on Halloween. I really think you should get a patent on your new fasteners. The biology instructor informs me that these are usually found on old trails or roads that aren't safe after dark. I'm recalling the good-bye. Went to church at 5:30 this morning. Aren't I good? Was down to the big oil fire yesterday PM. A sight worth seeing. Halloween party last night. Pumpkin pie & cider. Am in Sociology class now – worrying about French. See you in time for "benediction." Til then – Daisy

There was indeed a serious fire at the Roosevelt Oil Refinery in Mount Pleasant on Halloween 1933.

Nov 7, 1933   CSTC

Dear Ellis — (11:45 PM) You can see what time it is & I've got about 3 hrs work to do on Psychology so I can't make this very long, but if you'll answer this anyway I'll write you a nice long letter over the weekend to make up for it if I don't see you. I've removed my glass eye & wooden leg & false hair & teeth etc. – time to retire – get a Fish. [?] Made some fudge tonight – put nuts into it & had to cook it more – result – nutty & burnt – didn't taste so good – looks nice – we'll feed it to the neighbors. Everyone else gone to bed & doors rattling n' everything. I'm going to be a nervous wreck in about 5 more minutes. Roommate diligently studying – what I should be doing. Just heard funny noises – thought it was hounds on a coon hunt – guess it's just night-birds. Mercier (Catholic student club) meeting tonight. Very inspiring speaker, Joe Schnitzler – "Problems of Catholic Teachers." Had hamburgers Sunday night. We were wishing you & Harry coulda come up for some. Boy, were they good – mustard n' pickles n' onions – all the fixings. Haven't heard from home yet – but then I haven't written yet – hope they get a cottage, don't you? Little snow here tonite – hard like pellets but melts altho road and tennis court white now. I hope you can decipher enough of this to at least get the general trend – if there is one. Been practicing the Mae West gait. Getting it pretty good. You liked that – didn't you? Yes. 12 AM – Feel pretty good & wide awake n' peppy, spite of all I must do. Guess I kinda better get busy now tho – by the way, what color are your eyes? Oooo! Screech owl. Uncannily yours, Daisy

P.S. I'm not gonna study after all – think it wiser to get my sleep.

P.P.S. 7:15 – Had my sleep & breakfast, fed, you know, like a pig, & now I feel just swell in spite of fact that won't have my psychology. Beautiful morning & chrysanthemums from home still pretty. Gotta write a letter home before 8. Candy gave me bad dreams last nite. Write. Be good (like I always am), Daisy

1934 Mercier Club

Nov 13, 1933   CSTC

Dear Ellis – (6:30 AM) It's 6:30 and does my bed ever look good. This was the weekend I was supposed to stay here & study & rest. Well, in a few words, I went home with Helen, so you can imagine how much I studied & how much less I rested. Hit the hay a quarter after 7 Saturday AM. But it really isn't as bad as it sounds. I had a grand time. It would have been perfect if you'd been along. I've heard you say that you'd like to see how I act when I'm tight – well, you should have seen me about 1: Sat AM – only I wasn't tight. I'll tell you about it so you won't be scandalized. Got back 8:45 last night & your letter was waiting for me – almost as good as seeing you. I haven't heard from the folks yet about the cabin, but the very minute I do I'll let you know. Gee I hope it all works out all right, don't you? I wish on the first star every nite & I just hope everything will be all right. Oooh, it's cold outside. The wind sounds so shivery & mournful. It's still dark. As for the new V.P. of Mercier, I think she might like to meet you some time just to be obliging if you really want to see her so badly. Must close now & go to breakfast. You'll hear from me again soon & I hope it's good news. Here's hoping, Daisy

P.S. I don't know whether all those colors would fit into my "horrorscope" or not. What do you think?

P.P.S. We want you at our house for Thanksgiving so you won't make other plans unless you have already, will you? I hope you wanta come & can.

Helen Critchell was Mom's roommate for all four years at Central. She was from Williamsburg, up near Traverse City. They remained close friends and stayed in touch throughout their lives.

Nov 21, 1933   CSTC

Dear Ellis — (3:10) I'm awfully, awfully sorry, but it doesn't do any good to cry over it. Got a letter this morning. Clarence has been sick all last week & they're not going hunting except maybe just my dad & Clarence will go up for a couple of days. I was very disappointed when I read the letter but my motto is, "Never say die, say dam," so I just said, "dam! dam! dam!" until I felt better. I'm sorry that I got you all pepped about it too & I hope you can go somehow or something so you won't be terribly disappointed. I suppose I really shouldn't go anyway. I should stay here over the weekend and study. The prospect is so thrilling! Maybe you can go anyway over the weekend. But if you won't be going, how would you like to come up Sat nite? There might be an all-college dance – I'm not sure. If there isn't, we can get late leave & go somewhere to a dance, you & I and Harry & Helen. What say? We'll find something to do – interesting. Or – if you don't come Sat, Sunday afternoon or Sun nite would be all right – in case you don't go hunting & have nothing else to do important. It surely is cold here today – more snow last night & an icy wind this day. Slid out of the dorm yesterday. No ill effects. Let me know what you're gonna do – if it concerns me. Your pal, Daisy

Mama wants to know if you're coming Thanksgiving – she told me to be sure & ask you. You are, aren't you? D.

Nov 23, 1933   CSTC

Dear Ellis — (11 PM) Received your most (?) letter this afternoon & I'm so sorry that we'll have to eat pig's liver all winter, but what are you going to do with the rest of the pig? I suppose you didn't even think of pickled pig's feet, did you? Just came home from the lyceum course – "The Singing Boys from Vienna." They surely were good. I'm eating toasted roll & jam – tastes pretty good. My roommate's making her evening "cup o' tay." It's been awfully nice weather here this week. Hope it stays so for Thanksgiving. Got a letter from the folks yesterday. They're up hunting at the Rollway Camp near Hale. They decided to go at the last minute – Saturday morning. They're going to stay til they get a deer or until Sunday. Only have one class tomorrow, 8 – am I glad or am I glad. But oboy! am I busy. Right now tho I feel comfortable & warm & lazy & I hate to move. But I've got to wash up and get to bed. Looking forward to Sunday nite. But I'm sorry there is no more doing than usual. Sometime you'll have to come on Saturday nite & we'll go out in the country to a real dance & I'll get late leave! But just think – it's been three whole weeks since you've seen me & you really need to be polite, should say that "it makes no difference to you whether there's anything happening or not, you just wants see me." Oh yeah – worked in the dining room last night & served at the boys' football banquet in the cafeteria & went to the Co-ed Prom last night. More fun! Oh well, I'm awfully sleepy now. Good-nite, Daisy

P.S. I almost forgot the real purpose of this, to tell you I'll be in any time after 6:30 PM Sunday evening Nov 26, 1933. And so, for the second & last time, Good-nite. Very sleepily yours, Daisy

---

Dec 4, 1933 CSTC

Dear Ellis – (7:45 PM) I just think it's so nice of you to come up Saturday nite that I'm going to tell you so. I think that you didn't believe half the things I told you Sunday nite; but if I remember now everything that I said, I didn't tell you anything that wasn't really true. And as to what I was thinking about you, I'll tell you sometime when you ask me. But really, I was in Owosso Saturday nite with my folks. You probably believe that; of course that doesn't excuse me at all because I was even the one who suggested that you come on Saturday nite instead of Sunday. It was mean of me & I think I felt worse than you did. (I don't know whether you felt bad, but I really did.) Anyway, I told you I was sorry, didn't I? You didn't even say whether or not I was forgiven. Am I? I wouldn't have blamed you a bit if you had done just what you said you would Sunday. But I'm glad you didn't. Think how I would have felt then (& now). And just to show you how repentant I am – I've canceled two dates for this week & I wouldn't even go to see "Duck Soup" with Neil when he asked me. I'm saving myself for you. Are you? Am I still your "All Right"?

P.S. (9 PM) Of all the people I'm the most absent-minded. I want to thank you for bringing me back. I'm so sorry I forgot to thank you last night.

Thank you just awful much. I'll do something nice for you sometime. & P.S. Do you really think I'm so awfully sarcastic? I don't mean to be. You tell me when I'm being sarcastic & I'll take it all back. Don't take me too seriously. I've got so much work to do & I'm so sleepy. I don't know which way I'm going, if I am. G'night, Daisy

DUCK SOUP, with the Marx Brothers, was brand new in November 1933, and one of the most popular and highest grossing films of the year, despite the harsh times of the Depression. 'Neil' was probably Neil Hoover, a boy she'd known at Chesaning High School, who would have been around during Thanksgiving break. (This was the last known letter from 1933.)

Jan 3, 1934   221 Ronan Hall, CSTC

Dear Ellis — (12:30) Just an interlude between classes. After I made a firm resolve not to write to you this week, I find I can't resist 'penning' you something or other. (Almost choked on a piece of Xmas candy.) You like candy, don't you? I hope your stomach ache is better. My headache's all gone, but it took til this morning to get rid of it. I came back rather unexpectedly Monday afternoon. Thought I might not get here in time Tuesday, so packed in a half hour & hit the trail. Margaret & Hilda came with us. Changed rooms – 221. Got an east view now. Rather like it. Can see the sunrise but there hasn't been any yet. Taking only 4 subjects & a gym this term, 8-11 & 1-4, one 2-hr class – Psychology, 8-10, a whiz. French 10-11, English 1, Latin 2 & Gym 3. I feel pretty good today. How about you? Got 2 weeks back caught up in my diary, now gotta start over again. I hope your drive home wasn't too bad Monday morning. I was going to write you Monday nite, but I was feeling rather blue & lonesome & tired & I thought it was no use making you feel more tired than you probably did anyway so I didn't. And anyway I know you don't like to write letters. Well, the point of it all is – I didn't write then, but I am now. Just about time to go to English. There was more I was going to write but I can't think in such a short time. Until I see you. Love, Daisy

---

Jan 6, 1934   CSTC

Dear Ellis — (Sat 8:30 AM) You'll think I'm crazy after you read the other letter enclosed, but I'm really quite sane this morning – this is just by way of reassuring you. It's marvelous what eight hours of sleep & a good breakfast can do for one. But the night did seem so long. I read Helen to sleep last nite & made myself wider awake than ever. Went to bed at 12:15 and up at 8:15. Great large flakes of snow are falling this morning & the ground is white. Makes me feel at peace with the world, except I've still got heaps

13

of work to do. But I must have taken all my meanness out on that letter last night because I feel so good this morning. I am enclosing the striped jacket picture. I feel more now like that looks. Once from what you said I thought perhaps you might like it. You know that if you don't want it, you can always send it back. It isn't what I would call a beautiful picture but it looks just like me. So just forget all about that other letter & remember that I'm all over it now & won't feel that way again for a long, long time. I hope everything is just fine with you & don't let anything get you discouraged or down in the dumps I know it isn't a very pleasant way to be. And so, I kiss your ring, my dear. With all my heart, Daisy

There is no other 'enclosed' letter.

Jan 12, 1934   CSTC

Dear Ellis — (8:15 PM) I've wasted over an hour doing nothing at all & I've got stacks of work to do – Psychology & French & Latin books piled all around me. I just hate the sight of them – I suppose everyone feels this way once in a while. Do you ever feel as if you didn't care whether the world kept on going or came to an end tomorrow? I wouldn't give a d--n if it ended right now. I guess I don't even know what I'm talking about. I don't care anyway. I'm tired of everything & everybody around me – but most of all I'm just plain tired. I usually never write letters when I feel like this but I'm just bad enough right now to take my spite out on somebody else – and as long as you're not here to talk back, I can say anything I want to, can't I? This isn't a very nice letter to get, is it? I'm sorry, but why don't you write to me? I don't think you like me well enough even to write me except that you're too much of a gentleman to not answer my letters. Just for spite, I hope you've got a sore throat so you'll know I wasn't 'stringing' you – because I really did have one Sunday morning, tho it was nearly gone at nite. I'm sorry, I'm sorry, I'm awfully sorry. Don't believe a word of what I've said. I'm not responsible. I'm going to bed tonite & sleep until I wake up – then I should feel better – here's hopin'. I shouldn't send you this at all – you've always been so perfectly nice to me; you've never done anything I didn't like – there's no reason at all why I shouldn't write you a perfectly lovely letter & tell you how many "hundred bushels' worth" I like you, except that maybe just a little envelope wouldn't hold it all. Please don't let this make you feel bad – I'll be all over it by the time you're reading this & thank heaven I don't feel this way very often. Now that I've got that all off my mind, maybe I can get some work done. In fact I feel better already. Yours with love, Daisy

Jan 15, 1934 CSTC

Dear Ellis — (11 PM) I'm so sorry that you've had (or have?) a cold & sore throat & (such a coincidence) it happened that I had one too the first of last week. Isn't it odd? I must have been experiencing the worst effects of it when I wrote you that awful letter Friday nite. I'm ashamed of myself. If it is excusable, will you just please forget about it? Just remember the things you want to & forget the ones you didn't like. I wish you would do that all the time because sometimes I say or do things I don't mean & forget about them myself. I hope that everything comes out in favor of you in regard to the lumber for the CWA gym. I'm afraid I don't realize how much other people have to worry about when I'm away from everyone up here with a bunch of crazy instructors trying to imbue me with the idea that Latin, French, Psych – or what have you – is the most important thing in life, but somehow I can't believe them even if I am going to teach it. I may earn my living by it but I'm not going to live it. I seem to have wandered from the point – if there is any point. I guess it's that I'm sorry that I bothered you with my troubles when you had plenty of your own to worry about. Anyway, I liked your letter & I'm glad you're not sore. And such a splendid martyr in the cause of – somethin' or other – B.A., or Shakespeare – do you know I've spent an hour writing this letter, it seems I can't think of what I want to say. Paper is so inadequate, so I guess you'll just have to read between the lines (but not too much). Much as I hate to, I'm afraid I'll have to figure out some graphs for my 8:00 sike class. A hundred years from now it won't make any difference, but just try and tell Marshall that. It seems rather trivial now, but at 8 o'clock – and it's 12:15 now. I sincerely hope that your illness is all gone now. (Sounds as if I thought this would cure it.) But all joking aside, I hope your business dealings will all be crowned with success, & sometime when you're not busy, think of me, I'll be thinking of you. As always, with love, Daisy

The "lumber for the CWA gym" may have been about a Civil Works Administration construction project, though I've no idea what Dad's role might have been in that. The CWA was part of FDR's New Deal, a jobs-creation program to put people back to work during the Depression. It only lasted a little more than a year, in 1933-34.

Jan 28, 1934 CSTC

Dear Ellis — (11:30 PM) I don't know where to begin. I think of so many things I want to tell you, but I don't remember them long enough to put down on paper. For instance, little things like – there was a big ring around the moon Friday night with one star in it and I wish I could have been out under it with you. I'd like to save up all the heavenly nights and gorgeous sunsets and beautiful music and the perfectly divine chocolate peanut butter fudge I made today until we could enjoy it together. Sounds like I might be tight, doesn't it? But I'm really very normal and wide-awake. Got lots of sleep over the weekend and had my fortune told in my tea leaves. I just hate tea, but to be courteous I drank a whole cupful without making a face – just so I could learn the future. And who do you suppose was in my cup – a tall, blond young man & she said the nicest things about him – oh, my! Helen & I spent a grand weekend – just eating & sleeping & reading & loafing. Oh, it's so stormy & blowy & blizzardy out tonite – the wind howls & moans & whistles – a perfect night for a murder. Guess I've been reading too many ghost stories, etc. I'm so glad you didn't come tonight, not for my sake, but for yours. You would have frozen going home with no one to snuggle up & keep you warm, wouldn't you? Did you have a good time in Detroit this weekend? I hope you did & how is the Kid Brother getting along? Did you know that Joe Stasek is working for Mormon now? Joe Bila has got a job in Flint now. Mr John Stasek is in the hospital having a silver plate put in his leg where the bone didn't heal. I guess he was pretty bad last nite. (12 AM, Jan 29) A young man's athletic club has been organized in the Oakley Parish (proceeds to go to the church), officers – Joe Stasek, Jay Kleo, George Kleo, etc. & Jack Stasek (sergeant-at-arms) & Louis Walls, president. They're going to play baseball, I guess, dunno what else. Been eating toasted pork sandwiches with mustard & pickles, & bean sandwich, brownies, apples, candy, etc. & oh, my indigestion. But I always sleep well so I won't worry about that. Oh dear, I had so many things to tell you & now I can't think of a blessed thing except I wish you were here to kiss me good nite. Love, Daisy

P.S. Maybe if Carol O'Connell still hasn't any objections to meeting Helen, you could bring him with you to Oakley Feb 17 – maybe? Just a suggestion – not even sure yet we'll be there. There, I went & spoiled the nice ending by that P.S., didn't I? So just to show you my thoughts are all of you, I still wish you were here to kiss me good nite. With all my heart, Daisy

The "Kid Brother" would be Dad's youngest brother, Bernard, nineteen years younger. Joe Stasek worked for Dad when he was managing the elevator in Oakley. The other names and news probably came from letters from home.

Feb 8, 1934   CSTC

Dear Ellis – (7:30 AM) I hope you won't be too awfully disappointed when you read this. I'm so sorry, but I find it impossible for me to attend the J-Hop.

Helen had already asked me to go home with her that weekend. I sincerely hope that this will not put too much of a crook in your plans. As for Carol O'Connell & his girlfriend, it is perfectly all right for them to come, & he might like to know that all bids must be bought by Wed, Feb 14. Bids are $2. Please don't be angry with me, but it's only for one night anyway. Don't work too hard. Very sincerely, Daisy

---

Undated   CSTC

Dear Ellis – (10PM Sun nite) I wish we didn't have to have a beginning to letters. I could think of lots of things to say if I could plunge right into the middle of it. Guess I rather made a mess of my last letter to you, didn't I? I know it sounded terribly abrupt & stiff, but I really didn't mean it that way. It was lack of time, not sentiment that made it that way. I hope it didn't make you angry. I don't know what your reply is yet so I can say what I want to. You see, the J-Hop comes in Lent and I do not want to dance then. But after all it's only one more formal party and there'll be the Women's League Formal in the spring and that will be so much nicer & we can have a lot more fun then. That's what I'm looking forward to. There'll be no more dances or shows for me for six weeks, but then it will be spring and won't that be grand? Swimming & picnics n' everything. We're going over to June & Shirley's to get some candy when they get it made. Not even candy or peanuts after Wednesday but maybe it will be good for my figure. Will I be seeing you next Sunday nite just the same or are ya mad at me? Please say you're not. Daisy

A Valentine card is enclosed with notes from her friends

> *"I'm on your side." – June*
> *"Sure she's being good. Her phone number is 895 – Call her up sometime." – Shirley*
> *"Why dontcha' come some time n' see Daisy n' Harry n' me." – Helen*

... Don't mind them – just greetings from my fellow inmates. The candy turned out swell. I scraped the dish. Daisy

---

Feb 12, 1934   CSTC

Dear Ellis – (5 PM) It is a perfectly lovely Valentine gift and I thank you for it. But in spite of the label, I don't think they are very deadly. I have tried them on a number of people and all are still alive, well and experiencing no ill effects. I just love Peggy Jones chocolates and it was very kind of you to send them before Lent so I can enjoy them with a clear conscience. I am asking a favor of you. I just came from a meeting for those seeking campus jobs under the new FERA. We had to fill out questionnaires and give names for references as to our "need." I hope you won't think I was presuming when I gave your name. They will probably never write anyway, but just in case they do, you'll know what it's all about and you can tell them what a good character I have, etc. and that I really deserve it. Now, don't you think so? And will you do that little thing for me? What I thought was going to be lovely spring weather when I woke up this morning and heard the birds singing has turned into a regular old time snow storm. Makes me wish I had nothing to do but sit by the fire and read. I've been reading "A Farewell to Arms" & if you've not read it, I'm telling you that it's no story for little boys to read. They are collecting me for dinner so I must be leaving you now. Daisy

P.S. (10:00) I think it was awfully sweet of you. I am retiring. We are certainly enjoying the chocolates. Good nite, Daisy

> FERA was the Federal Emergency Relief Administration. It was replaced in 1935 by the Works Progress Administration (WPA). Hemingway's novel, A FAREWELL TO ARMS (1929) had already been adapted to the screen in 1932, starring Gary Cooper and Helen Hayes.

Feb 23, 1934   CSTC

Dear Ellis – So sorry to have waited so long to answer your letter, but I've been busy and I have also been doing a lot of thinking. About lots of things – in general and some in particular. I hope you enjoyed the lovely cool moonlight nights we have had. There was a ring around the moon tonite – I hope you enjoyed it as much as I did. I am working now – so I can write on company stationery too. I am doing stenographic work for Mr Parker – athletic director here. He is just grand to work for & he is a very nice man – I think. It's too bad it's so cold. I was going to ask you to come up on St Patrick's for the dance & we were going to have you stay over for a dinner party on Sunday. It would have been so much fun. But then – do you suppose it will be any warmer after Easter than it is now? I wonder. Will you write & let me know, so I'll be sure you're not coming – St Pat's? Yours truly, Daisy

---

Feb 25, 1934   CSTC

Dear Ellis – (11:15 PM) You can't say that I made any quick decision in your case for I had a whole week in which to think it over & give you the benefits of any doubts I might have& perhaps I have even been too liberal. Do you think so? Of course I was rather disappointed when 7:30 & 8 came & no Ellis, & then I was glad you didn't come because it was awfully cold

& it probably wouldn't have been worth it anyway – isn't that what you thought? And I know you weren't sorry – & didn't regret it. But "The only things that I regret are the things I haven't done." Please don't take that too literally. I've been pretending to myself all week that I was angry when I was really only a little bit hurt – I suppose. My reasoning always comes to the rescue & hard as I try sometimes I never can (or have) stayed mad at anyone any more than 2 hours at a time. I only wish that I could have seen you so we could fight it out while I was still in that mood. Maybe you'll give me a chance to after you read the enclosed letter. I just thought that up & it was too good to keep & I was afraid it might prove disastrous if I didn't explain so – this. Anyway, you know how I feel now. Kinda lonesome & sleepy, Daisy

---

Mar 4, 1934 CSTC

Dear Ellis – (8:30 PM) This is my second attempt & this goes regardless. The first was consigned to the waste basket on account of because it was a cross between a weather report & a record of the amount of sleep I have been getting & would like to get (very little & very much, respectively). I have been working very hard & I am very tired. I have very much studying to do & would very much like not to do it. That is not the right attitude at all, is it? I know it, so don't tell me. My folks were up to see me this afternoon & I was kinda glad. I haven't been home for five weeks & won't go home for three more. I guess they thought they'd better come up & see what their daughter was up to. The CWA workers have been laid off for 30 days & Joe Stasek has got a job in Flint. From what I hear, if it's true, everybody & his little brother have jobs in Flint. Must be a prosperous town. Mama brought me some apples & bananas & oranges & we're surely enjoying them. We're not eating between meals in Lent, but on Sunday nights we just extend our lunch time as long as we have anything to eat. It isn't as cold up here now as it was the last time I wrote. I mean the weather. Much as you would be inconvenienced, you very kindly offered to come up before St Patrick's "if necessary." I hate to disillusion you, but I find that after 4 weeks I'm still alive & likely to pull through. I'm still quite healthy & happy. So I will not ask you to lose any more sleep on my account until St Patrick's. Now, please, don't take me too literally. In other words, if I were to say what I really mean, I have been lonesome for you and I'm looking forward with great pleasure to St Patrick's Day and a dance if you still would like to come. As for dancing in Lent, St Patrick's isn't considered as Lent anyway. And you should take a Dutchman as he means & not as he says. And now I am going to bed. So good-night – I'll see you in my dreams. (Quite) sincerely, Daisy

Mar 9, 1934   Oakley

Dear Ellis — Just to show you that I'm still your pal and my "Dutch wit" works in less than two months, I think I will just knock you right off your feet and answer your letter right away, especially since it didn't even require an answer. I thought also that I would set you right on a false impression you got from my letter. I didn't mean that I thought you were losing any sleep just thinking about me. I meant that you wouldn't lose any sleep on Sunday nites coming to see me. Thoughts never kept anyone from sleep when they needed it if they are nice thoughts. It was rather mean to say that, I know now. You came because you wanted to see me, didn't you? I hope. And if that's right you wouldn't regret losing sleep. I can appreciate your situation & your long cold rides all alone. I came home tonight with the Apple Blossom Club on their bus, 4:20-7:20. Just about froze. They were going to Henderson & dropped me right at my door – just me & my purse & gloves – absolutely free of all baggage – new way for me to travel. Listening to "The Personality Kid," the "Little Theater off Times Square." Kinda good. Seems nice to be home – bread fresh from the oven & hot baked beans. Mmmm! Do I make you hungry? I'm going to bed now & sleep until noon tomorrow & dream about you. Good-nite from Your Pal, Daisy

The Apple Blossom Club was a choral group at CSTC that traveled around the area giving performances. I can't remember if Mom was a member or not. "First Nighter" was a popular radio drama in the 1930s that created the illusion of opening from that "Little Theater off Times Square," but it actually originated in Chicago.

Mar 20, 1934   CSTC to Wayland (Dad's home town)

Dear Ellis — It is 9:30 in the evening & I am very very sleepy & I must hurry & get this written before the sleepy feeling wears off so I can go to bed & sleep until 12 & then get up & work. I am surrounded by the forebodings of tests in Latin, test in French, tests in English & tests in psychology. But I rather enjoy this week. I'm living on a dream & a hope – a dream of last weekend with you & a hope of catching up on lost sleep next week when I'm home. I slept 9-1 last night & studied 1-5:30 & slept again until 7. We should have stayed up & studied Sunday nite but neither Helen nor I wanted to break the spell so we went to sleep at 10:30 – the end of a perfect weekend – for us anyway. Did you enjoy it too? I didn't want to spoil the memory of it by schoolwork & it's still intact, altho I might not be by the time this week is over. I want to wish you good luck & all success in your new job. I know you can do it. If anytime you are afraid to tackle anything (but maybe you never are like I am), you know that praying always helps. I have always prayed for what I've got & wanted. I couldn't do anything without prayers. This sounds awfully like a sermon or some kind of paternal or maternal advice but I am just telling you what my own experience has proved true for me. Probably you discovered it for yourself long before I did. Now I am going to say my prayers & pray for you too as I do every night – pray that you will keep on liking me as much (& more?). Just like I like you. With all my heart, Daisy

And now of you I have only your ring. You don't really want to trade again, do you?

I think Dad's "new job" was the one he was starting as a traveling sales rep for General Mills. Up to this point, he had still been working at elevators of the Christian Breisch Co chain, in Carson City and Middleton.

Ellis Bazzett's General Mills sales truck

Apr 2, 1934   CSTC to 1327 Sherman St SE, Grand Rapids, Michigan

Dear Ellis – (11:15 Mon nite) Received your very welcome letter this morning after two hours & a half struggle through registration & it was a fitting reward for all my troubles. I like to get letters like that. It made me feel just heaps better. After I'd been cussing everyone all over the place it was rather soothing to my tired nerves. I'm glad you like your job & your "boss" & I'm sure that you will "click" with him if you get acquainted, 'cause I know he'll like you. I would like to see you in your red truck –

pretty ritzy, I'll bet. Helen was wondering if there would be room for her & Harry in the back of it. The fellows' landlord kicked them out from their apartment & their gang is all broken up. Harry is staying at Brown's just across the street from the dorm on Franklin. It was dear of you to remember me on Easter. I hope you had a nice homecoming on Easter Sunday & lots of Easter eggs. The last week of school we lost so much sleep that I spent practically all vacation in bed & on the davenport. We got about 4 hours sleep a nite. Wednesday nite I stayed up all nite doing my term experiment for psike. At 4 I was downstairs in the kitchenette typing it. I slept from 6-7 in the morning, wrote a psike test at 8, French at 10, English at 1 & Latin at 2. But I wrote the highest one in psike, got A on my experiment & an A out of the course so I didn't care anyway. I got B in natural drawing & I'm prouder of that mark than anything. I got B's in English & French. I won't say what I got in Latin but it wasn't so hot. This term I'm taking: 8 – Current History, 9 – Education, 11 – Psychology, 2 – Latin Methods, 3 – Adv Natural Dancing. One hell of a schedule, but there's nothing I can do about it. It was nice, warm & springy today after all our snow & rain & the campus looked like an Easter Parade. I like first days. I wish there were about 4 more & a weekend before classes began but at 8 we'll be on the job in the morning. Wish me luck – I'll need lots of it this term. It's going to be terrible – I feel it in my bones. The weather will be so nice I won't want to study or do anything. And then I'll get lonesome for somebody too but he'll be so far away it won't do any good. And I won't be able to sleep it off either. I'll have to study & concentrate. You can imagine all the concentrating I'll do. I just hate to think of this term. I'll be glad when it's over. I'm going to try to get a job in the canning factory in Owosso then. Okay – I'm a lady of leisure this term too. That's why I was cussing everyone this morning. But perhaps I'll be working again in May. I hope so. The FERA jobs are being rotated. I only hope they get back to me pretty soon. All the kids in Oakley had whooping cough when I was home except Harold's kids & Dorothy's. Gee, they're all so darn cute. Jimmy is into everything. Friday nite I kept him at home while the rest of the family went to church. He cried just about all the time they were gone. I still think kids are cute but I guess I'm no good at taking care of 'em. The Easter Bunny came up to Harold's on Easter Eve & Rosalie brought me an Easter egg he laid. I told her I thought he laid a lot of eggs for just one bunny but she said the fairies helped him. It must be the fairies. There are no new arrivals in Oakley as yet except me. Agnes & Kenneth Kettler have a baby girl about 2 weeks old – I've forgotten her name. They live in Oakley now, in the white house by the schoolhouse. Virginia Hill is going to get married soon too. I guess that's all the gossip I can think of now. Too much already anyway yet, I guess, huh? I'm getting a little sleepy & it's dangerous for me to write letters then because I'm liable to say most anything & not be responsible for it. I don't know what's making me write so small tonite but I guess it's because I haven't had any practice for so long. I had to catch up two weeks in my diary & believe me that was fun. Two years ago today I was bridesmaid at my brother's wedding. A week ago today I saw my first robin (& the only one I've seen yet) & that one was way up in the top of the tree & I could only recognize it by its song. As I said before, I will close now, and will you write me another nice fat letter like that, please, if you're not too busy – or tired? If you know how I love to get them, 'cause I miss you, really, a lot. Good nite from your Daisy.

For those who don't know or remember, a "davenport" was a couch or sofa. A curiously Midwestern term, perhaps.

Apr 12, 1934   CSTC

Dear Ellis – (11 PM) Nice weather we're having here, how about it where you are? If you'd like some snow, we have plenty of it & just itching to give it away to someone. And have you been in swimming yet? Somehow the idea doesn't appeal to me now. I'm feeling a bit stiff from strenuous exercises in natural dancing. But I like it a lot. There are fewer in the class this term & it's more fun. There have been a group of 18 foreign students from Ann Arbor on the campus yesterday & today, & tomorrow visiting classes, etc. The YW brought them here. They conducted an open forum discussion last night & were guests at a party for them tonite. They represent China, Japan, Persia, Iraq, India, Bolivia, Peru, etc. Very odd & interesting. Helen just went to bed, damming Harry all to hell. I guess there has been some misunderstanding & a lot of stubbornness on the part of both of them. I guess maybe they see each other too often. Sometimes I wish you lived closer so we could be together oftener but I wouldn't want it to be that way if we'd have fights all the time, would you? Do you think we would? I'd rather have it like it was Sunday, if you only came once a year. You brought the spring with you when you came, I guess, but it didn't stay. I wish you'd bring it back again. Harry was disappointed because he didn't see you. He was asking all about you & was going to ask you to spend the night with him, I guess. I hope you didn't try to jump any more ditches going home. I should be sorry that I kept you so late when you had so far to go. But really, I can't truthfully say that I am. I was with you all the way home – in dreams. Did you know I was there? I don't have much to write about tonite but I thought that if you came back to Grand Rapids Saturday night, you might be disappointed if you went clear there thru the park and didn't find a letter from me. Perhaps I'm overestimating it. But there is another reason too, why I'm writing – I wanted to. Anyway, I hope you do get this this weekend 'cause I'll be thinking about you. Don't worry about answering if you don't get this soon. Write me when you're not too tired and have some time. I'm going to bed now & get some sleep so I won't be an old woman by the time you see me again. Work hard & sleep a lot & don't get too fat – I don't like fat men. But I do like you – so much. Good nite. Love, Daisy

---

Apr 17, 1934   CSTC

Dear Ellis – (9:50) I've come to the conclusion, for the present at least, that it's a pretty good world to live in. I'll tell you why. I'm eating chocolate-covered graham cracker cookies and an apple (3 seeds) and I'm never so contented as when I'm eating – and I've got on my new blue pajamas my momma made for me – and I'm going to retire to slumber land presently and I've got a letter from you (just one thing wrong with that – it wasn't long enough – but I liked it just the way it was). So, for all the aforementioned reasons (especially the last), don't you think I should feel pretty well satisfied with the world? I do enjoy feeling contented & lazy once in a while but I have a guilty feeling when I think of Latin verb conjugations, etc. I caught (hell) in Latin class today because I couldn't say a synopsis of (poto?) in the 2nd person plural, subjunctive active as fast (or as accurately) as I should have. I'm afraid I don't care as much as I should, either. So I suppose I'll get up early in the morning and study my conjugations and probably know less about them than I do now. Helen is just going to bed & she says to tell you hello for her & that she & Harry are fighting as usual. And she thinks Harry is the stubbornnest fellow that – she didn't finish it, I guess the last sentence wasn't meant to be repeated anyway. Personally, I think 2 people are stubborn in that case. Oh dear, I'm getting sleepy. Guess I'll never get caught up on the sleep I lost last term. I just happened to think that maybe sometimes my letters don't seem very clear on account of no paragraphing. I really do know how but I guess I'm just too lazy. Anyway, you can paragraph them to suit yourself. I'm leaving Friday morning (get out of one day's classes) for model League of Nations at Ann Arbor & returning Saturday nite. Guess I'm all set for it now. I think it's going to be kinda fun. We had election of officers at Mercier meeting tonite & we elected Helen president & I am social & program chairman for next year. Kids dashing in here looking for her roommate – and to borrow brown thread, etc. Wish they'd go to bed like they should. O, I almost forgot to tell you what I caught (& it was from you?) – impetigo contagioso – that's the way it sounds anyway. It's something like a skin disease, I guess. I've got 2 spots that big – O – one over my chin in the middle – and one right on the side of my nose – two white patches on 'em & everyone thinks my roommate has been abusing me. But I'm taking good care of it & it'll soon be gone. So you should be glad you can't come to see me now, 'cause you couldn't kiss me – you'd probably catch it. Would you be sorry? I wouldn't let you even if you wanted to, 'cause I wouldn't want you to catch it – it burns like hell every time I put antiseptic on it. I guess a page is enough for that – too much. I think I'll go home next weekend, or the next. I haven't been home yet this term. Aren't you going to see Mrs Gower soon? That strawberry shortcake made me hungry, but we had ice cream with fresh strawberries on them Sunday. My cookies are all gone & it makes me hungry – for strawberries – not ice cream. A new restaurant opened down by the theater Saturday & on opening day (the Broadway Café) gave a free soda, sundae, etc. with each one paid for, so Helen & I in the course of the afternoon & evening had four apiece – oops! And as if that weren't enough, we had a treat for Sunday night lunch – very generous, luscious, rich banana splits. It was just too much – we couldn't take it. Last night we ate mince pie just before we went to bed & did I have bad dreams last nite – the most awful ones about you & everyone under the sun. Well, I must get up early & read about Austria, and Food & Drugs Act & the WPA for Current History. Kinda like that class. Best one this term, except Natural Dancing. This letter is positively too long, & I apologize profusely. You're probably bored to tears by this time so I'll end by saying, "Don't work too hard – that's what makes so many old men." & don't judge me by just what I write – I think so much I never put down on paper. I can hear you say, "Well, thank heaven, she doesn't put it all down." Good-nite. Love, Daisy

P.S. I get awfully lonesome for you sometimes even if I don't say it. D.

Apr 27, 1934   CSTC

Dear Ellis – (2 PM) Ain't it a grand & glorious feeling? Nothing to do this afternoon - that is - no classes. Last class over at 10 this morning. Of course, there are many, many things for me to do this weekend. Whether or not I do them is another question. You know, I'm going home next weekend. Isn't it a "coincidence that we're both going to be in Oakley at the same time? But I hope it will be warmer than today. Sun shining but a cooold wind! I had a grand time in Ann Arbor. I started to write you when I was there, but I never finished the letter. I was just dead when I got back. We went in a crazy old bus, started at 5:30 Friday morning – back 10:30 Saturday night. But it was a lot of fun. As to treaties, none were formally drawn up - but I stand firm with the other nations on the question of disarmament - "no disarmament without a definite guarantee of security." "Wonder Bar" is here Sunday night & we are going to see it – couldn't miss it. If it's as good as "Rip Tide" – it'll be worth it. Saw that last Sunday nite. Norma Shearer, I think, is the best actress in the movies today. "Rip Tide" surely was grand. I'll be at home looking for you Saturday nite – May 5 – okay? I don't know what will be going on as I'm not in very close touch with the place anymore – but you know the expectations. However, I'll do my best to entertain you. Helen is sending you her love, too – on account of she hasn't given any to Harry lately. Now, I'll begin the very pleasant task of doing nothing (useful) remainder of the afternoon. So, so long. Love, Daisy

"Wonder Bar" was a 1934 film adaptation of a Broadway musical, starring Al Jolson, Kay Francis & Dick Powell. And "Riptide" was just one of many films starring Norma Shearer, a very popular screen actresses of the 1930s.

1934 at Shirley Allen's farm near Clare, Michigan
Jenn Shelander, Shirley Allen, Daisy Whalen, Helen Critchell & Mildred Stirling

---

May 7, 1934   CSTC

Dear Ellis – (Mon – 1:15 PM) I hope you didn't have any more bad luck & got home not too late & safe & still healthy & weren't too sleep this morning. I think of you having to go to work so early & then I feel like I'm rubbing it in when I tell you that I slept 'til 11:30 this AM. I'm afraid I haven't any word of honor because I didn't go to the doctor this morning as I said I would, but I'm being taken care of by my friends & heating-pad & Ben-gay & gargle, etc. Had my lunch in bed & I'm still here (in bed) propped up with pillows & behaving like a real invalid. But please don't worry. I'm not really so very ill as it may sound. I'm just staying home & getting doctored up today so I can start in new tomorrow. I guess the wood I knocked on yesterday wasn't very good wood after all. I'm really sorry I kept you here last night when I knew you wanted to stop in Carson City & get home early. I guess my mind wasn't functioning very clearly & I didn't exercise my reasoning power. Maybe my natural intelligence was all used up. I just knew that I wanted you & I didn't even consider anyone else. All I can say is – you were a darn good sport – & that goes for all the time. Now I think I'll take advantage of my invalid state & sleep the rest of the day. I wish this letter could reach you as quickly as my thoughts – for they're loaded with Love, Daisy

---

May 9, 1934 CSTC

Dear Ellis – (Wed nite) It was dear of you to write me so soon. I'm sorry that I didn't realize I was causing you worry or I would have written you Monday morning. I think I could have stayed awake that long – for you. I'm quite all right now and feeling fine. A little sleep at the moment, I will confess, but otherwise perfectly sound, mentally & physically. I'm still getting lots of sleep & not much work done. I guess it's just a habit but I surely do enjoy it. I'm going to stay here this weekend & hold the dormitory down while most of the kids go home. And guess what – I'm going to make me a dress. That is, I'm going to attempt it, anyway, & if I make a mess of it, there'll be no one here to bawl me out but myself. Had a test sprung on us in psike today – it wasn't so bad, but we're going to have one in Current History Friday which is very likely to be "not so good." I should study it tonite but I'll probably go to bed & not even worry about it. Rained here this morning & almost had a thunderstorm – lovely this afternoon & tonight – ooh – it just made me lonesome – for somebody a long ways away. My eyes are getting so heavy. Guess I'll just have to say – Good-nite – without even a kiss from you – except in my dreams. Love, Daisy

P.S. As to the League Formal, you don't really think I'd like to go with someone else, do you? 9 or 9:30 or any time will be OK with me, if it's all rite for you; but if it would be better for you & you'd rather wait & come Sunday, that's all rite with me too. Any time. But I like Sat nite too. Love, Daisy

---

May 11, 1934 CSTC

Dear Ellis – (Fri 2 PM) I must say that I am quite overwhelmed by all the correspondence, and sympathy expressed. It made me feel rather guilty & ashamed of myself for not having been sick enough to deserve it all. It also made me wonder what would happen if I were to be really ill. Guess I'll have to try it sometime & find out, shall I? But, seriously, I really did appreciate your thoughtfulness (& do). And even when I was feeling awfully good, it made me feel lots better. Wanta dance & sing & everything. I will devote my excess energy to my work this weekend and see how much I can accomplish. (Don't hold your breath in expectancy.) I hope this reaches you Saturday nite & have a good time when you're home. Do you know what I liked best about your messages? It was the last word. And I'm sending it back to you. Love, Daisy

---

May 12, 1934 CSTC

Dear Ellis — (Sat nite 11:45 PM) You're a perfect darling - but, honestly, this is getting too funny for words. I'm looking forward every day now to see a message of sympathy awaiting me in the mailbox when I get home. I'm going to stay sick so I'll hear from you every day. It would be worth it. If you were the judge, I could be drawing on my health insurance policy. But really, darling, I love to get them. I wish I could do something besides getting sick, so you would write me every day. It's lonesome as the grave here tonite - only two people at this end of the hall. Just about 20 people left in the whole dorm this weekend. I'm working in the dining room & - it's 12, and I promised myself to be in bed by 12, so good-nite. With love, Daisy

(10:20 AM Sun) Dear E - going to church in about 2 jerks. Love, Daisy

(12:15) Back from church & starting to clean house. Rainy, but the air is warm & sweet. Got breakfast all alone this morning for all the girls in the dorm (about 12 came). There's nothing so lonesome (or so scary at night) as a big empty building. Now I can really understand how it is for you to go home all alone every nite with no one to talk to. I'd just about pop if Helen weren't coming back this afternoon. I'll probably talk so much I'll drive her away again. Must get busy now. I find that work is the best cure for loneliness. (To be continued later.) Love, Daisy

(9:15 Sun nite) Dear Ellis - I guess I've talked everyone to sleep. Helen is all tired out & went to bed & I've talked a leg off from everyone else too. But gee, it sure is grand to have someone to talk to again. The solitude was getting me down. However, after a week of companionship again, I'll be back to normal. Went to the library this PM with Denno when she came back, & Bob Webb & Clarice & their younger brother & sister were here this afternoon to see me, & Shirley came back at 4:30, & June & Helen & family at 5:30. Helen weary from her weekend at home, you know, & a couple flat tires coming back (real ones - her brother brought her). They've got the sweetest little girl - Carol Joan - lively as they come & into everything - same age as Jimmy. Down to Harry's place tonite with

Shirley for a hamburg & just got back. Only 9:25 now but no one's left to talk to so guess I'll go to bed & get up early with lots of zip & pep & energy, etc. all ready to start a new week. Feeling fine now. Makes me feel better every time I read your cards again. Just like a tonic. O, you were awful sweet to me. I'll be seeing you soon, won't I? But it won't be soon enough, so I'll send you my – Love, Daisy

Although I could find nothing online about a "Harry's" in Mt Pleasant in the 1930s, in an earlier letter to her folks, Mom enclosed some clippings from the Central Life newspaper, and on the back of one was a small ad for "Harry's Sandwich Shop: Hamburgs & Red Hots, Best in Town." There was no street address, but I assume it was very close to campus, as Mom and her friends went there often.

May 24, 1934   CSTC

Dear Ellis – (2:30 PM) It certainly is a grand day now. A half hour ago I was inclined to think it a bit cool, but since I discovered we don't have Latin class today, everything is rosy. It's positively ridiculous to see the spasms of joy everyone goes into when she discovers class doesn't meet. Anyway I'm feeling fine now. I wrote to you last night, but the letter's so crazy you wouldn't understand anything in it. We have been attending the music festival here, May 22, 23 & 24. It has been fine so far & expect it will be fine tonite. Tuesday nite was Mt Pleasant Civic Chorus, 135 voices, & Mt Pleasant Symphonic Band, 90 pieces. Last night was Central's a cappella choir & Lillian Knowles, contralto; William Miller, tenor; Helen Freund, soprano; & Barre Hill, baritone. Barre Hill was by far the best. He was the last half of the program (& 6

"Church- found" South Portico Ronan Hall

encores). Helen Freund was awfully sweet & is here again tonite & Knowles & Miller. I'm enjoying it all especially as instructors have considerably lightened their assignments "in order that we might attend" (as if that would stop us if we wanted to go). It was such a nice letter from you yesterday. I'm glad you like my picture. But weren't you kidding me just a little about "the blues & lonesomeness"? An attractive & unattached young man like you really shouldn't be lonesome. I think it would be just grand for everyone concerned to have the cottage at Reed's Lake. And, by the way, do you think you'd have it by June 9? You know my roommate & I are coming to Grand Rapids then – and does this junior executive have a ball & chain? Or might there be possibilities – for my roommate? Helen & I are going to Flint Saturday morning & shopping, etc. & return Sunday. We were downtown bumming around & enjoying ourselves this morning 10-12. We served at a dinner last night in honor of Mr Grawn, former president of CSTC. I'm glad you enjoyed the House of Rothschild. Surely you don't think I would recommend any picture not beneficial to you, do you? Don't take me too seriously. I must go to Natural Dancing class now & if there's anything I haven't said, it's because I'm in a hurry. But I'm not too rushed to send you – Love, Daisy

---

May 27, 1934   Flint, MI

Dear Ellis – (Sat PM) I'm here, having a fine time. Came down with Sup't of M.S.D & visited school for deaf. Went to the circus last night. Haven't seen anything of Dillinger yet. Your pal, Daisy

This is a postcard of Genesee County Courthouse

MSD was the Michigan School for the Deaf. When it first opened in 1854 it was called simply The Michigan Asylum and also had blind students. It officially became the MSD in 1884 and is still in operation today.

May 29, 1934   CSTC

Dear Ellis – (Sun nite 12m) The end has come to a grand & glorious weekend. And part of what made it so was your letter waiting for me when I returned today. We went to Flint Friday at 2 with Mr Gilbert, the Superintendent of the M School for the Deaf, who spoke in assembly in the morning. We stayed with Ida May Clapper (she went here last year). Friday nite we went to the circus given by the Homedale School (6 grades, 1,000 kids) where Ida May teaches. A regular circus in miniature – it surely was clever. Bed at 11 & we were going to get up early & go shopping the next morning, but at 9:30 Ida May woke us & brought us breakfast in bed. Pretty nice. She was just swell to us all the time – Sat we spent all day shopping around & at 4 we visited Helen's cousin & family (family consisting of one 7 ½ lb girl, Patty Sue). At 7 we had dinner with Ida May & the Rands (where she stays) & at 8 took in a show & dance & beer garden. You can supply the details there. We came to Owosso with Mr Rand in time for 9:15 Mass this morning. Breakfasted at Rose's Sweet Shoppe & began our first experience at hitch-hiking. A total of 4 rides & no walking brought us to the dorm at 1 PM, tired but happy. Dinner, bath, library, nap, lunch, shampoo, etc. has constituted the rest of my day. I must admit that my eyes are a bit heavy now & I have done no studying for tomorrow but I don't regret a moment of the weekend. Still, there was something lacking that would have made it complete. Can you guess? If everything comes out OK we're going to Grand Rapids June 9. Are you going to be there then & if you are, would you like to come over Sat nite, you & another fellow, or do you still think I'm kidding? I'm not. Wednesday, I guess, we're going home with Shirley to Clare & spend the day. I'm going home this weekend, I'm quite sure. And just three weeks from now I'll be home to stay. I'll be so glad. Then I can go to bed & not worry about anything. I worry so much now, you know. I'm afraid this isn't an awfully nice letter but I'm so sleepy. Your letter was so nice & I appreciated it. If this letter isn't so nice, will you forgive – Your Daisy, with Love

Homedale School in Flint opened in 1913, closed in 2004 and was demolished several years later.

May 30, 1934   CSTC

Dear Ellis – (nite) Here's hoping you're feeling more comfortable than I am now. Had a perfectly perfect day & now I'm paying for it. But in fact I'm more lightly touched by Old Sol than the other 5 of the party. Went home with Shirley yesterday to spend Decoration Day & how we did spend it! Shirley lives on a farm 7 miles from Clare in the nicest big house – about 12 rooms. We all went to the show last night – "Stand Up & Cheer." I liked it. Then had ginger ale & crackers & bologna & pumpkin pie & to bed at 12:30. Up at 9 & to the river– Helen & I lying on the fenders – swimming – a weenie roast, potato salad & cherry pie – Mmmm! I really tried to keep out of the sun – I was cured last year, but I just couldn't keep out of the water. So now I resemble a boiled lobster – or something of the sort – anyhow, awfully very red. A sheep & lamb got into our lunch. Otherwise everything lovely. Oh – mosquitoes too, but they don't bite me. Back to Shirley's – Allens' – at 3. Slept on the davenport 'til 5. Dorm at 6. And – a picnic lunch. Instead of regular dinner it was put up in form of picnic boxes. Nice though. Downtown to buy lotion & June Current History (so we could study). Sundaes at the Inn & here I am. Now that that's all over – probably gained 5 pounds. I'm going home Friday for another weekend. Seems like weekends have been coming thick & fast around here lately. I don't mind a bit except I'm never here long enough to get anything done anymore. Read the book that's been hanging over my head all term on Monday nite & gave my report on Tuesday morning. It's such a relief. Now I feel as if I've nothing to worry about. I hope your Decoration Day was

*just as enjoyable as mine & that you can read this so you'll know I'm hoping
so. I'd hardly know what's written here myself if I had to depend on reading it
I guess. But I'll tell you – if you can't read this, you keep it & I'll transcribe it
for you sometime. Harry would like to come to Grand Rapids next weekend if
he can & I think he will. The Ronan Round Table is going on a picnic/weenie
roast tomorrow nite & Helen & I compose the entertainment committee. We've
decided to make it an old-fashioned school picnic & play games, like poison
tag, cheesit, Farmer in the Dell, May I, etc. What do you think of the idea? Tell
you later how it works out. Maybe you think I'm sending a lot of envelopes
with not much in 'em too, but I like yours when this is in 'em – Love, Daisy*

The Ronan Round Table was a "literary society," a forerunner of
sororities. "Stand Up and Cheer" was a 1934 musical, consisting
mostly of song & dance numbers. It was a breakthrough film for Shirley
Temple, who went on to make ten more films that year.

June 5, 1934   CSTC

*Dear Ellis – (Tue nite 11:30) At last, after much debating pro & con, we
have made up our minds that the most sensible thing we can do is stay here
this weekend & devote our time to studying. We are very busy at this time
of year. This weekend we must read 2 Latin textbooks & write a review of
them, read a couple books on disarmament & other things too numerous to
mention. I'm working now, 2 FERA hours a day & my schedule is absolutely
full. The Physical Education Department is giving a program in assembly
Friday & our dancing class is putting on a dance & we practice every nite.
It's a winter skating dance only we don't wear skates. Couples – 8 of us,
Carl Larson is my partner, you know him – "president." Harry is coming
down Friday afternoon. I gave him your address, and ours, 26 Dickinson
SW. I said that the most sensible thing to do is for us to stay home, but did
you ever know us to do the most sensible thing? We're coming Saturday
morning, so we'll be prepared any time you come Sat nite, as early as you
want. And there will be no "hours." I'm having a lot of fun peeling my
sunburn. It was rather sore for a while but it was worth it. I had a nice
time when I was home this weekend. Steph & Pete are our neighbors now,
in Adams's house. Free show Friday nite, but I didn't go. The heat has
been almost unbearable for the past week. Here's hoping we'll have some
pleasanter weather this weekend. 'Til then. Love, Daisy*

Just a note: "Going to the show" almost always means the movies. It
was a phrase passed along to me and all of my siblings. We used it too.
You will note from Mom's letters she went to a lot of 'shows.'

June 11, 1934   CSTC

Dear Ellis — (Mon nite 12m). I'm not going to write what I intended to after all, I guess. I'm afraid you might take me up on it & I wouldn't want you to. I've been thinking & thinking 'til my head is going in circles so I'm going to quit thinking & accept things as they are. They are not now as they have been. I'm afraid they'll never be the same again. After one misunderstanding, it just seems that people can't return to the old levels again. I'd give anything in the world if I hadn't said the things I did. I don't know what made me do it. I guess in the first place I wanted to get it off my conscience. There's a great relief in confession – that's what that was intended to be – but in this case I think it would have caused a lot less heartache if I had just forgotten the episode completely. I've only had two dates with the fellow & I'll probably never see him again I hope. There might have been too an element of cattiness – wanting to make you jealous – but I don't like to think so. I'd like to blame it all on the beer & I was so dreadfully tired. I still am. You must have been awfully tired last nite too after driving all the way back. I do hope you don't have a "tough" week. And thanks again for bringing me home. When I think of all the times we've been together, I can't believe you'd be so willing to give back my ring. I guess I've just been kidding myself along probably. But I pride myself on being a good sport too. I can take it. You have said that you'll leave it all up to me. Now I'm putting it up to you. I want you to tell me – honestly & truly – if you are tired of me & I don't measure up to what you might have thought I was. If in any way I have disappointed you – please tell me. You know how I feel; don't let that influence what you have to say. I'll send your ring back to you if you want it. And if you're tired of looking at my picture, you can send that back too. I can't give back to you all that you've given to me, & no one can take it away. Now I'll probably cry myself to sleep, 'cause I guess I did write what I intended – but though I didn't have the courage to – but I'll get over it eventually. Meanwhile you may accept it or not as you wish, I'm sending you my – Love, Daisy

---

Jun 13, 1934   CSTC

Dear Ellis — (10) It was a sweet letter from you today, & I'm sorry I wrote you before when I was so tired & it was so late. I don't remember just what I wrote, but it must have sounded rather childish. I wish that if you haven't read it yet, as a favor to me, will you tear it up & throw it away? I know you must have been awfully tired & when I get letters like that from you it makes me want to be with you. I appreciate them just that much more when you write them then anyway. I'm just stealing a few minutes now when I should be doing something else. We've been cleaning our room – we're *going to have company tomorrow. Clarice Webb from Chesaning is visiting me tomorrow afternoon & going to dinner with me. And Ida May Clapper whom we stayed with when we were in Flint is coming tomorrow & staying overnite 'til Friday noon, when she & Marshall (her fellow) are leaving for Chicago & the Fair. Helen is somewhere studying with some kids for our Current History test tomorrow. I should be too, but here I am. We have a test in Health Ed tomorrow too. I suppose I'll have to study something for that too. The Cliophiles were going on a picnic tonite & we had our bathing suits all ready to go swimming & then we had it in Prof Larzelere's back yard, a lovely yard tho & a nice picnic – croquet, etc. We ate dinner here at 5:30 & there at 6:15. Can you imagine how I feel? Worse than that. But really not so bad now. I don't feel so bad tonite – kinda all straightened up with the world & everything seems to be working out OK. I've been getting to bed at 1 about every night for two weeks (except one – remember?) & up at 6, so I'm getting used to the hours & really think I don't need so much sleep. Six of us had a hamburger party last night (used my "griddle") – celebrating four June birthdays – & were they good! Mmmm! (The hamburgers I mean.) I've been working for Miss Ryan 2 or 3 hours a day FERA. And must put in about 8 hours more Thurs-Fri. We're going to have a show rush tomorrow nite – Jack Oakie & Spencer Tracy in something. Afterwards Miss Omlor has invited Helen & June & Shirley & I down for a party. We've been wasting gobs of time running around having people sign our Chippewa's & signing theirs but I think it will be worth it sometime. I'll be glad to get home Friday nite & get into the habit of sleeping again. I don't think it will be hard, & then my address will be Oakley. The RRT had our ice cream social Monday nite & it rained cats & dogs while the abbreviated Senior Swing-out took place – so we made $1.15 on the social. We're having tests in Natural Dancing today & tomorrow – accomplishment tests on the floor. Don't mind it so much. It'll be Saturday nite when you get this so I'll say I hope your week was successful & the next one will be more so & then too I want you to know that I'll be thinking of you now like I do every nite & all day too. With love, Daisy*

P.S. No. 1 – I want to thank you too for the grand time you showed me in Grand Rapids & thanks for bringing me back. You just didn't want me to be a tramp, did you? I appreciate your solicitude. Really. And I'm sorry I rather spoiled the last part of the trip back. I won't every again. Love, Daisy

P.S. No. 2 – If you're ever planning to come to Oakley, don't wait for me to ask you. I want you anytime. Just let me know when you're coming so I'll be there. Love, Daisy

P.S. No. 3 – I guess you'll need your glasses to read this.

Larzelere Hall is a residence dorm for CMU honor students, named for Mom's history professor, Claude S. Larzelere.

Jun 17, 1934 Oakley

Dear Ellis — (11:30 PM) It's good to be home again, quite grand anyway, that is, from all angles but one, & I'm just as well-situated here as I was at Mt Pleasant from that one. I guess I rather messed that up, didn't I? I didn't make it very clear what I intended to say. I mean once you were here, but you're not now. It's hard to say just what I mean, but you get the point. It's not very easy to write, lying on the bed either, but it's comfortable, if not very convenient. We had our annual St Michael's parish chicken dinner today & it really was a marvelous success. It was held in the barn & 4 tents in the back yard of the parish residence, much better than it sounds. We had a very large crowd, & Keno & beer & everyone went away satisfied. I served from 12 to 3:30 & came home, intending to sleep a half hour & go back, but I didn't wake up until 7 & everything was all over. Nobody missed me anyway. Momma & Steph baked about 300 biscuits today & they surely were good. But I'm sorry to say she didn't use Bisquick. I guess the purchasers of the materials just didn't appreciate true quality. I'm sorry I didn't tell you about the dinner today if you wanted to come, but honest, it just slipped my mind. I know it just breaks your heart to miss it, doesn't it? I got home at 9 PM Friday nite & slept 13 hours straight, believe it or not. But that's not hard to believe knowing how well I like to sleep. I'm getting caught up enough now so I can enjoy staying up & luxuriate in the thought that there are no lessons for me to worry about. I guess it must have been the worry that was getting me down – the loss of sleep anyway – no matter what the cause. My nerves were on edge & I was irritable & I'm afraid not a very pleasant companion. I'm feeling much better now & - cross my heart – I'll do my best to be amiable & agreeable when I'm with you (& it isn't at all hard) & I hope it will be soon. All of which rather lengthy discussion brings me to the point of my whole letter. There is to be a party Saturday nite (June 23) in Bendis's "sheep shed," given by the Bendis boys in honor of Harold's Rosalie's & my birthdays. I would like very much for you to come if you would like to & find it not too inconvenient. The time – any time Sat nite – place – I'll be home. I hope you can come. You know I won't be offended if you don't, for I understand how circumstances are sometimes. But I'm hoping just so hard that you will. Love, Daisy

Bisquick was one of Dad's bestselling products when he was a traveling salesman for General Mills.

 PIECES OF A LIFE

Jun 26, 1934   Chicago

Dear Ellis — (Tue 8 PM) Thank you for the lovely gift. I'm enjoying it immensely. Had a grand swim this morning & guess we'll swim all day if it doesn't stop raining. Just ready to go. Take care of yourself. DCW

This is a postcard of The Avenue of Flags at Chicago's 1934 International Exposition

Jun 26, 1934   Chicago

Dear Ellis — (Tue 2 PM) The arrow points to where we are. Came from the other tower on "Madam Queen." On top of the world, but wish you were here too. D.

This is a postcard of The Skyride's twin steel towers at the Exposition

Jul 1, 1934   Oakley

Dear Ellis — (11 PM) Well, here I am, all set & can't think what to start with. You said you like to read so I decided when we were coming home tonite that I'd write & write & write so you can read & read & read. I thought of just oodles of things to tell you but I think them all out & forget them & when I do write my thoughts get so far ahead of my pen that I don't say ever all the things I've meant to & here I've wasted a whole half-page saying what adds up to absolutely nothing. I meant to save this for the end but I won't remember it then so I'll say it now – my intention is to write you such a long letter that you'll get tired of reading it & then write me a long, long one so it'll take me a long time to read it & I won't have any time left to write much. This is nonsense but you asked for it. I haven't written in my diary since June 13, I owe letters to June & Shirley & Helen, but I had only one stamp so you see you're the only one I'm faithful to. Helen is going to summer school & Harry has been working in the Hotel 'til this weekend, is quitting Friday. She wanted us to have a reunion this weekend if you & I could have come & would have stayed over but I didn't get her letter until Thursday nite & that was too late to do anything about it. It would've been fun tho, wouldn't it? And that reminds me - I didn't get the letter I was looking for - telling me you were coming Saturday nite which you vowed so religiously that you wrote. But I guess that makes us even now, doesn't it? Only I really did write a letter even if I didn't send it. I'll bet you didn't. But I'm so glad you came anyway - surprises are always so nice - especially when the surprise is you. I was feeling just a little blue about your not coming & not writing. I prayed that you would come anyway & another time my prayers *were answered. You must have been right here in Oakley while I was on my knees. It seems rather funny now to think about it, but it wasn't a bit funny then. I guess I didn't talk very much, did I, but it wasn't because I wasn't glad. There were a million things I wanted to say but I couldn't & anyhow it didn't even seem necessary or important to say anything. Please don't regret what has gone by. It doesn't seem right to have memories tinged by regrets. Life is too short. Trite, but true. I loved having you with me & I'm sorry if it wasn't as perfect as it might have been. Sounds awfully philosophical, etc. but I really mean it. To get back to earth again – I did have a nice time at the Fair & enjoyed it a lot, but, frankly, I was rather disappointed in it. I don't know what I could have expected – magic, I guess. Of course we didn't even see a good sample of it in 2 days spent there. We really had nice weather too. But Thursday when we came back it was "102 in the shade" – as they told us when we stopped for a cooling drink – of course that made us feel lots better. We stopped at the House of David & ate our lunch there & went back into their park – really cool & nice there. We camped at Manhattan Beach Park on 75th Street on the Lake in Chicago – nice beach – wish I'd had more time to enjoy that part of it. (Stop for refill & guess I'll have to quit pretty soon. Bet you wish I'd quit before I started.) We're not going to St Ignace this week I guess. Mother & Dad got rather tired at the fair & decided they'd rather wait & so later we're going to spend a week at a lake & I can have Shirley or June or someone with me. I like that idea better anyway. So we'll be home the 4th. We'll probably go to the St Charles parish picnic that day. There's a "Carnival Dance" in Oakley the 4th too. Prizes given – beer & eats. I'll be good & stay home probably. Clarence was home last nite & today & according to reports still likes his job. He's been promoted already – $24 a week starting tomorrow. I think I'd like that too. O dear, afraid I'm getting a little sleepy. Did I hear you say, "At last!"? If the "Big Boss" knows Ellis very well, I'm sure it wasn't his "walking papers" he was bringing. But I'm really sorry that you don't like your job & I hope you'll find something that will make you happy. If it's California, the best of luck to you & my most sincere wishes for your success. Honestly. But I should think it would be hot enough for you in Michigan. It has been nice today tho, & just right to sleep tonite. We were up to Ronds's discussing family inheritance, reunions, etc., etc. And tomorrow is wash day. Oh well, I really don't mind it. Now that I've written all this mess, I'm sorry if I've bored you & I hope you cans still read it, tho it doesn't matter much if you can't. There, caught myself napping – must be closing time. Good nite, my dear. Love, Daisy*

And come & see me when you can, won't you? You've no idea how lonesome I get. But maybe you do too. Love, Daisy

Jul 17, 1934   Oakley

Dear Ellis – (9:45 PM) I just had to read your letter again – it was such a nice letter. I'm glad you've moved in with Bud. I'm sure you'll fit it a lot jollier living with someone like he is. You can have a lot of fun together & you won't get lonesome when there someone around to talk to when you come home. You'll find that a compatible roommate is a priceless thing. There's nothing like having someone around to make you snap out of it when you get blue & "down in the dumps." And when you both feel that way at the same time, it's so funny when you begin condoling together that you can't help laughing. Helen & I used to always get broke about the same time & grieve together until we'd both realize it was just a big joke & laugh. Once we were telling each other about our dogs we used to have – dead now – & we actually both cried – then it was so funny we had to laugh. Well, I didn't start out to write so much on that subject but I really mean it. I hope that you & Bud will stick together & be as good pals as Helen & I have been for two years – and hope to be for two more anyway. And it'll not just be "blue-ing" it together – you'll have grand times too. I'm going to Central this weekend for a reunion with our gang – Shirley & June, Helen & I, & are we going to have fun! O boy! Will the dormitory be glad to see us back – mostly old dames attending summer school to renew teaching certificates. Leaving Friday & returning Sunday or Monday. It surely will seem grand. Shirley isn't coming back next year – going to business school in Detroit. So we'll raise the roof for one grand & glorious weekend as a farewell for Shirley. We had a thunder shower tonite at 9 – but it's all over now, I guess – rained quite hard for a few minutes. Have seen two good shows – "Little Miss Marker" – with Shirley Temple – 5 year-old star. It was really worth seeing, I thought – story of the racing game & a little girl who was taken as a "marker" & then her father killed himself because his horse lost. Really good. The other was "You Made Me Love You" – Thelma Todd & Stanley Lupino – a scream from start to finish – best comedy picture I've seen in ages. Down to Dorothy & Alfred's last nite & Jerri & I had a big ball game – score 9-2 – he won – rather novel method of scoring but we had fun anyway. Harold & Helen were down to dinner Sunday Jimmy getting more devilish every day & Rosalie more angelic (when she sleeps). For once in my life I seem to be out of material to talk about. I'm getting rather sleepy. I hope Katherine has a nice trip thru Europe. I know she will. I suppose dear Miss Barnard will be there too. I'm sticking close to Michigan, again – rather like it too. My eyes won't stay open a moment longer, dear, so now I guess it's my time to – dream – a visit & Loads o' Love from Daisy

Dad's new roommate was a fellow salesman with General Mills, Helmer Joseph Vidar Brorby, but he was always just "Bud" to Dad, and to our family. They remained good friends throughout their lives.

Jul 19, 1934   Oakley

*Dear Ellis — Well, ol' pal, how's tricks? Hope the world's treating you as
well as it's been treating me lately. Don't mind the weather at all when I'm
busy, & when I'm not, I just keep cool. Excuse - please - going to show,
"Baby, Take a Bow." - 10PM Shirley Temple & it was just very awfully good
- even better than "Little Miss Marker," I think. Just had a piece of fresh
cherry pie "a la mud" & was it good! Mmm. Not so good for the digestion
tho, I fear. When I started to write this I'd just come from an Altar Society
PM gossip circle at Steph's. Pete has been laid off for a couple of weeks
now & just came from a trip north with a load of plow-points this AM.
The "Highway Comm." I haven't seen for a couple of weeks, but he got his
first check Monday morning & I suppose he's still walking on air. Went to
band concert & free show in Chesaning last night. Had the Chevy up to
75 & not wide open on the way to Owosso tonite. More fun. I had a grand
time last weekend. Went up on Friday & back on Monday. St Louis Friday
nite - Crystal Saturday afternoon - swimming, toboggans, etc. - dance -
Bass Lake to dance - nice pavilion there. Good orchestra - then to Winn
at the good old-fashioned dance we looked in on one night & was it fun!
Home at 1. And not a minute too soon. 9:00 Mass Sun AM & 10:30 church
at Methodist church. Had to do something to even up the score. The Rev's
sermon was "God Almighty & the School Teacher." In the PM we slept &
read & recuperated for the evening. Coldwater Lake in the evening - dance
at the "Wigwam" there. Best time of all. The place was lousy with oil men
& the surprising thing was that no one was drunk & they were all so nice.
I don't mean to suggest that they weren't nice at all the other places too. I
saw all the others off Monday & didn't leave 'til 4. Helen & I had a good old
long talk together 'n' so ended a grand weekend. Helen & I wanted us to be
together - you & Harry & she & I - next weekend - 28th & I wish we could,
but I couldn't on account of our reunion being then, etc. Margaret Clark
has got scarlet fever. Just found it out today. Hope the whole town doesn't
get it. I'm glad you enjoyed the game Sunday. I almost got there myself.
Have you got anything on for next weekend? If you haven't & would like to,
I would like very much to have you come out to Palmer's Park in Lansing
Sunday where our reunion is going to be & join in the festivities, etc., or
if you would like, to the ol' home town on Sat nite - & from there Sun - if
you've nothing else you'd rather do. R.S.V.P. Momma says thank you very
much for the present, & when you come out she will serve you sugar &
cream from it. Sorry you don't like the "cleaning up" - but it does have to
be done, doesn't it? Isn't that comforting? And so to bed - "to sleep - aye to
sleep - perchance to dream" - but I'll be 2 cents that even Bill Shakespeare
couldn't sleep on a nite like this. Yours, with love, Daisy*

Jul 30, 1934   Oakley

Dear Ellis – (Mon nite 9:45 CST) C.S.T., in case you're curious, is "conscience-saving-time" – by my clock, an hour or so slower that daylight savings time. It makes me think I get up very early in the morning & go to bed very early too. Tonight I saw the Baer-Carnera fight picture, round by round, & "Monte Carlo Nights," the first-mentioned better than the last. It is a very dark night & the stars are all out in their glory – & no moon. So I takes my little star-map & goes out star-gazing, intent on finding Bootes & Cassiopeia's chair, etc. etc., but the Big Dipper was cockeyed & there were a million more stars in the sky than there were on my chart, so I gave up & had some apple pie for consolation. I did locate the North Star tho, and the pie I remembered to put salt in the crust (my pet failing) & almost sliced my thumb in with the apples, so I enjoyed it very much, even if it will keep me awake. But I'm rather sleep rite now & my arm aches. Please excuse the penmanship. I'm very comfortable myself, but a penmanshipper would never advise this position, I think; very apt to get ink on the sheets too ... 15 min later – especially when one goes to sleep with pen in hand as I just did. You must be having a grand time with such a full summer social schedule. I hope you are – the summer is all too short anyway, isn't it? When you go to Crystal & Lake Michigan, take an extra swim for me, will you? Wish I had a lake at my back door. But hasn't the cooler weather been heaven sent? Last night we had an electrical storm that left the whole sky alight for minutes at a time, it seemed. Clarence was home for Sunday – next week he does not work & will be home all week. Sorry you couldn't come Sun. It was OK, of course. You probably wouldn't have enjoyed it much anyway, usual family affair. I've been collecting info for a paper on the history of the Oakley school, which will be read at the school reunion Saturday. Kinda fun interviewing people, etc. Thursday the Ladies Altar Society meets here & I guess they're going to tie a quilt. Next Sunday, Aug 5, we have 13 Hours Devotion here. I'm so sleepy I must close before I make a blunder. I'm glad you're with Bud so you won't get lonesome anymore during these lovely summer evenings. And may an "Old Friend" send her love to an "Old Friend"? Good-nite, Daisy

The Max Baer vs. Primo Carnera fight (June 14, 1934 at Madison Square Garden) was for the heavyweight championship. Baer creamed Carnera, knocking him down nearly a dozen times before the referee stopped the fight in the 11th round.

Aug 14, 1934   Oakley

Dear Ellis — (Tue nite 9 PM) Gee, it was no nice to see your letter waiting for me when I got home Sun nite about 9, tired & dirty & brown as an Indian. I'd been spending the week at Bay City State Park camping with 9 Oakley girls - Helen Jones, Audrey Owen, Betty Smith, Norma, Betty & Ruth Dearman, Gertrude Mormon, Emily Hill & Mary Ellen Jones. I'm not sure that it was because of or in spite of the crowd, but I had a corking good time, mostly in the water. Had one exciting day Wed, when the wind blew so hard one or our tents came down & it rained in sheets - but some kind neighbors put our tent up for us & we all survived. Left here Sun Aug 5th & returned Sun Aug 12 & came home 6 shades darker - 5 when the surface layer was washed off, & so tired that even the alarm couldn't affect me Mon morning. I meant to write you last nite but you wouldn't have enjoyed the kind of letter I'd have written. I saw "Here Comes the Navy" - James Cagney - darn good, & I nearly went to sleep, but I'm feeling lots better today & by tomorrow should be quite myself again. In the morning I'm going to start making me another school dress. We went to Saginaw this afternoon - saw Clarence - he was home all last week while I was gone - he might go on the marker (tar) this week & if he does he'll go to Muskegon. Next week we're going on a trip to Kentucky (caves, etc.) & Virginia. If Clarence is home, he'll go, & if he isn't, I'm going to take Betty Mae Smith along. We had some fun here a week ago Thursday when we had the cyclone, hailstorm & cloudburst here. The Ladies Altar Society was meeting at the house & you can imagine the rest. There wasn't a great deal of damage done around here. Everything is greener now than it has been since spring. I'd changed my mind about coming to G.R. this summer but Tom & Aunt Stacia were here while I was gone & want me to come, so I might be out the first week of September. Are you still gonna come over & see me then, or are you "mad" because I waited so long to write? I'm sorry. After getting up at 6 AM to go swimming every day for a week, I think I'll spend a few days joining in your sleeping game, & Brother, you'll have to be darn good to beat me. Hope you have a microscope handy so you can read this. Love, Daisy

P.S. The dirt wasn't on my nose, it got on the picture. This is how I look now. Brown. Taken Sat nite Aug 11 [no photo found].

From Mom's earlier comment about the "Highway Commissioner," and Clarence's extended absences with time off, the Marker [truck] and 'tar,' working in Saginaw & Muskegon, it's probable that her brother was employed on a road construction and repair crew that summer. He would have been 20.

Aug 19, 1934   Oakley

Dear Ellis – (11:30 PM) Just a week more & oh gee, I'll be so glad to see you. It seems ages & the summer has gone like lightning too. It's been so cold here the last few days. Feels like a frost tonite. I do so hate to see summer die so quickly. I hope it's warm next week. Sounds like a discourse on the weather, doesn't it? Back from our trip Sat afternoon. Thru Ohio, Kentucky, Virginia, West Virginia; back thru Ohio to Michigan. Mostly thru the mountains. We had a grand trip, & the best of it, as usual, was coming home (& finding your letter– nice one too). I surely would have liked to be with you for the Fair & this week, but, you see, I just couldn't. It seems that my time at home this summer has just been "in-between weeks" – getting over one jaunt & ready to go on another. We're all going to Aunt Stacia's Sat & stay over Labor Day. Come over whenever you have time & I'll probably be there. I had a number of things in mind to tell you when I began this but now I just can't remember them. My eyes persist in going shut when I'm not looking. I'm propped up with pillows here, in bed with an Indian blanket (Ol' Faithful) around me to keep warm & I guess I'm too comfortable to be conscientious. So Good-nite, my Dearest Dear, I'll be looking for you to drop around in Grand Rapids. Love, Daisy

---

Aug 26, 1934   Oakley

Dearest Man I Know, Ellis – (Sun nite 10:15) Grand Rapids & you have spoiled me now. I want to go right on seeing you as often even when I know you're a hundred miles away. But if I can't see you, I can do the next best thing, & I'm doing it now. The sky is so bright with stars tonight –rather unusual. I'm glad it isn't raining, because then I know I couldn't stand it. I'm not really lonesome tonite tho. I feel so happy & breathless, as if I'd just left you somewhere. I know I'm going to miss you & want to write to you lots of times when I won't even have time to write, so if later I don't write you so often, you know it'll not be that I don't think of you. Please don't read that twice. I know it sounds rather asinine but it isn't supposed to make sense. I really thought of some nice things to say before I got my pen out but now they've left me. I want to thank you for being so nice to me in G.R. & bringing me home & everything. You've been awfully sweet to me. The girls tell me to take all I can get & not give anything but I've always felt that I want to give as much as I'm getting. I hope sometime I can make you as happy as you've made me for a week. I hope you're having just a grand time in Detroit & can get loads of sleep when you get back, 'cause if your eyes droop like mine do tonite, you need it too. Dorothy & Alfred & 2 kids came for dinner today & we went over to Flushing & saw the new coal mine. Maybe I'm going down in it sometime too. Then tonite we saw "Dames" & – "spotty" or not, I surely enjoyed it. When we came out there was a waiting line for the balcony halfway downstairs. My mouth won't stay shut & my eyes won't stay open so what can I do? I know you won't get this 'til Friday but I couldn't wait any longer to send you something you left me with & I'll be waiting for you to send back – Love, Daisy

P.S. Loads of it, but none for anybody else but you.

(Mon 11 PM) – Dear Ellis – Just saw "Dragon Murder Case" & "Tillie & Gus" – Not bad. It's been a lovely day. We don't have rain in Oakley. But I think of you even when the sun shines & the stars. Love, Daisy

Tue 7:30 AM – I beg your most humble pardon, my dear. It's raining here this morning too. L, D

Sep 11, 1934   Oakley

Dear Ellis — 9:45 Tuesday night & I haven't mailed your letter yet, so thought I might as well add to it now. Had a thunderstorm this afternoon about 3 & oboy did it rain! & thunder! & lightning! I went to sleep in the middle of it – slept right through the rainbow & the sun was reflecting on the clouds in the east when I woke up about 6:30. I had sweet dreams too – dreamed about you. Joe Bila & Agnes were married Sunday afternoon & are having their dance, etc. Saturday nite. Steph is having a shower for them tomorrow nite. Pete is having his party tonite – pheasant supper & beer. Steph came & invited us over but we didn't go. I got a letter from Helen this morning. Almost knocked the pins from under me 'cause I'd only written to her Friday & she always waits at least 2 weeks to answer. But she's an invalid now & didn't have anything else to do. She sprained 2 tendons in her leg when she was pushing the car trying to get it started. But she'll be up soon & back to school all right, I think. I guess our thoughts about Harry & Helen were just wasted. They seem to have 'busted up.' From the tone of Helen's letter I guess something happened to change her opinion of Harry. I'm really sorry. Helen said to say "hello" to you from her, so "hello." I'm making me a brown wool crepe dress. Cut it out this morning & basted part of it this PM but it got so dark I couldn't see to sew so I went on strike – at least until tomorrow. I'll bet you wish I'd go on a strike & not write so much. I guess you'll have to read this in shifts. I like to write to you tho, it's almost as good as talking to you. I can picture you to myself, & hear what you say to me too, but when it's late & bedtime, sometimes I wish the picture were a bit more substantial – so I could kiss you good-nite. I still have one for each nite this week & next, but what'll I do when I run out? Then your ring will have to do, unless you send me some. Love & kisses, Daisy

Sep 19, 1934   Oakley

Dear Ellis — (Wed 8:45 PM) I wouldn't for the world disappoint you if I can possibly help it, so I hope this is waiting for you Friday nite when you get in. it really isn't much to look forward to but I'll make it the best I can by sending lots of Love right at the start. You're just as dear as you can be & I'm sending you a kiss for every day of the week too - xxxxxxx & x one to grow on. Seems rather early for me to be retiring but I must take my sleep while I can get it - just about 3 more nites of it. I had to search my old Current History notebook for stationery & just looking at it gave me the jim-jam jitters. I'm trying not to think of anything like that until I can't get out of it at all. Sounds terrible I know, but - it could be worse, I guess. Dear, I'm awfully sorry that your eyes are troubling you & don't put off getting your glasses. And if this will help any, I know I'll like you just as much in "specs" as out of them - maybe more - who knows? We were up watching the stone-crusher tonite - Harold's working there. It's so noisy that you have to scream to make yourself heard. I don't think I ever could work there. I'd die I know if I couldn't talk. Clarence came home last Thursday nite - got to St Charles & we had to go & get him - had a broken axle on the car. He decided he'd be better off without a car, so it's still in the barn. We went to the Saginaw Fair Friday afternoon & nite - exhibits good & floor show at nite better. But you know all the things one eats at a fair - well, they didn't all or any agree with me & I didn't sleep so well. And that was the night of the last free show in Oakley & I missed it - tragic. Sunday at 2 the WLS Barn Dance Crew were at the fairgrounds & gave a performance. They weren't much better than what we saw at the Capitol. Hal O'Halloran, Mac & Bob, 3 Neighbor Boys, Skyland Scottie, 3 Harmonica Hounds, band & a girl whistler. I haven't done much of anything but sew this week & last. I made me another dress & a lot of little odds & ends that take time when there's a lot of them to do. I was down to Lily Madden's this afternoon. She's leaving for Florida Friday morning & is all upset packing, etc. I guess she isn't ever coming back. It gave me a rather funny feeling to think I'll probably never see her again. I like her a lot. I'm awfully glad that you & Bud got the prize in the sales contest 'n' keep up the good work too. I'm glad you had a good time in Carson City too. I'm sorry but I can't excuse "body & arrangements, content & form" of your letter. I want them just like they are. There's the most gorgeous moon tonight. It seems the moon is always here when you're not. If I could only have it, and you too. I guess you & I & the moon never can get together - but I can do without the moon. Love, Daisy

1935

1935 Chippewa

Sep 25, 1934   221 Ronan Hall, CSTC

Dear Ellis — I was almost afraid to hope for a letter so soon, but there it was – & I think I ran all the way upstairs. I'm sorry you were so lonesome & blue & I hope you felt heaps better the next morning. Sunshine does make a lot of difference, doesn't it? After Sunday we've had lovely weather here. It has been warm & nice just like summer yesterday & today. Sunday it rained & I didn't feel a bit pepped up about coming back & Helen felt the same way I discovered when I arrived so we didn't make each other feel any better. But after we had unpacked everything we went down to Harry's & had a hamburg & saw "Chained" with Joan Crawford & Clark Gable, & Olympia afterwards. That helped a little but the feeling still persists. Yesterday we just bummed around seeing some of the old kids, instructors, etc. In the afternoon we went downtown & got us material for bedspreads but we haven't got them made yet – probably by Xmas. I'm going to work for Mr Lantz in the new Training School – office work 1 ½ hours every day – 3:30-5 & 4 hours Sat morning. Guess that means I get home just about once this term & work 8 hours some Saturday to make up for it. There was a women's mixer last night in the gym but – as usual – Helen & I went to sleep about 7:30 & when we awoke at 8:30 decided we'd rather go to bed – so we did. Tonight there's an All-College Conclave – Central's Fall Roundup – in the gym, & I guess we'll get to that – if we don't fall asleep on the way. I don't know whether you could call this starting out with a "wham" or not – right now I don't feel so "whammish." Everything was going along fine. I had my schedule just like I wanted it – & gym 2-4 – heavy apparatus & tumbling & badminton – & I wanted to take it awfully bad but I found I had to go to work at 3:30, so that was all off. Then I went looking for Helen on 3rd floor & Miss Loughridge called me in to ask me why wasn't I taking French & tried to mess up my schedule so I could get it in & bawled me out in general so of course I felt just fine by that time. I just have to take the methods course now to get a minor in it but I'd like to drop it entirely. I disliked it enough before I finished my last course in it & she doesn't make me like it any better now. But if I dropped it, it would be just my luck to have an offer of a job teaching English & French or something. It's a mess any way you look at it. I kinda like my schedule now tho: 8 – English – Comparative Lit from Harry Miller. 9 – English Literature from Dr Beck. 10 – Home Ec from Miss McNinch. 1 – Government from Lazerlere – kinda dread that, but I'm glad you'll like me just as much if I fail. Miss Rogers is trying to organize a class in Beginning Tapping & if she succeeds & it fits my schedule, I'll take that. The Dorm dining room isn't open this year at all. The people from the Harmony have closed that & have taken over the college cafeteria, so now we eat there or the Inn – not much choice. I prefer the cafeteria. Helen is working there too. We called on Fr Mulvey Monday PM & he was awfully nice to us. We're going to use the church basement for a reception for all Catholic students some nite next week – the Mercier – Helen's president & I'm social chairman. We're going to try hard to make a real success of the club this year. Hope we can swing it. Our first football game is with Univ of Detroit there Sat nite. Oct 6 we play Ferris here. We have 8 games scheduled – 4 here – Oct 6, 13 & 20 & Nov 10 – Ferris, Hillsdale, Ypsi & Kazoo. The Mercier & the YW are giving a breakfast Sun at 8:30 for all new women students & we helped write invitations this afternoon. Besides that, haven't had much to do this afternoon. It's the hardest work I know – doing nothing – but that doesn't mean I'm at all anxious for classes to begin so I'll have something to do as some of the freshmen are saying. And if I recall correctly, I was once that nutty myself – but just once. This is getting more like a book, so I guess I'd better think about stopping soon. June's coming for me to eat in 10 minutes. Shirley isn't back, & June's way up on 3rd rooming with a freshman. Doesn't seem at all like old times. Shirley's going to Business College in Saginaw. Oh, & I have a new cousin, born Saturday nite Sept 22 on my folks' silver wedding anniversary – William Edward Clark – 6 ¼ lbs, curly blonde hair, & blue eyes, & is he sweet – & are they proud of him. Clarence was home Sunday & helped bring me back. Saw the best show Sat nite – "Death on the Diamond" – it sure was good – baseball picture – Robert Young & Madge Evans. Glad you beat Bud. Keep it up. You can do it – & have a good time at Don's. I'll probably be studying my gov't. Afraid it's going to be a bug-bear. And as far as worrying about all A's – did your ever know me to worry about anything like that? I'm so busy worrying about whether I've got a clean pair of hose without runs that I don't have time for anything like that. Next time maybe I'll have time to write you a letter instead of just a note like this. I do hope you won't be feeling lonesome & blue when you get this Friday nite, 'cause I'll be thinking about you with a heart full of – Love, Daisy

---

Oct 2, 1934   CSTC

Dearest Dear – (Tue nite 11 PM) Eleven o'clock & there goes my 10 o'clock resolution – but there are special occasions you know, & this is one of them. Your letter was so very nice that I just couldn't go to bed without answering it. So here I am, at your service, sir, & not very sleepy either, altho last nite it was 1, Sun nite 11, Sat nite 2, etc. And I don't waste any time anymore either. I'm so busy during the day that I don't even have time to get sleepy. I leave the dorm at 8, classes 'til 11, eat in cafeteria & study in the library until 1, Government class, study in library & work until 5. Home for 2 minutes, back to eat at the cafeteria, library until 8:30 & home to study until 11 & so to bed, & start all over again the next day. It's a full schedule & I'm working harder than I ever have here, but I like it. I'm more satisfied & contented this term than any term I've been here. Maybe there's a moral somewhere. I'm doing extra FERA work this week tho, so I won't have to work on Saturday. I'm going home Friday with Lucille Coppernal from Chapin & my folks will bring us back. Then I won't get home again until Thanksgiving. Your letter made me just a trifle homesick. I'm anxious to get home & make some fudge – & I'm gonna bring a lot back with me too, by gosh. I made a batch of peanut butter cookies (Aunt Stacia's recipe) just before I came up here on Sunday & I came away & didn't bring any with me. Wasn't that a shame? I think your card is cute, kinda nifty too. Nice to hear news about Don & Isabel. I'm glad you enjoyed your visit with them & that you thought of coming to see me, but when you lost, someone else lost too, I'm sure. I probably wouldn't have been here tho, Helen & I "went West" Sun nite – Mae West in "Belle of the Nineties." I don't think that's censored, is it? Anyway, I liked it & I like Mae West too, & a lot better than Joan Crawford. We spent a very busy weekend. Saturday I worked from 8 to 1, had lunch & slept until 2:30. Then for practically the remainder of the day & nite I printed dainty little programs for the Mercier & YWCA Sunday Breakfast, & of course we would have to have 4 pages to the things & we didn't finish them until after 1. Then Helen & I had to compose our speeches for the Bkfst, as of course, we were on the program too. But we felt well repaid Sunday at 8:30 when a hundred gals came & all the places were filled. Everything was a success & we went to 10:30 Mass & came home & made our bedspreads from our gingham plaid, bound in red tape & they're kinda cute too, we think. Wish you could come up & see them. Last nite we had a pajama party 10-10:30 in the dining room. We danced & had frost-bites & "we new officers" were introduced (ahem!) & a good time was had by all. We attended the faculty reception last Thursday nite, a rather nice affair & enjoyed it a lot. I guess that's about all that's happened since last I wrote. But do you know what was the nicest thing of all? It was something that made me postpone my bedtime a half-hour tonite, but I wish it could happen every nite. Honest I do. I dashed home at 11, just long enough to get your letter & read it & if you can imagine anything dryer than studying government, after reading an epistle like that, I don't know what it is. But I waded thru it & got to class & discovered I'd done tomorrow's assignment too. So you're going out for football. I hope I won't feel like that after my first gym class tomorrow. Maybe I would if it were tumbling, the class I wanted to take, but it's tap-dancing & I think it'll be a lot of fun. We're making plans now for a Mercier party Tuesday nite next & a reception in the church a week from Friday. We've been invited to join the Home Ec Club too, now that we're minoring in that, & their meeting is Thursday nite – a party honoring the freshmen girls. But I'm looking forward more to Friday nite when I'll be getting a good night's sleep – I hope. You said once you'd come to Oakley some weekend when I'd be home but I guess that & Thanksgiving & Christmas will be the only times. We'll be seeing each other sometime tho & don't think that I'm saying, "What about me," because I know what a long cold drive it is, especially alone, & I'll be thinking of you, ever so hard & kissing your ring over & over again each nite because you're not there. Love, so much I can't tell you here. Love xxx, Daisy

---

Oct 7, 1934   CSTC

Dearest Ellis – (Sun nite 10:45) I really worked hard to get my work done early so I could write to you but I'm leaving a special report for English until morning 'cause I don't have any 8:00 class & now I've forgotten everything I was going to say. I came back from home about 4:30 & unpacked, ate lunch, washed my hair, took a hot bath & then I had to study – home ec, etc.- only have 3 classes tomorrow tho, including tapping. Gee, I guess I'm too sleep to write this now. Guess I'd better go to bed & finish it tomorrow nite, but I just wanted you to know that I'm thinking about you, like I do every nite – & day too. With loads & worlds o' Love for Ellis from Daisy

> Parts of the letter below are smudged or indistinct, so 2-3 words missing will be rendered as '2-3M'.

(Mon nite 11 PM) Ellis, my dear – This is like a continued story. I should send it to you in installments too. I've been reading the Koran, the Mohammedan Bible – most-read book in the world & of all the assininity – I can't get

head or tail to it but I guess no one has ever been able to anyway & I'm no exception. I have also the Ramayana & Mahabharata from which I should read selections. Maybe – but I'd rather write to you than read – except your letters. Clarence came home over the weekend. We went out on Sat nite & went to the show – pretty good. Church at 8 Sunday. Went to Harold's – they've moved up to [2-3M] lived & Joe's moved into [1-2M]'s house. Of course I had to [hold] the 2-week-old Clark family addition, he's gained 1 ¼ lbs – weight 7 ½ pounds. I had time to make some peanut butter cookies & were they good! Mmm! My only regret is that I didn't have time to make any fudge. I felt so darn dead & tired when I got back & Helen feeling the same way. We sat around together until finally we gave up & went to bed. I guess we may be getting tired of school or something – not so hot as it might be. I finished my report this morning & [1-2M] have to give it. I don't like to have [1-2M]. I hope he gets to it tomorrow [several M] anything about it, but she wouldn't tell me what you did. I rather enjoy working with the freshman files – their application blanks with their records, recommendations, life stories, etc. Fun reading some of them. Quite a few freshmen here from Carson City, I've noticed. We have a Mercier party tomorrow nite & we're gonna play Bunco & Fr Mulvey's coming & we've invited all the students interested & I hope we have a good turnout. Are you working in Grand Rapids this week? Wish the weather weren't getting too undependable for hitch-hiking. Gee, it's been just grand here this week – just as warm & nice & trees just beginning to turn & an autumn haze along the horizon & I guess I've got "autumn fever" – a parallel of spring fever, if there is such a thing. Helen & I went downtown this afternoon & it was so nice. We've got a new dime store here so now it'll take us longer to make the rounds each trip. We skipped tapping class to go down & get some tap shoes. I worked 3:30-5 & ate & stayed in the library 'til 8:30 & came home & gossiped, studied, etc. & that brings me up to now, I guess, which reminds me my diary is just about up to last Thurs & after I catch up on that I may, can, & will retire & dream about you. Love X, Daisy (P.S. To be cont, maybe)

Oboy oboy, would I like it & how! Just rushed back here to see if I had a letter & I'll be walking on air the rest of the week now & just dying for Sat nite. Love, Daisy

---

Oct 14, 1934   CSTC

Ellis, my Dear – It's been such a perfect day (or as nearly perfect as it could be without you) that I just had to write & enjoy it with you because then it makes me twice as happy. I'm afraid I don't appreciate you nearly as much as I should when you're with me. I must tell you how much I enjoyed your company last nite & thank you for a lovely evening. I hope you enjoyed your day today as much as I did. Helen & I saw "The Barretts of Wimpole Street" tonite. It was really wonderful, one of those shows that you don't want to talk about after it's over. It made me cry sometimes, but I'm so glad it ended happily. And the advertisements I think now I have completely committed to memory. The weather continues grand & I think I wouldn't have had such a satisfying day if I hadn't had 10 hours sleep last night. We were up at 7 & brushed our teeth for 7:30 Mass, up at 8:30 & combed my hair for 9:00 Mass & at 10 we really did go to Mass, but only because there isn't a 12:00 Mass here. It was so warm & nice we didn't even wear a coat to church. We went to communion & came home & had a combination breakfast & dinner & cleaned our room & took a nap & studied in the library 3:30-4:30. Had lunch at 5:30 & went to the show. Got back at 9 & learned a selection of The Rubaiyat of Omar Khayyam for English. "The moving finger writes; & having writ, moves on. Nor all your Piety nor Wit shall lure it back to cancel half a line, nor all your tears wash out a word of it." To make the day complete I thought I'd share it with you. I have only three classes tomorrow – 9, 10 & 2 – and I'm all ready for them, so I'll be in bed at 10:15, dreaming of you. With love, Daisy

12:30 – Dear Ellis – Just so you'll know I was thinking about you. I've had a rather full evening. At 8:15 I flew the Atlantic with Amelia Earhart & it was thrilling. She was here for a lecture course program & she is just darling – so cute & a most delightful speaker. Her pictures do not do her justice. Then we went to a spread [1-2M] went downtown & danced 'til 10:30 & then came home & studied. 2 tests tomorrow, but let 'em come, I'm ready. I worked until 6 tonite & was awfully tired but after a bath, etc. I felt better & had an enjoyable evening & I'm still up but getting a trifle sleepy. The [2-3M] simply too good to be true. Every morning [2-3M] I hold my breath for fear it will [end of letter missing] ...

Yes, she's talking about THE Amelia Earhart, who was doing the lecture circuit then.

Oct (21?), 1934   CSTC

Dearest Ellis – (Sun 1 PM) I guess I really haven't got anything to tell you – I just feel like writing. I hope you don't mind. I'm just about in the middle of my weekend now – it didn't start until this morning, but I'm thoroughly enjoying it. It's quite cold today – wish I had my winter coat here. We went to 7:30 Mass & really got there on time – we caught a ride down tho. I worked 11 ½ hours yesterday: 8-11:30 in the training school, 1-5 downtown in the city offices typing for a democrat, & 7-11 typing at home for an oil man. It was kinda fun tho. Tomorrow I'm going to work downtown all afternoon again. I only have two classes, 9-11. And I work 8:30-10 PM in the training school – there is a parent-teacher meeting there then. We had our first snowfall yesterday – if you could call it that – it turned to rain before it reached the ground & wasn't nice at all. Last year our first snow came on October 24th. I wish it wouldn't snow for another month. Everyone says that this winter is going to be colder than last – cheerful thought. A year ago today we went to the Cathedral Woods & had a marshmallow roast – Harry & Helen & you & I – remember? I wish I could turn the calendar back a year, just for today. Gee, it's nearly Halloween again. Halloween doesn't mean a thing to me anymore, it seems. I wish it were Thanksgiving & time to go home. It seems so darn far away. I wish you could come out Thanksgiving weekend, if it isn't too cold & you wouldn't be doing something else. Wishing, wishing, and wishing! Guess I'd better stop & sleep a while. I'm getting so sleepy – I'll dream about you. Love, Daisy

---

Oct 24, 1934   CSTC

Dearest Ellis — (Wed nite 10:50 PM) I'm sorry that I can't make this a continued letter now but I hope you'll get just as much of a "kick" out of it anyway. I'm very comfortable – this is on a box on a pillow on my lap – in the rocking chair with feet propped up on the radiator & pausing between every other word to bite a Baby Ruth. Helen just filled my pen for me 'cause I'm too lazy to move. Isn't my roommate nice to me? We went to a marionette show last nite – in the auditorium – "Ali Baba & the 40 Thieves," by professionals from the W. Fair. It was cute n' everything & we enjoyed it but it was so warm & we were so sleepy that we left in the middle of it & came home & ate dill pickles & went to – to dream about everything under the sun. Bed at 10 last nite, 10 Monday nite & 9:30 Sunday nite. Isn't that a record? For us it is anyway. I guess nothing's happened this week worth telling about – and that, too, is the reason for our early hours. I don't know tho whether so much sleep is doing me any good or not. It makes me want to sleep all the time. Yesterday I came home & slept from 12:30-1 & had a test in gov't & got 20 (of 25) right in the middle of the C group. Tonite came & slept 6:45-7:30. Had a test in Home Ec yesterday – got second highest. I like that class now – altho it is rather boring. We're studying the [1-2M] now in Comparative Lit, rather interesting too. Getting the inside [1-2M] on all those 'rare' stories too. We sell candy bars in our room for Ronan Round Table & it's such a temptation. We usually buy about [1-2M] every day. Good for our figures, I know! Got a letter from Mama & she said Clarence is at home every nite this week. He's working on the compressor & he brings it to Oakley & leaves it at night [and comes?] home. Gee, it's raining. It rained today about 11:30 & cleared up this afternoon & now it's raining hard. But it's kinda nice – the rain – when [XM–a couple lines missing here] about Latin – & French. It seems so good. I just can't get used to it. You know, it seems a long time 'til Thanksgiving – 5 weeks yet. Well, by gosh, here I've rambled on for over 2 pages & said nothing. I tell you so many things in imagined letters that I can't remember to tell you when I really write. I want to thank you for inconveniencing yourself so much as to come up & see me Sunday. Really, that wasn't meant to be sarcastic. But I appreciated your coming more probably than you thought I did. You don't know how much comfort I get out of your company & afterwards too. It's so nice when I'm tired (& when I'm not) to just lie down & rest & think about you & day dream & it's awfully nice to know too at nite that – in Benton Harbor, or Muskegon, or wherever you are, you may be thinking of me too. I like these quiet evenings at home. Sometimes I even have time to indulge in a novel. I hope the rest of the term will continue like this. I'm so sleepy. I guess I'd better stop now, but not before I send you my very best. Love, Daisy

---

Oct 29, 1934   CSTC

Dearest Ellis – (Mon eve 5:55) Would you believe it? I was home fully a half hour before I found your letter. I'd just sat down in the rocking chair & read your Fri's letter over again when I spied this one, stuck in the mirror where Helen had left it so I would see it. I could hardly believe my eyes. Pretty darn nice surprise, I'd say. Now I can go to work again feeling as peppy as I did at 1. I work from 6:30-8:30 typing at Miss Myers's house, & 8:30-10 in the training school. I was going to study 'til 8:30, but I thought you deserved at least one page & I need the recreation anyway. Helen went downtown with me today & we were both so happy (she got 2 letters too) that everyone said hello to us whether they knew us or not. I ate at Harry's & walked home alone – just a taste of snow in the air & cold enough to make me want to walk fast & I did enjoy it so. I wish I could work in town every afternoon – if only for the walk down & back. I'll bet you did have a grand time at your Grandmother's. Reminds me of Aunt Stacia's. Wish I could spend a weekend with her before it gets too cold. Was it Bud's wedding that he had to attend & [1-2M] married already? I think I know how you felt Sunday. Guess we all feel like that sometimes. You're [1-2M] honest about it. Right now I wouldn't in the least mind lying down to sleep for hours & hours & let the rest of the world go by or go to hell. I'd best be getting ready to go to work again so – Love, Love, Love, Daisy

(Mon PM) Dearest, Dearest Ellis – To whom, first of all, I'm sending my very Best Love! Did you ever feel so happy & pent-up inside that you just knew if you didn't let it out some way, you're going to burst sure as

anything? Well, that's the way I feel now & I just had to write you before I lost it. Your letter was so awfully nice – it was a sort of crowning touch to everything. Things have been running so smoothly & I came home & found a letter from you & from my mother too – and I hope you understand how I'm feeling – otherwise this would sound rather silly. I'm glad you're in GR now so I can write anytime & don't have to save everything up until Friday nites. It was so sweet of you to write so I'd get it Saturday & I appreciate it really. I would have gotten it but only packages are delivered from the P.O. here on Sat afternoons. I could have stopped for it on my way home Sat if I'd known it were there but I liked it just twice as much today. It was snowing just a few minutes ago – a real white snow flurry but it's all gone now & the sun is smiling again. The world's all right, isn't it? I hope it's as "Right" with you when you get this as it is with me when I send it. I'm going downtown to work at 1 & I'll mail this when I go at the P.O. I don't know if it'll go any sooner but my intention is good anyway. Yesterday after I wrote you I read until 3:30 & went to sleep until 20 to 6. Then Helen & I went downtown & had supper at Harry's & had the nicest walk home afterwards. We do so enjoy each other's company. I don't know what I'd do if I didn't have Helen for a roommate. We were going to the show but we didn't think we'd like it especially – "Peck's Bad Boy." We spent the evening typing invitations – 50 of 'em – for our Tuesday nite Mercier meeting & retired at 11. We ate together this morning at the cafeteria & didn't have class 'til 9 & at 11. I ate lunch with June – which practically brings me up to now – 12:30 & as have to be at work at 1, I guess I'd better step on it. Momma said Clarence isn't going to be home this week & she said Jimmy talks all the time now. I'm glad you're going to weekend with your grandparents & I wish I could go along too, but if next weekend is as nice as this one was, I can't ask for anymore. Have a good time anyway Sunday I know you will & eat some pancakes for me too. It makes me feel so good to know that you're "for me" no matter how I do in my school work. I think about that when I get down – way down – & then I don't feel so bad. I hope you enjoyed the show Friday nite & I'm sorry if you don't care for Katherine's girl friend. You know, it's more natural to like people than it is to not like them & I wouldn't like to feel that I had anything to do with your not caring for her. I sincerely hope that you didn't give her the "run-around" on my account. I'm afraid I'm writing this in too much of a hurry to get across what I mean, but I hope you get the point. I don't know what you were real sorry about in your letter. I hope you weren't sorry for anything you said 'cause I liked it all & here's to you – may your thoughts "ever be happy thoughts," & again I'm sending to my very Dearest Dear my very Best Love Always, Daisy

My Dear — (Wed 11:45 AM) O gee, right now I'd like to be tucked in bed with a hot water bottle at my feet & nothing on my mind & about 6 hours of sleep to look forward to. But no matter how much I'd like to do that, it doesn't in the least change what I have to do. I've got the kind of a cold that makes me feel miserable & at odds with everybody. I don't know where I could have caught it. But this doesn't make you feel any better, does it? I should have answered your letter last night when I was feeling better, but I'm afraid that drowsiness got the better of me & I didn't even have my lessons today. I worked 'til 6:30 last nite & library 'til 8:30, so I didn't get your letter 'til nearly 9 & it made me feel just twice as good because I wasn't expecting it. I'm glad you had such a good time at Mick's. I wish I were home now for about a week, where I could sleep in peace & do nothing the rest of the time. I got a letter from Momma this morning & it made me feel kinda homesick. Guess I better quit that before I turn on the sobs. I must get busy & study my government pretty soon anyway. Hope you have a good day for hunting Sunday. How far north do you think you'll hunt? I wish – but I wouldn't want you to do that, altho I would promise to send you home at least an hour or 2 earlier than you [1-2M] Carson City Sunday nite. Love, Daisy

(Cont'd) Dearest Ellis – Well, I'm feeling pretty good again. My roommate & I are tight on cider. We've got a quart that we [2-3M] dance a week ago last nite. It's just [1-2M] so it doesn't taste sweet anymore. We tasted it from spoons & it turned our teeth & tongues all black. If we're dead in the morning, we'll know what killed us. I did about the only thing there is to do when one has nothing to do. I washed my hair tonite & then it rained tonite too, but it's over now I guess. I worked from [1-2M] today & when I've worked 3 hours tomorrow, I won't have to work anymore this week. Friday & Saturday is Homecoming & there'll be a game, & breakfasts & luncheons & the parade & dances, etc. Ida May Clapper is coming to stay with [XM line or two missing] be here for Homecoming. Helen hasn't heard from him, but we just thought he might. Gee, here it is 12:00 again. Maybe we could retire an hour earlier – but every nite we go downstairs & dance 10-10:30 & then it takes us about a half hour to get settled down again. I'm afraid I'll just have to stop because I haven't anything more to say – at the moment – Good-nite and Love, Daisy

Clarence "Mick" Churchill was a friend Dad made when they worked together at the Carson City elevator. Mick was probably twenty years older than Dad, but they remained friends, and, in 1945, they became partners in buying the Kent Elevator and Seed Company in Reed City. Dad bought Mick out several years after that to become sole owner, until he sold the business in 1965.

Oct 31, 1934 CSTC

Dearest Dear — (Wed Eve 6:30, Halloween Night) I'm so lonesome, my roommate won't be back for fully a half hour so I decided to pay you a visit by letter. I went for a walk all alone in the dark – it gets dark so early now – & it was just what I liked. Next to being with you or with Helen, I like to be alone. I guess I'd make a good hermit. And I was thinking too, perhaps my letter to you sounded a little bit "preachy" – I didn't mean it that way, really. Am I forgiven? I have your last letter in the edge of the mirror yet. Every time I come in & see it again, it reminds me of how good I felt when I saw it first. I'm going to leave it there 'til I get another one to put in its place. Wouldn't it be nice if I could change them every day? I wrote steady with a pencil for 3 ½ hours this afternoon & it practically made a bruise on my thumb & 2nd finger – training school office. I was supposed to work tonite at Miss Myers's again but she wasn't home at 6:30 so I came back. I'd much rather stay home tonite anyway. I'm just a little tired. Guess I've been working too hard (if you can imagine me doing that). I have a test at 8 in the morning too – English. Got our Friday's test back again – in the C's. I'm so glad you'll love me anyway. Tomorrow nite Kryl's Band again on the lecture course & [1-2M] attend that. Signin' off now with – Osomuch Love, Daisy

Bohumir Kryl (1875-1961) was a Czech-American financier & bank president who was most famous as a musician, band leader and early recording artist. He toured extensively with both popular and Bohemian bands. Enclosed with this letter was a CSTC football schedule for 1934. Their opponents that year were: University of Detroit, Ferris Institute, Hillsdale College, Michigan Normal [Eastern], Wayne University, Western State, Kalamazoo College and Alma College. The schedule was printed courtesy of Hi-Speed Service Stations of Mount Pleasant.

Nov 5, 1934 CSTC

Dearest Ellis — (Mon eve 11 PM) Guess I kinda forgot to send my last letter to you & I've been wondering why in the world you didn't answer it, but it's coming to you tomorrow morning just as fast as love & a 3-cent stamp will carry it. I've been reading my Bible tonite – the Book of Job – if you've ever read this all thru when you're sleepy & wanna go to bed – you'll know what it means. I vowed I was going to bed at 11 tonite rain or shine, but it's neither raining nor shining so here I am yet. We've had a real snowstorm here already, last Thursday, I guess, the snow stayed on all nite. It's been kinda nice here tho – I didn't have anything to do last weekend & I did exactly nothing too. Saw "Cleopatra" Sunday nite & it really was one grand picture. Claudette Colbert was Cleopatra & Warren William Julius Caesar. I worked

3 hours 9-12 Saturday & went to Confession & downtown in the PM & fooled away the rest of the weekend I guess. Had to get up early this morning & prepare my assignment for the one class I did have today. Went to work at 1 today & at 4:20 had to come home & sleep. These weekends with nothing to do simply wear me out. Helen's Bill from Western was up to see her Fri & Sat nites. And my dear, if it's something I said in my last letter that has retarded your answer, I'm so sorry. I'm kinda sleepy. Wish you were here just for a minute so I could kiss you good-nite, but I'll just make believe & send you my Love – my Best Love, to my Dearest Dear – from Daisy.

Nov 13, 1934   CSTC to the Vincent Hotel in Benton Harbor

Dearest Ellis — Don't you just enjoy telling me about all the good things you had to eat & making me hungry! But I'm nearly even. My Dad & Mother came up Saturday & stayed all afternoon & went to the game with me & brought me a great big chocolate cake & apples & bananas & candy & my winter coat n' just everything nice. So I guess we both enjoyed our weekend, didn't we! Boy, you said it. Did we ever beat Kazoo – & how! And I'd just love to have you come up & see us beat Alma. The game, I think, is scheduled for 2:00, at least that's when all our home games played. I don't think I can meet you in Alma, altho I'd like to – so I'll be in Mt Pleasant. If you get to Alma too late to come for me & see the game too, I'll look for you after the game. I do hope the weather is fine & the Detroit supervisor doesn't show up. Oh, I must tell you – Clarence's democrats all won out in the election, so his job is thriving & apt to improve any time. The folks are going deer-hunting next week, I guess – up to Lake St Helen's with John & Cory & stay with their relatives there. There's a lot more news I could tell you but I'll save it 'til I see you Saturday. Anyway, I'm a wee bit sleepy – only had 9 hrs Sat nite & 3 hrs Sun afternoon & 9 hrs last nite & a cat-nap tonite after the added exertion of a shampoo & bath & preparing all my lessons for tomorrow – reading of one poem. I'll be looking for you awfully hard Saturday. Best Love, Daisy

P.S. If you haven't answered Harry's letter yet, you might let him know that you're coming up this weekend, please, for Helen's sake, Amen. Good-nite, Love, Daisy

---

Nov 18, 1934   CSTC to the Occidental Hotel in Muskegon

Dearest Ellis — (Sun nite 11 PM) It's raining steadily, such a nice rain. I like it. I'd be perfectly happy now if I had our fireplace, our davenport & you. But I can talk to you anyway, can't I. This has been such a lovely

weekend that I want to hang on to it as long as I can. It has rained all day, off and on. We went to 9:00 Mass & Mr Carey brought us home, right to the door, where we found the Sunday paper & proceeded to read that. Then we had lunch & read, slept, entertained company, etc. until 5:30. We had a nice walk between showers & ate dinner at the Downtown. Saw "Affairs of Cellini" & rode back with Mr Frances, one of our bus drivers, had a "mud" sundae at the Inn & came home. Today didn't at all measure up to yesterday but it was a pleasant afternoon. The show was not quite as grand as I expected, but it was darn good comedy. I expect that it's on the disapproved list – there's some kick in it. A few minutes ago it was thundering & lightening & I was afraid the lights would go out – it's all over now I guess. I hope you had a nice trip home today & a successful trip to Muskegon tomorrow (today or yesterday?). And again – I'm so glad that you came – & I hope you will be with us at least for Sunday dinner Thanksgiving weekend. Just a little sleepy. I'll be dreaming soon (of you). Don't burn up too many waffles & take good care of yourself because – I love you, Daisy

The "disapproved list" Mom mentions here was undoubtedly a reference to the Catholic Church's National Legion of Decency, first formed in 1933. This organization regularly published lists of the latest movies with ratings of – A: Morally unobjectionable; B: Morally objectionable in part; and – the WORST of ALL – C: CONDEMNED by the Legion of Decency. This film 'rating' organization had changed its name & ratings system a few times, but is still around. In the 1950s I remember Mom clipping the latest listing out of the Our Sunday Visitor newspaper each month and posting it on our refrigerator.

Nov 19, 1934 CSTC to the Occidental Hotel in Muskegon

Dearest Ellis – (Mon noon) Monday noon & my classes are all over for today. All I have to do now is work from 1 to 5. But even that can't get me down. I like my work anyway. It's just gorgeous out today. Seems that winter has forgotten to come & we're going to have spring instead. I suppose you've been out haunting grocery stores all day. Hope you had a good day today & here's to a good one tomorrow and every day to come. I told my story in English class this AM & came thru OK. Had our tests returned in Home Ec & came out on the very top of the pile. We're studying reproduction & child care. We have our baby up to a year old now & tomorrow we're going to start raising him to be a man. Have to read five books for that course & write a review of each one – have until Christmas to do that but I haven't started yet. Must get busy. Also have a hell of a mess of a chart to do for government. I don't care what I get out of that course (or curse) just so I get thru it. That isn't the right attitude, I know, but nevertheless, it's mine.

Well, I don't know what brought on all that outburst! We'll just forget it. Tomorrow night is the Co-ed Prom, called the "Amazing Amazon Ambush" this year, football banquet the same night for the men – prom for the girls. Oughta be fun. Sorry I have to stop now. I could write on for ages. I'm sending you my very – Best Love, Daisy

(Mon nite – 6:30) Dearest Ellis – It was so sweet of you to welcome me home tonite with a letter& it does pep me up to start the week with too. I wish you could be here for just about two minutes every time your letters come. I always want to hug you (with one exception – but that's all forgotten now). I worked in the files at the general office for 4 hours steady this PM gathering statistics for Mr Lantz & I felt so dusty & dizzy & all "in a daze" when I came home & found your letter – so I'm still in a daze – but a nice one. I'm going to study now until 9:30 – then a manicure & bath & bed at 10. Isn't that a nice program – my ideal – from 9:30 on. So now I must begin – & close. Good-nite. With Love, Daisy

It's obvious from the last few letters – addressed to hotels – that Dad was, at least briefly, back out on the road again, peddling General Mills products – cereal, flour, cake mixes, Bisquick, etc. – demonstrating & pitching to local grocers around southwestern Michigan. He did not like being a traveling salesman.

Nov 21, 1934   CSTC

Dearest Ellis — (Wed nite 11 PM) "Rain, rain, go away" – it probably will tomorrow – and there'll be snow. I hope it isn't raining & dismal & lonesome when you're reading this. I guess the kids upstairs must have insomnia – their beds are squeaking like nobody's business. My roommate is sleeping peacefully and soon I will be too. I've said my prayers & can hit the hay as soon as I say good-nite to you. Kinda sleepy too. I didn't go to the Co-ed Prom last nite – suddenly became very ambitious & stayed home & studied – took advantage of the silence resulting from the absence of most of our neighbors. We've been going calling & having visitors all this evening so far & didn't get much done – but there's always another day. Guess I haven't any news to tell you. Nothing's happened but the weather & even that gets monotonous. So I'll say good-nite, My Dear, & My Best Love I'm sending to you. Daisy

P.S. Will you add your prayers to mine & Helen's for a special intention, please? I love you. Daisy

Dearest Dear Ellis – (Fri nite 12m) I just got it all figured out that you'd be in Grand Rapids this week – so if you don't mind the smears, penmanship, etc., here goes. I'm wondering if you'll be baking waffles tomorrow nite – boy, wouldn't I like to see you! Oh gee, I did have lots of thoughts but I'm getting sleepy, they've left me & now that I know you were just kidding & will really believe me, I feel safe in saying Good-nite now & will continue later. So good-nite from a very sleep girl who loves you. Daisy

(Sat nite 9:15) Dear Ellis – Just feeling kinda lonesome & I don't mean to take it out on you but I know you'll understand how I feel. Saturday nite & nothing to do but study. There's one thing worse than having lots of studying to do & no time to do it – that's this – time on your hands & nothing but studying to do. Down to confession his afternoon & through stores all decorated for Christmas & that surely does make me lonesome & homesick & in need of someone's shoulder to cry on [2-3M] I won't. Doesn't do any good that I have to read tragedies for English [2-3M] tragedies – & who in hell wants tragedies out of the past to read when there's enough of them in the present – all we have to do to find them is look around. This afternoon we saw a woman on the street with about [2-3M] all under school-age & another on [1-2M] & all cold & half of them crying & I felt so darn sorry for her – but I guess there's nothing one can do about it. I'll bet I'm cheering you up a lot. Sorry. There's no use in making someone else feel as bad as I do, is there. So just forget what I said & I'll try to be more cheerful. Went to the show Rush [1-2M] – "Our Daily Bread" & I liked it so much but the other kids didn't seem to think it was so hot. Maybe there's something peculiar about me but I did like it just the same. What did you think of "Affairs of Cellini"? I do hope you approve of my choice of recreation. [whole line M] on account of there is a party at the HS tonite & we couldn't sell very many tickets we postponed it & I'm glad of it too because I don't like to sit & play bridge with some fiend who always insists on explaining to you just why you should not have played that card that you did. Helen just came in & said I look "industrious or sump'n – mostly just sump'n." that's the way I feel too. I'd best stop now before I get started again – I'll write you some more later maybe. So 'til then, X Love, Daisy

(Sun nite 10:30) Dearest Ellis – I'm feeling much better tonite, thank you. Have had a very busy day & feel good because of it, I think. Last nite I began to feel better after I'd written to you so I bought myself a Snickers & read "The Child from One to Twelve" until 9:00 & retired in a much better humor. Went to 7:30 Mass & communion this morning & had breakfast over the morning paper at the Olympia. Came home & finished reading my book & dinner at the cafeteria & worked like the devil until 5 on my book

*report – not as simple as I thought it would be. Hamburgers at Harry's &
had a lot of fun seeing "The Merry Widow" – I do hope you won't censor
my amusements – & a Coke & home again & people coming in to buy candy
& to say good-nite – & also just on general principles until I was typing
¼ 's for p's & everything else & gave up in despair until tomorrow. I am
very wide awake now tho – for a wonder – I have an 8 o'clock class in the
morning too. I spent about an hour this afternoon doing a repair job on
my typewriter – had it all apart & used nail file & scissors & tweezers &
various other little useful instruments on it – more fun – but it's all fixed
now – good as new. I have only 4 more books to read & write reviews of for
Home Ec & when I have my government chart done too – I'll have a load off
my mind. I'm going home at noon Wednesday. Won't that be nice? Momma
wrote that they had a venison supper at home – Pete got a deer & Joe &
Agnes named their baby William Henry. This is Helen's ink – that's why it
changes color back on the first page – way back there – do you remember?
My mother has also for about the third time extended you an invitation for
Sunday dinner & all that goes with it – Dec 2 – after Thanksgiving – maybe
we'll have some turkey left. But I don't mean to scare you away. I want you
to come & I hope you'll want to come & can come & I know Oakley will be
glad to see you & I wish you could come Saturday nite but Sunday anyway
& will you let me know & if you can't come you know I won't be angry
ever – just disappointed & awfully sorry & my Dear – don't try to read this
sentence all in one breath – I fear there might be dire consequences if you
do & I wouldn't for the world have anything happen to you ever because I
love you – so much. Daisy*

Mom's comment about the woman in town with all the crying children
might be construed as her first 'sideways' mention of the difficulties
of the Great Depression. And then too there's her support for the film,
"Our Daily Bread," which is directly about the hardships of the times.

Nov 25, 1934   Oakley

*Hello, Ellis – Have been looking f 2 your visit. We rcvd your card at last – our
address is 502 S Main. Rcvd a very pretty syrup pitcher from Betty Crocker
cut glass. Please thank her for me and will thank you too. Yours as ever,
Belle Gower*

This is a postcard found with Mom's letters. It is to Dad from Mrs. Belle
Gower, who was his landlady when he lived in Oakley in 1933, the
summer he met Mom.

Dec 3, 1934 CSTC

Dearest Ellis — (Mon nite, almost Tues morn) There are any number of kids burning the midnite oil tonite – term papers & things. I could have been in bed at 12 but I feel that I owe you a letter – don't mean by that that I'm writing from a sense of duty – never that. But you've been so sweet to me & leaving you so early Sunday nite bothered my conscience almost as much as keeping you until 10 does. You see, I resolved that if you brought me back I was going to let you go right away so you could have time for a nice visit in Carson City & still not be too late getting back to Grand Rapids. I hope you'll understand that my intentions were good, even if I did come dangerously near weakening – it really wasn't easy – & if you'd stayed 5 minutes longer – it probably would have been 10:00 in no time at all. I love you. We had a real snowstorm today – about 3 hours this PM & about 3 or 4 inches of snow still on the ground. I worked from 1 until 6:15 today – and then I came home and went to work. I wish I could get as much accomplished every day for these last two weeks of the term as I have today. But I fear my ambition isn't going to last. I've got a sore head today too, from banging it against the door like a nut. How are you? I just stamped the envelope upside down – purely an accident – I've had nothing stronger than water, I assure you. Perhaps, tho, that's an indication that I should retire – what think you? Then if we both agree I'll say Good-nite, Dear Ellis. Love, Daisy

Dec 7, 1934 CSTC

Dearest Ellis — (Fri nite almost 10) I told myself I'd have to read a whole book through before I could write you – I'm over half through it now & I couldn't keep my mind concentrated on it anyway – so here I am. But I must finish it before I go to bed – so you won't keep me too long, will you? Gerry is coming down for me to wave her hair when she comes from the show and every time someone knocks on the door, I'm all set to see Gerry & it's someone to buy candy or to borrow a razor-blade to trim paper, etc. etc. "College Rhythm" is on tonite & I saw the previews & I didn't think I'd care very much about it. If we get our work done (& probably even if we don't) Helen & I are going Sun nite to see Greta Garbo in "The Painted Veil." It promises to be interesting. Dr Beck very kindly today bestowed upon me the privilege of reading a new biography of Cicero that he has just purchased so I can make a report to the class Monday and in [1-2M] really give him an idea of the [1-2M] of the book without his having to read it. He doesn't have time really [2-3M] luckily for him, perhaps, didn't let him know how much I appreciated this distinction. I have only four books to read and write reviews of for Home Ec. "Understanding the Adolescent Girl" is the one underway [1-2M] done, & 3 more to go. I've just completed "The Child from One to Twelve." I've been thinking about what I'll take next term – the new schedules are out today & I'm going to be taking 3 English courses & since the Home Ec I want comes at the same time my Eng's do, I think I'll take Agriculture – won't that be [1-2M] I'm coming to summer school & take Home Ec and. Typing – then I can be a full-fledged stenographer, office-girl or what have you. I'm going to church in the morning and [possibly a couple lines M]. Pool was the most fun tho. I really did get about six balls in the pockets in the course of the game, & my "banking" was most spectacular, I'm sure. Do you like to play pool? I wish the girls had a pool table in the dorm. I had more fun playing that than anything I'd done in ages. Is pool supposed to be just a man's game – or is it for women too? Whether or not, I like it! Gerry just came down & said she'd be ready in a few minutes for me to wave her hair so I expect I will presently be leaving you – temporarily at least. Helen wrote to Bill (in Kalamazoo) tonite & sent him your address so I suppose you'll be hearing from him soon. I gather from the reports that previous to, during & since vacation he has hounded her for it – ever since she told him that you lived in Grand Rapids. It would be nice if he & you could come up together sometime during the basketball season to a game, wouldn't it? Bill is just crazy about basketball too. And he doesn't smoke, and he doesn't drink beer & he only attends shows that are on the approved list in the Sunday Visitor, & Sister Petronella is his special confidante & has been since he started school. But I guess for all that he isn't as bad or as "good" as it sounds. Anyway you'll probably hear from him & don't hold against him anything I've said. Just waved Gerry's hair & I'm back again but I guess that was all the news I had anyway & Helen is sleeping so peacefully that it makes me sleepy too. Gerry was all pepped up about the show & was humming snatches of the hit numbers – "Take a Number from 1-10," "College Rhythm," "Stay as Sweet as You Are," etc. At night when I come back to the dorm & it's dark & so cold, I think of you just coming in from work all alone, & I always hope that my letters will help to cheer you up & make you feel better instead of depressing you. I try not to write when I'm in that mood & if some of my letters sound rather "down," just regard it as a passing mood. Well, I didn't mean to write an essay on "My Letters," I just meant to say that I'm awfully glad if you like my letters & I hope you always will. It is mutual, you may be assured. There are always a few paragraphs in your letters that I read over & over, & love you more every time. I'm sorry your friends weren't at home in Middleton & Carson City Sunday nite. I'm afraid my noble – what should I say – intentions & actions resulted in just the opposite way from what they were designed for. That sounds rather "dutchy," but the idea is there if you can find it. Maybe next time you won't have such a long way to go home & won't have to leave so early. I'm looking forward with LOVE – for you, the Dearest Dear in the world. Daisy

I never knew my mom had ever played pool, but there it is – and she liked it.

Dec 18, 1934   CSTC to Middleton

Dear Ellis – (9 PM) On account of because we ain't got nothin' to do but study for final exams, we're writin' ya a letter to tell ya that tomorrow Tuesday night we can stay out 'til the outrageous hour of 11 o'clock, so if you get this before Tuesday nite, you can come up if ya can't find nothin' else better to do & you can come just as early as ya wanta & stay just as late as ya wanta providin' it ain't after 11. This is being written in partnership & mostly under the dictation of my dizzy roommate who is sick from eating too much candy at a party just because she was on the refreshment committee. I think because once before ya wrote me a letter once in the morning & I got it in the afternoon that ya might get this yesterday afternoon & have come up last nite - or this afternoon & tonite if ya get it this afternoon. If ya don't get it be sure & let me know so I'll know ya didn't come. Helen was gonna write this but her leg is so lame from playin' shuffleboard that she couldn't.

Different handwriting here

> *Ya - that's rite, it's such an effort to write. We'll be seein' you tomorrow nite ... Helen*

It was really a civilized party we went to tonite. It wasn't nothin' we had to drink but we just feel pretty good on account of because we been averagin' about 5 hours sleep. I hope I'll be seein' ya but in case I don't - Merry Christmas & I'll see ya sometime anyway. Daisy

December 17, 1934: Ellis at White Cloud, Michigan

Dec 25, 1934   Oakley

Dearest Ellis — (9:15 PM Christmas) Bing Crosby is crooning – the lights are dim – it's Christmas night & I'm lonesome – how are you? I do wish I could be thinking how soon I'll be seeing you but I'm not coming to Grand Rapids this weekend. I'm so sorry & disappointed too. You see, Aunt Stacia & Tom are spending the holidays out here – in Owosso. Oh, I do wish you weren't so far away. You know how I'd love to have you come out, but when I think of the long, cold ride for you, it makes me shiver. However, if you would dare to brave the elements, a most cordial & hearty invitation is extended to you for this weekend or New Year's Eve & Day – whichever would be most convenient for you. Will you think it over anyway & let me know of your decision? You know that I'll understand & sympathize most heartily if your answer is no, but on the other hand I'm not trying to discourage you. Clarence comes of age on New Year's, you know – 21 & he'll be a man. I hope you had a pleasant Christmas at home today. Harold & Helen & family were down & with a truck banging around in the house & a doll that goes to sleep & must be taken for a ride, everything was quite complete. We went to 6:00 Mass, & I've forgotten when the last time was that I've been up as early as 5:30 – except when I was up all nite. Which reminds me – I received my marks yesterday for the term & they were just what I expected – C in Government, B's in English, A in Home Ec. I'm glad I have such a nice long vacation before time to go back – the 7th seems a long way off now. Did you know we have two new babies in town? – a boy, Max, Dec 24, at Person's (Va. Hill) & a girl, Dec 12, Dorothy Marlene, at Steph's & Pete's. And the youngest member of the Clark family is as sweet as he can be. Saw a good show Saturday nite – Loretta Young & John Boles in "The White Parade," a story about nurses. Margaret was over this afternoon & we spent about an hour in close harmony – it may have sounded more like noise than music, but we had a lot of fun. Then I took her for a ride on her bobsled, only dumping her off a couple of times. I took Gerry for a ride Sunday when we were down to Dorothy's & of course he thought it was more fun going in the very deepest snow & I enjoyed it immensely too. I've been keeping myself pretty busy shoveling paths, baking cakes & pies & cookies, etc. getting ready for Christmas, & tomorrow I'll be getting over it probably. Gee, this sounds rather disconnected & senseless, doesn't it? But I mean all right. So again – I'm sorry & I hope – & I am Your Daisy

P.S. With all my heart. D.

Dec 26, 1934   Oakley to Grand Rapids

Dearest Ellis — (Wed morning) Just received your letter & again I'm sorry. Glad that you had such a jolly vacation. I wondered if you have this coming Monday off too. If you have it would be nice if you could come here from Detroit Sunday nite. Just a suggestion. If I don't see you, I'm sending you my best Love just the same. Daisy

Christmas card with penguins & Greetings

Jan 3, 1935   Oakley

Dearest Ellis — (Wed nite 11) Just finished my diary account of three happy days, not including yesterday & today - I'll do those later - I don't want to break the spell. It was so perfect & you were so sweet, but you always are anyway - only 'specially so this time it seemed. It was dear of you to come & I want to thank you. I hope you arrived safely home & warm. It was more than a hope - a prayer. I saw "The Mighty Barnum" tonite & it quite came up to my expectations. I talked to you on the way home & told you everything that will be in this letter & more. No, I'm not crazy - just living in a land of make-believe, a carryover from childhood perhaps, but it's really lots of fun. You say to me just the things I want you to say so I can reply just what I want to say. I can talk to your picture now & it can't talk back (sometimes an advantage?). Really tho, thank you again for just the nicest thing you could have given me. I love it & I always will, because I love you. I could tell you more but it doesn't seem necessary tonite. Are you going to be in Grand Rapids this coming week or ? - so I'll know where to write you. Good-nite, Pal, Daisy

---

Jan 8, 1935   CSTC

Dearest Ellis — (11:30 PM) I wish you could step out of your picture & hear what I'm telling you. You look just as if you could but you're saying you're sorry but you really can't. I'm sorry too. Anyway, Hello, Ellis. You're so dear. I've come to the end of my first full day this term. Left here at 7:30 & worked 'til 8, classes 'til 11, worked 'til 1, classes 'til 3, downtown, class meeting at 4, worked 5-7, library 'til 7:30 - home again - 12-hour day. How'm I doin'? I'm working in the cafeteria, temporarily at least, permanently I hope. I'm taking 5 subjects - when I signed up, I didn't think I'd have a job, but I can carry them, I think - 3 Englishes at 8, 9 & 10, Agriculture at 1 & Geography at 3. I didn't know quite what I was getting into in my 10:00 English class or I wouldn't be there now - we have to write a short story! In Agriculture I've learned to date that 4 or 5

65

bushels of corn = about 1 pound of hog. I'm going to be up to my neck this term in work I'm afraid. Here's hoping I don't go under. You were formally introduced to Bill this afternoon, although you had been together for two days (on the dresser) & were getting along famously. You're on the desk though now, right in front of me & I keep talking to you & forget to write, so if I leave out anything, you'll know I told you anyway. We're having our J-Hop Feb 9, Sat nite, we decided in our class meeting today, & I want you to come. Please don't say no. Bill is coming up to go with Helen & you could come up together & wouldn't get lonesome. Won't that be nice! You'll probably hear from Bill before long. It will be the nicest party of the year, & I do so want you, you will come, won't you? I got back about 4 Sunday. We had 10:30 Mass & the Rev didn't get there until 11 – then we hauled in all the dirt for the sidewalk & painted the church & when I came home at 10 after 12 he hadn't started benediction yet. Sunday was like spring & it's been raining ever since. We practically waded downtown today. Did I send you our basketball schedule? I don't know myself what it is now. I'll send you one if I can find it. And if you'd like to come up & see a game, just let me know. Maybe you & Bill can get together on a game. I was feeling pretty down yesterday morning when I came home after enrolling & didn't have any job or letter or nothing, but you said – "Don't take it so seriously, it won't do any good to feel bad about it," so I slept a couple hours & woke up feeling better, thanks to nobody else but YOU, & now I'm going to kiss you good-nite (please don't mind a smear or two – I polish the glass every day) & retire to rest. So Good-nite, darling. Love, Daisy

Ellis Edward Bazzett 1935

Jan 10, 1935

Dearest Ellis – (Thurs nite 11:10) Time out to breathe. I've been wading through a chapter on diastrophisms, anticlines, geosynclines, etc. – Geography – and how! I was going to answer your letter last nite but it was 2:30 when I finished my two English themes & various other assignments – so – I didn't. But I wanted you to get this this weekend. Thought you might be looking for it & I'm sure that I'd rather disappoint Harry Miller & Dr Beck tomorrow than you – any time. Heard another number on the lecture course last nite – Miss Bertling – a soprano, Mr Darcy – a baritone, & Mr Hughes, pianist. I quite enjoyed it – more than I expected. The weather, etc. seems to be drying up & it's been so nice today. When we went to work this morning it seemed like a summer morning before the sun comes up – but not that warm, of course. I have a most inspiring assignment to read for English tomorrow – entitled "Un-Burial," being a discussion of various methods of disposing of people – after they're dead. I'm progressing marvelously in the cafeteria – I make salads & I really like it. Hope Miss Ronan lets me stay on – but I "hae me doots." She wants me on a typing job but I'd much rather do what I'm doing. However – it's neither here nor there tonite & I'm so sleepy I don't care whether I work anymore or not so I guess I won't. I don't feel in the mood for an urn-burial tonite anyway. So you'll be in Benton Harbor this week coming. I thought you were there or Muskegon this week or I would have written you sooner – but I'll make up for it next week. Meanwhile I send a great deal of love & I'll give my kisses to your picture & your ring & good-nite, my Dearest. Love, Daisy

---

Jan 13, 1935   CSTC to the Hotel Vincent, Benton Harbor

Dearest Ellis — (Sun nite 12) I hope you had a good day & here's a kiss for you X & a great big hug O. Gee, it seems just ages & ages since this term started & since I've been home & especially since I've seen you. It doesn't seem possible that we've only been here a week. It isn't that time drags because there just aren't enough hours in the day for me to get done what I should get done. But when I think back it seems like we've been back at least 3 weeks. It's been 13 days since I've seen you. This is the 14th now. I wish I could turn back the clock about 16 days. But then I'd have to live the rest all over again too, altho I think it'd be worth it. We were going to see "Flirtation Walk" tonite & changed our minds & just went down to Harry's & got a hamburger. The place has been enlarged again & they've got some kind of an electric Victrola that works when you put a nickel in the slot numbered with the song you want. We played "A Little Angel Told Me So" – 'member? – & "Stay as Sweet as You Are" & another one I don't remember. It was so nice walking downtown. It snowed all night last nite & we've got about 6 inches of snow today. The streets had all been cleared this morning when we went to 7:30 Mass & we weren't late. I've put a red ring around today on my calendar so I'll remember it. I finally did find a basketball schedule in an old paper (Nov 21) & I'm enclosing it. I had a later one – it was just the same, I think, only it had the Alma games on it & I guess I lost that. I got a letter from Mama yesterday & she said Helen

(Whalen) is in Saginaw Hospital & has had an operation & a relapse & another operation but I guess she's getting better now. I feel so darn sorry for those poor kids. They finally were getting started & Harold had steady work & something had to happen. Harold is staying in Saginaw this week too, of course, but he was coming home today I guess but Helen must be still there. Saturday morning 3 of Helen (Critchell's) friends from Traverse City came down for extension classes & got us up about 7:30 so they could come up to our room & change their clothes. They wore ski-suits. They said there was lots of snow up north but there wasn't any here. Gee, I hope you can read this – some scrawl, isn't it? Someday I'll write you a real nice letter in my best penmanship that you can keep for a souvenir. I've got my Agriculture assignment all done – a week's work & don't have class tomorrow. I have my 8:00 English & Geography off tomorrow too. Won't know what I'll do with so much time. We're planning a sleigh-ride party (Mercier) Tuesday night if we can get sleighs & get the kids together. I hope we can. I haven't been on a sleigh ride since I went to the Oakley school & think it's just heaps of fun. If you were here I could talk to you for an hour, but guess I'd better sign off now. Station CHATTER. Be good, won'tcha. 'Cus I'm always good, aren't I. Anyway, I loves you. Daisy.

The "nickel in the slot Victrola" was obviously an early model of what came to be called a 'jukebox.' A few companies were already marketing them in the early thirties. Most of these early machines could only hold ten to twenty 78 rpm records. While I found it intriguing that there WERE jukeboxes then, most kids today would probably wonder, "What's a jukebox?" Full circle.

Jan 14, 1935   CSTC

Ellis Dearest — (Mon nite) Please don't be alarmed if this is short but I'm just so awfully tired & I wanta go to bed by 10:30 it's 10:15 now. The other kids are at House Meeting downstairs & I didn't go. Your letter was waiting for me tonite when I came home, a nice fat one propped up against your picture where my roommate so thoughtfully left it for me. As for the J-Hop, I'm going to hold the date for you anyway, & if your sales-meeting comes then, it will be too bad but worse things have happened than missing a J-Hop. I do know how you feel & please don't worry about it. Good-nite with Loads o' Love & Kisses, Daisy

Jan 16, 1935 CSTC

Dearest Ellis — (Wed nite 12:30) I'm afraid I'm not minding very well – about the sleep – tonite anyway. But I guess I'm really not studying too hard. I should study more tonite – I just think, though, that I'll drop my English 203 & only carry 4 subjects. My Little Merry Sunshine roommate is very encouraging & tells me that I'll surely be a nervous wreck at the end of the term if I continue to carry 5 subjects & work too. So perhaps I'll follow her sage advice. What would you do? A few minutes ago she was moaning that she's "just living, just putting in time" – but she's putting in her time sleeping now. You know what an Irishman's conception of heaven is, don't you? – "a long row of beds with me in every one of them." Well, I guess that's mine too, right now anyway. I wrote my "duty letters" & I felt like writing to you & I hope you won't get tired of me practically "waiting on your doorstep" every night when you get in. I'm just hopin' & prayin' that your sales-meeting will be the 2nd or some other time. Can't you use your influence with the "Big Boss"? I'm sure if he knew why it should be not the 9th that he'd _____! Anyway maybe you can come up to a game after that date, if you miss out on the 9th – or then too. That doesn't mean, tho, that I want you any the less for the J-Hop. O no! We played Alma here tonite & it was a hard & fast game & close – tied about every 4 points but we didn't win, 38-41. Our Frosh beat the Alma American Legion team by one basket – 25-27 or something like that – I didn't see that game. We play Wayne University this Saturday nite – wish you could see that game. Nite before last, after I wrote you I went to bed at 10:20 & to sleep to the tune of Helen's typewriter & made salads furiously for 3 hours & got up at 1:30 all tired out thinking it was morning & discovered it was the middle of the night & did it feel good to get back in bed again – oboyoboyoboy! Gee, I hope you don't have to work so hard & so late every day. You'll be all tired out. So you mind me & get your sleep, won't you? Boy, did that apple turnover a la mode ever sound good to me – especially when I know that I won't be home 'til the first of April – it's things like that that make me feel kinda homesick sometimes. A couple days ago when I got your letter I don't know what it did to me but I just flopped down on the bed & cried like a baby – it wasn't anything in your letter that made me do it – guess the tears were all ready to come anyway. But I felt lots better afterward. Gee, I don't know why I'm writing all this but o well. If I'd keep a copy of my letters to you, I guess I wouldn't need a diary – haven't written in it this week anyway. It isn't so long but it seems like ages. Oh, this is just nonsensical chatter. I'd best say Good-nite – to an awfully Dear Pal. Love, Daisy

Jan 17, 1935

Dearest Ellis — (Thurs nite) I'm dropping you a line on account o' cuz I had a envelope what I addressed to G.R. last nite & a loose stamp & also on accounta cuz I'm askin' you to tell me where you'll be next week - you know - I might write to you. Wouldn't you be surprised to get a letter from me? I'll have lotsa time to write now. I dropped my English Comp class today & I feel so relieved that I'm taking it out on you again as usual. I've been to hell this afternoon in Geography class - thru the volcanos & I've gotta go to Hell again pretty soon & learn about Satan & his fallen angels ("Paradise Lost"). They don't teach me anything about Heaven up here. I hope I don't get sent to the place I learn most about. Guess you'll have to come up and show me "Just a little bit of heaven" before I'm completely lost. G'nite. X Daisy

Jan 24, 1935

Dearest Ellis — (Thurs morn 12:30 AM) I'm so glad that you can come. I think sometimes praying helps too, do you? I could have been much more enthusiastic about it at 3:30 tho, when I got your letter, but I had to go to work after I took room inspection - church at 7;30, spread at 10, etc. & that's the way it's been all week. I'm making the mission here this week - 6:15 mass every morning & 7:30 services every nite. Fr Miller & Fr Coughlin of the Servite order (Servants of Mary) are holding the mission - women this week & men next week. So we didn't have our sleigh-ride party Tuesday nite on account of having to go to the mission after running around & getting the sleigh & everything. But after the mission 7:30 services we had special Mercier services in the church basement. Practically all day Sunday we spent making invitations for our rushing party what had to be out Monday morning at 8 & they were cute too. We made them in the shape of an artist's palette & splashed paint on the outside & wrote the invitation (in verse) on the inside & tied them together with ribbon. I'm on the decorating committee too, so I suppose I'll be doing that this weekend - our party is Monday nite & I have a date with the dentist too Saturday PM - pleasant thought. There were 18 kids tonite at the spread - 8 RRT kids & 10 rushees - & I ate so many toasted sandwiches, fiz's etc. that I feel a bit upset. 5:30 isn't so very far away, so even if I'd rather not, I must close & again I'm just so happy that you can come! Love, Daisy

Good morning, Ellis dear, it's 7:30 & we've been back from church a half hour. I think it must be about 15 below - and has been all week - we got a ride home tho, so it wasn't so bad. Must go eat now but wanted to say "Good Morning" with Love, Daisy

Jan 25, 1935   CSTC

Dearest Ellis — (Fri nite 11:30) I'm so sorry if I seem to have been neglecting you this week after last week's outburst of letters. What I've been doing this week tho is supposed to be doing my soul good. I have my doubts. According to the priest, I'm afraid my morals aren't quite up to what they're supposed to be. However, I do know that the mission is doing my college work a minus quantity of good. All week I've slept through my classes. Tuesday we slept thru the alarm & skipped our 8:00 to go to mass. Yesterday I skipped my 9:00 & came home & slept 'til 11:40, worked 12-1, classes 1-3, worked 4-7:30 making cabbage salad, mass production, & serving at a banquet, heard first quarter of Westminster Choir (world-famed chorus from England) program, came home & took a bath & went back & heard the last quarter of the program & served punch at a reception given the choir by the a capella college choir & got home at 11:30 – an 18-hour day – excepting the 2 ½ hour nap. How'm I doin', keed? I'll bet you can appreciate how I feel though, 'cause you've probably been working harder than I have. I do sincerely hope that the broken ring isn't a bad sign. Are you superstitious? If you are, just remember too that your ring (mine?) is still intact, except perhaps the design is wearing down a little – can you guess why? Gee, I hope you don't slide around anymore & go into the ditch or anything. It surely has been slippery tho, & still is, altho now there's some snow packed on top of the ice & it isn't so bad walking down the road. But boyoboy, was it ever cold at 5:30 in the morning – skidding & slipping down the icy road & just about get thawed out in church in time to come home again. These missionary priests have got some narrow-minded viewpoints in some things tho, I think, & they cited some of the most horrible examples of sin, from the altar. Maybe I'm getting too far gone. I'm afraid I feel myself slipping & I don't know whether the mission has done me more good or more harm, but it has made me think. I'd like to listen in next week & see what he says to the men. I was just reading over one of your letters where you said, "hadn't you better count me out on the J-Hop" – now aren't you glad I didn't? I am! Just awfully glad that you'll be here in just 2 weeks. O, I can hardly wait! But if those weeks drag like these first 4 have, it'll be a year. The J-Hop is more formal than the sophomore party but the dress is optional for men as then. Some wear tux's & some don't. It doesn't make any difference. Have you heard from Bill yet? I know he wrote to you 'cause he told Helen in a letter. We (4) ought to be getting around to knowing each other through these letters pretty soon, hadn't we? You'll be in Detroit Monday nite – before you get this, won't you. Hope you had a good time – a little pleasure along with the business, you know. There was a mission in Oakley last week too – a Fr Marion – & Mama sent me a little gold crucifix that's set up on the dresser & it's so nice. Helen came home from the hospital Monday & is getting along fine. Mr Hill & Mrs Welch's father are dead now. Everybody, including the Clarks, Thurbers, etc. all attended the mission in Oakley, & Clarence is still working in Saginaw, & I guess that's all the Oakley news. I'm so sleepy & I'll pray for nice weather 2/9 to bring you safe to Your Love, Daisy X

Jan 27, 1935   CSTC

Dearest Ellis − (Sun nite 11:30) When I close my eyes & dream about what's going to happen in just 2 weeks, I can hardly believe it's true & I'm praying that nothing can happen to spoil it. It's easy to imagine myself there now too, 'cause there's the nicest soft, sweet music coming over our radio - our newest & most prized possession & probably another reason why we won't get any studying done. But it's so cozy & homey to have a radio in our room & we got it yesterday – no, we didn't win it - we decided we didn't want the kind they're giving as a prize so we bought ourselves one yesterday – a Monarch - but we're going to exchange it for a better one this week, I think. We finished the mission this afternoon at 4 when we renewed our baptismal vows & received the papal blessing. Last night I went to confession to Fr Miller & he was just awfully nice. I felt so pure & exalted & at peace with the world afterwards & I still do. I told him that I'd gone to immoral shows (he said on the altar that it was a mortal sin to see shows on the C-list) & I told him that I didn't they were terribly immoral & he said it wasn't a sin as long as they didn't make an impression on me & if I kept my mind clean – but now I don't even feel a desire to see a C show. Someone's singing "When I Grow Too Old to Dream" – I hope I'll never get that old. You dream too, don't you, Ellis? It doesn't seem as if there'd be much left to live for if we didn't have our dreams. It seems that you're in all my dreams now. I love you so much, Ellis, & I pray to God that He'll keep you safe & after 2 long weeks – I'll be seeing you. I get all thrilled just thinking about it! You are planning to stay over Sunday, aren't you? O please do. I wish there were some kids here you could stay with. If you don't want to stay at the hotel, I'll ask one of the fellows to get you a room at a house – I know he could. You've probably heard from Bill, haven't you? I hope you like each other & don't have a fight before you get here. I have no fears at all that Bill will like you, but I've never met Bill so I can't vouch for him. Don't you think it would be nice for us all to go to communion Sunday after the Hop - we're all Catholics & I think it would be so much nicer than going out & getting tight afterwards, don't you? – Not that we ever did, but some kids do. It was 2 below zero when we went to 7:30 mass this morning & we're going to mass in the morning too – weather reports say rise in temperature starting Tuesday – hope they're right. It's getting rather cold in here now – so guess I'll have to go to bed & get warm. Good-nite, Darling. Love, Daisy

The above letter was written on my birthday, nine years before I was born. Little did my mom know that in 1944 she would be giving birth to her fourth son in six years. And my dad used to sing that song, "When I Grow Too Old to Dream," around the house when we were growing up. Now I sing it.

Jan 29, 1935   CSTC

Dearest Ellis – (Tues nite 11:30) Pardon me, I mean it's 10 to 12 now – I've been trying to keep the radio adjusted to suit my roommate (& me). But O, it's so nice. I don't know how we ever got along without one (or how we'll get along with one). I suppose you're back from Detroit now & I hope you had just a grand time & beat 'em all at ping pong & won first prize n' everything that'll make you feel good. An' I'm for you every time, Big Boy! - 'course I am. There's a girl singing "Let's Be Thankful." I'm getting acquainted with all the new songs again now. We had our rushing party last nite & it was so nice but I'm glad it's over & we don't have to go to church this week so it's more leisure – if you can call it that. We're having Chippewa pictures taken now. Tonite at 9:30 we had our Mercier picture sitting. Hope it's good. Group pictures are always awful tho. I haven't even gotten an appointment for a personal sitting yet. Guess I'll have to get one tomorrow. Gee, I'll bet it does seem good to you to get back to G.R. where you can settle down for 2 weeks. I'd like to be settled there for about a week myself but I seem to be stuck here until April. But it really isn't that bad. We exchanged to an Erla radio yesterday & it works just grand. And guess what? This news nearly bowled me over – Helen wrote me that Clarence & Gertrude are going to be married! No comments necessary. I think you know as much about it as I do anyway. I was going to write you last nite but I lay on my bed in a nest of pillows & went to sleep & didn't wake up 'til 7:30 AM this morning – didn't even remember going to bed. I had 2 poppy-seed cakes just before & maybe they put me to sleep – they do that with babies you know. The reason that this might look a little crooked is that I've been lying down writing – & still am. I wish you & Bill could come up & see & hear our radio. If Mrs Porterfield would give us permission to have you come up for a few minutes, would you like to? So – to the strains of "Blue Moon" I'll say good-nite, my Dearest, Dear Ellis. Love, Daisy

The Chippewa was the CSTC yearbook. And the Monarch radio was an RCA product, while the Erla was a lesser-known model produced by the Electrical Research Laboratories Inc. Both were, of course, vacuum tube type radios.

Jan 31, 1935   CSTC

Dearest Ellis – (Thurs 1:15 PM) "If I Had a Million Dollars" is what he's singing now, but I know I wouldn't be any happier, or as happy, probably, if I had $1,000,000 & I'm glad I haven't. Deep philosophy for early afternoon, isn't it? However there's a reason. No Agriculture class today – at least there was no one in the classroom so I came home – and I had just the kind of lunch I like – & I don't feel so bad – & O yes I received a letter from one Ellis Bazzett in Grand Rapids & I always feel good then. Helen had a letter from Bill in the same mail & he paid you a very nice compliment. He said your writing is the most remarkable that he's ever seen & he's going to practice up on his handwriting before answering so if you haven't heard from him yet, you'll know the reason. I had my picture taken for the Chippewa at 10:30 this morning – I suppose it'll be a dilly. They never turn out like you think they will anyway. Yesterday I skipped Ag & went downtown & skipped Geology too, so I didn't have any afternoon classes. It wasn't the right thing to do, I know, but I didn't have my assignments done & there was no use going without them. I must go to Geo pretty soon now. Helen's alarm just rang & I almost jumped over the desk. I'm so glad that you arrived back home safe & didn't try to come all the way at nite on the slippery road. I haven't even been out on a road in nearly 5 weeks but I do know that the sidewalks aren't very good going. Congratulations on your winning the Wheaties prize, but don't wear yourself out working this week, will you? I gave some of your love to Helen, but Honey, I can use a lot too – & Bill sent his love to me too – did you get together on that? Am sending you a clipping about the J-Hop – as you've probably noticed. Must rush off now. Love, Daisy

> Enclosed is a newspaper clipping about the upcoming J-Hop, which would feature a "Winter Wonderland" theme and music by the 11-piece Duane Yates orchestra, out of Kalamazoo. And my dad did indeed have enviably beautiful handwriting (as too did Mom).

Feb 3, 1935   CSTC

Dearest Ellis – (Sun nite 11) A week from last nite is what I like to think of – not a week from tonite, 'cause then it'll all be over & I hope it'll be just perfect. Gee, I can hardly wait – but it's so much fun looking forward to the J-Hop – and you. I saw Shirley Temple tonite in "Bright Eyes" & it was just grand. Have you seen it? O, you'd love it too, I know. It's so wholesome & refreshing after seeing so many slinky, suggestive, immoral movies. The weather has been perfectly lovely this weekend & I hope it'll be the same next weekend – without the ice, if you please. Helen & I both

met up with the ice on our way home tonite. You won't mind if this is short, will you, on account of at 8 I've got to go over to the Science & study rocks for a test & I'll be seeing you soon anyway, won't I? Are you happy too? Love, Daisy

P.S. Can you figure out how – one can change a $5 bill but not a $1 bill? I mean – a man buys 5c worth of something & he has a $1 bill. The cashier says she can't change the $1 bill, but she can change a $5 bill. Can you figure it out? It's really a problem.

Feb 4, 1935   CSTC

Dearest Ellis – (Mon nite) 11:20 & I haven't got much of anything done, but I haven't many pressing thins to do – except one that was to receive my IMMEDIATE attention & I'm enclosing my attention. I received your most "luff-ing" letter this afternoon & I'm writing in regard to the J-Hop & I wondered what time you'll be coming & to say that we've engaged a room for you & Bill at Newton's – right across from the Inn where the Harmony was, you know. They're the people we work for at the Cafeteria & I know you'll like 'em – & will like it there & the room is right next to the bathroom. I know I'd appreciate that. When you come, you can go there & freshen up a bit – you'll probably want to after riding so far. If you come before 5 or between 6 & 7 or after 8:30 we'll go over to Newton's with you & introduce you if you'd like us to. Anyway, call us when you get in town & let us know you're here, won't you? Helen says, "Tell Ellis I'm saying my prayers" – but I told her it's too late to make a good impression now. Just between 5& 6 we'll both be working – I come home at 6. You'll probably be sending this back for a translation too, but anyway I'll be seeing ya soon & then we can talk about things I won't write about now. G'nite. Love, Daisy

---

Feb 12, 1935   CSTC

Dearest Ellis – (Tue nite 10:45) Heard today by way of Helen by way of Bill that you were practically in the dark on your way home Sunday nite; I'm glad that nothing serious resulted from it. I'd rather have had you leave at 4 & get home before dark if I'd known your lights were going to fail, but I'm afraid I just couldn't have seen that far ahead on Sunday. Also heard (via same source) that you & Bill had some serious discussion about religion, etc. Did Bill tell you what the questions & answers were that he wouldn't tell us? Wish you'd let me in on it – I'd like to know. This is the 6th week & we know it by the number of girls coming in to buy candy – to keep them awake while they stay up & study for mid-terms. I have only one mid-term due this week – wish me luck. Served at another banquet last night – 7-8:30 – Child Study Club – Lincoln's birthday scheme carried out in decorations – patriotic. It really was a nice dinner – 45 – & they complimented us on the service. I had a bit of a sore throat yesterday – I can't imagine where it came from because I wasn't out with anyone Sunday nite – but I gargled & gargled about every time I turned around & took a real hot bath last nite & went to bed & had nightmares all night – I was making fruit salad for everyone at the J-Hop – but I felt much better today & I'm sure that all the precautions were effective. I had my bed made for me today & expect to have it made each morning this week. We're initiating the pledges into Ronan Round Table this week & they must do whatever we tell them to do. Today they all had to carry umbrellas & raise them when going to & from classes. They also had to learn the definition of a knight & will repeat it to us on request. They have other things they have to do each day this week, such as supplying RRT members with gum & candy, etc. We had to go through it too, so we have no sympathy for their embarrassment. The announcer just said that the way to get the most out of life is to enjoy Wrigley's Spearmint Gum. Deep philosophy, isn't it? You must have made quite an impression on Bill from what he says. Besides other nice things, he said that you are the "cleanest & most sincere fellow" he's ever met & he thinks you're pretty swell. He's not the only one who thinks so either. I do. Mrs Newton said that you were "charming" & very nice-looking & Catherine voiced the same opinion. I wouldn't be telling you this if I didn't know that you can take it & I agree with them all, & may I add that they don't know the half of it either. I suppose Bud is all settled in Kazoo now & you're left quite alone, aren't you. It certainly is tough to lose a pal like that & I wish there were something I could do. I can only extend my sympathy, and hope, too, for a reconciliation. It was just awfully sweet of you to come clear up here to a J-Hop when everything was happening to make you feel bad & not at all in the mood for fun. I want you to know that I did appreciate it & loved having you here – every minute. Good-nite. Love X, Daisy

P.S. Let me know how you're getting along with your increased volume of work. Wishing you lots of ambition for it. X, Daisy

If Dad had a falling out with Bud Brorby, they must have patched it up, because, as I said earlier, they remained close friends for the rest of their lives. (Bud died in 1986 and Dad in 1989.)

Feb 13, 1935   CSTC

Dearest Ellis — (Wed nite 10:30) Your lovely Valentine gift was waiting for me when I came home tonite & I've been enjoying it so much, & so have my friends. Thank you, Ellis, it's so dear of you to remember me. I've been drinking hot lemonade. My roommate made it for me – for my cold – & Gerry greased me all up with Vicks & put a flannel cloth around my neck, so if I don't get over it soon, it won't be their fault. Kinda nice to be waited on though. I can't talk – much – & it's such a rest for my roommate, I know. It has just come on me today & it's in my throat & chest, but it'll be most gone by tomorrow probably. I know where I caught it (14, 371,000 germs & one of them is alive yet, but I'm not sorry – it was worth a dozen colds & I'd do it over again). Don't worry, will you. It was raining tonite when we came home from the library, & freezing & slippery & so nasty. I thought about you having to go out on the roads tomorrow & every day & I wish that you didn't have to. You'll be careful & take care of yourself, won't you? My instructions were to go straight to bed, so perhaps I'd best say Good-nite now – & thank you again. Love, Daisy X

P.S. This kind doesn't carry any germs.

P.P.S. But I'd still rather have the other kind.

Feb 17, 1935   CSTC

Dearest Ellis — (Sun nite 12m) I did receive your letter to have with this weekend "instead of you & your plagued cold." You're so dear, Ellis. Sometimes I wonder how your mother brought you up to make you so sweet & so entirely lovable. I hope you're made that way so you won't change. Your letter came shortly after noon Saturday & Helen nearly broke her neck & her leg getting it to me – I was in the library & when she rushed in & gave it to me my heart did a flip-flop – & when I read it, it gave a couple more. I thank you for your very kind sympathy, but really I'm sure you needed it more than I. I hope you're all well again & able to use your voice – not being able to talk is the worst of it, isn't it? Was for me anyway. I'm practically myself again tonite & feeling fine after a successful weekend. I'm caught up on all my back work & only have 2 classes tomorrow – one a test. I was going to write you Friday nite, but I was feeling rather down & the letter I would have written would be neither heartening nor enjoyable so now I'm glad I didn't write then, aren't you? I did my housecleaning this morning, got all straight with the world, took a shower & went to work & when I came home at 2 my folks were here & Clarence & Gertrude & they're not engaged, although the announcement was in the paper. Someone handed it in to the Press & they printed it – but without authority. (No comments necessary – I still have my opinions.) Momma brought us a loaf of bread, fresh-baked yesterday, butter, a pan of new-baked beans, & Northern Spy apples. So tonite Helen & I got the dish of beans between us & when we met in the middle we stopped eating. First time I've tasted homemade bread in 6 weeks & I did appreciate it. Your Friday's letter sounded so all tired-out & sleepy. I know you've been working awfully hard. I hope you don't have to work so hard this week & can get more rest. It was too bad that you had to come up here the weekend before such a hard week & lose sleep – and not feeling well in the bargain. I'm so sorry, Ellis, really I am. I know you didn't enjoy the party nearly as much as I thought you would, but there isn't anything I can do about it now except ask you to forgive me for almost forcing you to accept an invitation that you didn't especially want to in the first place. It did mean quite a lot to me, although of course not ever nearly as much as your health. But gee, now when I think of Sunday, I wouldn't have given it up for anything. I wish it were last Sunday now, about 6 o-clock. I'll just go to bed now & make believe that it is. Good-nite, my Pal X. Love XX, Daisy

---

Feb 19, 1935   CSTC

Dearest Ellis — (Tues morning 7:15 AM) We've just been listening to a preacher telling us how to live today so we won't be eternally condemned. It's kinda early for me, but I'm in a pretty good humor. I'll be so glad when the sun will get up before I do so it won't be a task to get out of bed in the morning. I received your letter yesterday afternoon when I was going to work at 4 & (just as all good news comes at once) Mrs Newton told me that I would have to come to work until 5 from now on. She has a new girl working by the week now so I won't have to work as long as I did & I can go home some weekends too. I certainly am enjoying this morning sermon but it disturbs me (my thoughts, not my conscience) so I think I'll turn it off. Your letter was so nice that I'm tempted to tell you I'm not feeling well yet. But I am & now I can appreciate them all the more & have more time to write you too. I'm so glad that Bud & Katherine are together again. I hope they don't run into any more difficulties. Is Bud a Catholic? I got 47 out of 50 on my 9:00 English test yesterday & feel pretty good about it. At 8 this morning I'll get the results from last Friday's test. Hope I'm as lucky. G'bye now. Don't work too hard & be sure to get your rest. Love, Daisy

Feb 19, 1935 CSTC

Dearest Dear Ellis – (Tues nite 11) I went to sleep at 4:00 today with your sweet little note & didn't wake up until 5:30 & I had the sweetest dreams. You're so thoughtful, Ellis, thank you for remembering me. I know that if I had been very sick, you letter would have me sitting on top of the world by now. Helen just tumbled into bed & said to tell you "hello" for her. We had a Mercier meeting tonite in the den & it was very successful – 21 in attendance & we played ping-pong & shuffleboard & pool & billiards & had a business meeting & made plans for a pancake supper to raise money to pay for our club picture in the Chippewa, & then we had punch & cookies & I served the punch. I'll soon be an expert. I didn't do too badly on my English test & feel pretty good about it. Tomorrow I have a test in Geography on topographical maps, to which I am looking forward with anticipation (?). I hope your days aren't as long & hard as they have been & I wish there were something I could do to help you but there doesn't seem to be. 100 miles is a long way so I can only send you my very best Love, Daisy XXXXX

Feb 21 & 22, 1935 CSTC

Dearest Ellis – (Thurs nite, Fri morn) We had a darn good game tonite with Northern (Marquette) & we won 21-18. Half the time it seemed more like a wrestling match & it looked as if the players were so tired they had to lie down on the floor – but – however – it was a good game. Now that I have my roommate all put to bed (but not to sleep) I can settle down & write. We fed 230 fellows in the cafeteria tonight in 15 minutes – I gave 'em pie & I never saw so much pie go so fast in my life. We had them all served in 15 minutes. The Men's Union gave the dinner & it was free for them. Kinda fun too. They made the freshman fellows carry out the dirty dishes & believe me we had dirty dishes – all over the place. Ronan Round Table had our initiation of new members tonite at Mrs Gibson's, & we took in [1-2M] girls – knighted them with all the ceremonies, etc. & then had cherry ice cream – half pint apiece & cookies & coffee & all went to the game together. I did pretty well on my Geography test yesterday & it made me feel kinda good. Hasn't been a bad day & I only hope that you're feeling as fine as I am tonite at the end of all your days. (1:15) How is business anyway these wintry days? Today & yesterday have been so sunshiny & cold & the nights are clear & starry. I like this kind of winter weather best if we must have winter but soon it will be spring & I'll be so glad! Helen is going home tomorrow & if Mrs Newton will let me off I'm going with her but I'm afraid she won't because the dessert girl is going away this weekend too. I wish I could tho. I always have fun when I go home with Helen. We'll go at 11, if I go. Gee, but I'm a trifle sleepy now, & if I don't go I can sleep. I only have one class Monday too, & that's something to look forward to. The music is so nice tonite. I wish you were here so we could listen to it together for a while. But since you're not I'll just have to go to bed & dream you are & send you my very best Love – & all the kisses I've saved & would give you if were only here. XXXXXX all these, etc. & ever so many more. Love, Daisy

P.S. (7:30) Dearest Ellis – I slept on it, & decided I'd best not go home with Helen on account of it will leave Mrs Newton short-handed & I'll have to skip Ag & Geography which I'd best not, & also I want to go home next weekend myself maybe & can't have too many off, so you'll probably hear from me again soon. Love, Daisy

---

Feb 24, 1935   CSTC

Dearest Pal o' Mine — (Sun 5 PM) I haven't been alone very much this weekend but I am a little lonesome now & I wish Grand Rapids weren't so far away. Your photograph is better company than none tho, even if it isn't very responsive. I wish you could see our room now. (In fact I wish you could be here.) I changed it all around Friday & slicked it up. I have the heads of our beds together with the radio between them & the desk & dresser on the other side of the room & just the desk lamp & dresser lamp on & it's so cozy & nice – like a fire-lighted room. I'll draw you a little plan of the room. The proportions may be a little screwy but just overlook that. I'll tell you about my weekend. I had all my classes Friday & worked from 10 to 1. I came home at 3 & juggled furniture & made beds, etc. Worked from 5 to 7 & came home & added the finishing touches, read a story in Good Housekeeping & went to bed at 9:30 luxuriating in the radio music that I had at my fingertips. Helen had left before noon & after weighing all the pros & cons I wasn't sorry that I stayed home. Mrs Newton wouldn't have let me go anyway – there were 3 of the help gone as it was & we had a rather hectic time Saturday noon with the extension students, etc. Saturday morning I awoke at 8:30 to a bright & sunshiny day & I typed English cards & studied until I went to work at 11. I was dessert girl & refill girl & worked on salads with Doris when I wasn't doing the other. I breathed again at 1:30 & came home, spent a social afternoon sewing & listening to the radio with Gerry for company & to work at 5. The crowd was light & it was really fun, not being very busy. At 7 I came home & went visiting, then went to the game with Doris & Vonnie & Marvel & Margaret Emery & Pauline Houseman & yelled ourselves hoarse. We played Hope & won 35-33. O, it was a very good game. I wish you could have come for it. You'd have enjoyed it I know. After the game the kids all came to my room & we had popcorn & candy & sat on the floor & listened to the radio & ate. Then Vonnie & I took Pauline home – she's Dick Houseman's wife, you know, & they live in that little tiny house over on Fancher. Dick had just come home from work (Kroger's) & was going to come after Pauline. They've been married a year & they're still sweethearts, living in their little doll house. It's awfully cute inside. We had some chocolate cake & came home at 11:30. June & Gerry & Doris were here listening to Jan Garber & Ted Weems until 12:30 & then I went to bed & was up at 7 to 7:30 mass. It was a lovely morning – with a breath of spring in the air & I enjoyed the walk so much but I rode the last few blocks with some awfully nice people & rode home with Bambers & ate breakfast at the cafeteria. Back to the dorm & cleaned up the mess from last nite & cleaned myself all up too. Made salads from 11 to 12 & was dessert girl from 12-2. Wasn't very busy this noon. Bee came home with me to see the dormitory & I showed her everything & we were up to Vonnie's & down to Margaret's & Doris's & after her tour of inspection she went home about 3, as "Kenneth" would be waiting for her – & it made me wish that there was someone to see me. But there wasn't, so I resigned myself & went to the library & brought home a load of books for me & for another girl. It snowed this afternoon & now it's winter again. I guess spring will never come. I was afraid Mrs Newton wouldn't let any of us go home again after this weekend, but I asked her today if I might go home next weekend & she's quite sure that I can go – so – I think I will go – next Friday afternoon. I have just one class tomorrow – at 9 o'clock, & at 1 I'm going to observe Margaret Johnson's Latin class. I'll probably be doing the same thing myself next fall & I really don't think I'll mind it. I only hope I'll still be in this frame of mind next fall. Helen isn't home yet, but she'll probably be along pretty soon. I hope she isn't snowed in or anything. Have you enjoyed yourself this weekend? I suppose you had more deadly ping-pong battles. I'd like to play a game with you. I'd probably get beat but it would be fun anyway. Kids are going to the show now & Margaret was in & asked me to go with them. It's "Clive of India." Somehow it doesn't appeal to me in the least. Since we have our radio, I'm just an old stick-in-the-mud, I guess. I'd just as soon stay home & listen to the radio as anything. Anyway, tonight I'd rather stay in where it's warm than go out in the cold & walk clear downtown on the slippery sidewalks. I'm going to read the History of Niagara Falls – for Geography now & so I'll close with Heaps o' Love & Kisses, Daisy xxxxxxxxxxxx

(10 PM) Dearest Ellis – Helen came home about 8 & woke me up where I'd fallen asleep on the Niagara River & a chocolate bar, which smeared me all up. She startled me out of about 7 years growth, because I didn't even realize I was asleep & I'd probably still be dreaming if she hadn't come. She appears to have had a very pleasant & successful weekend & saw a home-talent play which she told me all about & I told her everything I

did so I guess we're all caught up now & can go to bed. She brought back some chocolate peanut butter fudge & set the plate of it right on my bed with me – what else could I do? But I confess I do feel rather sorry now, but it's just grand candy. Good-nite now. Love, Daisy

Enclosed is a rough drawing of the layout of Mom's dorm room. Mom obviously had plenty of friends at work & in the dorm so was never lacking for company if she wanted it. And I was a bit surprised at her enthusiasm for a basketball game, and for her saying Dad would have enjoyed it too, because I can't remember either of them ever attending any athletic events when my brothers & I were in high school. Bill & I both played basketball and Bob ran track, but neither Mom nor Dad ever came to any of our games or meets. And Jan Garber was a very popular big band leader throughout the 1930s, and so was Ted Weems, whose "boy singer" was Perry Como, who had an unbroken string of hits in the forties and fifties, and later hosted one of the most popular variety shows of the 1960s.

Feb 26, 1935   CSTC

Dearest Ellis – (Tue nite 11:30) Gee, when I was coming home tonite, I was wondering if you were stuck in a snowbank somewhere & hoping that you weren't. Enough people have been in the last few days & I hope you weren't among them. Wish we could all stay inside & sleep when it's as cold as this. I think it would be a very sensible thing to do (I'm so sleepy now). We have it pretty soft here tho – the walks are all cleared off on the campus & we don't even have to wear boots. Served at a Rotary Club banquet last night – there were about 100 there & they had a floor-show afterwards. Helen & some of the kids stayed to see it, but I was sound asleep when Helen came home at 10:30 & didn't hear a thing altho she stayed up until 12 & had company & the radio on all the time. I have a test in English tomorrow at 9 o'clock & I've been reviewing for it, but not very thoroughly I'm afraid on account of my eyes won't stay open. I had a letter from my mother today & they're having measles & scarlet fever & whooping cough all around home. Clarence had been praying for snow & when it did come he had such a cold & sore throat that Mama wouldn't let him go to work. I'm going home Friday if someone comes after me & I think someone will. I'll pray that you won't get snowed in or stuck or freeze any parts of your anatomy, 'cause it is awfully cold, isn't it? Helen got a letter from Bill yesterday special delivery. I wonder if he got the idea from you. Great minds – you know. Your picture is all smeared up with kisses now – so I'll polish you & kiss you again. Good-nite, my Dear Ellis. Love, Daisy xx

Feb 28, 1935 CSTC

Dearest Ellis – (Thurs 10:45 AM, Library) I'm so happy. Everything is rosy & I'm just glad today. The sun is shining osobright just like it'll be shining for Bud & Catherine Saturday & every day afterwards I hope sincerely. It seems almost as if I know them too & I'd like to send my best wishes for their happiness. And you're going to be best man? That's what you think – but don't forget to remember the ring. I'm sorry you still have such a cold & I hope it'll be all gone by Sat or before. But you just think how much longer you'd have it if you hadn't given some of it to me. I got a card from my mother this morning too & they're coming after me Friday & Doris (Mickles), my cousin, & George Malesky are getting married Saturday in Detroit & they're coming to Oakley Saturday nite so I'll see the bride & groom too. It was 14 below zero at home yesterday morning & it was pretty darn cold here too. I was beginning to get spring fever last weekend but it was snowed under. It's coming on again now tho, & I hope the snow goes away soon. There was a robin in Mt Pleasant Tuesday, but I didn't see it. It's lucky that you were snowed in at home rather than out on the road somewhere tho. I don't expect to go ice-fishing this weekend. I'm not planning anything, but I will "take you with me in my dreams." I must get busy now. Was working on an Agriculture assignment but it was just too dry for words & I couldn't keep my mind on it. I'm chairman of a group who have to tell stories Monday in English class & I made the assignments today & now I have to prepare my own before I go home. "David Copperfield" is here next Sunday nite & if I have all my work done, maybe we'll go. We have to go out & celebrate sometime before Lent starts & we figured that as the best time on account of there's a lecture course number Tuesday nite & that wouldn't be a regular celebration. Have to go to work in about ½ hour so I'll close now with Heaps o' Love, Daisy xx

P.S. Sorry you're going to "lose a pal," but I hope he won't be sorry & you really shouldn't be losing one – but gaining another. If you'll be leaving G.R. I hope you don't get too far away. L, D.

Mar 4, 1935 CSTC

Dearest Ellis – (Mon nite 11:30) I wonder where you are now - if you're still located in GR or elsewhere. Wherever you are, I hope you like it there, & that this will reach you safely. I had such a grand rest over the weekend - & felt so full of pep & "wim & wigor" today that I wore myself all out. But my bath has revived me & I'm all ready to start in again. I didn't do much besides sleep when I was home except to go to a couple of shows. I saw James Cagney & Pat O'Brien in "Devil Dogs of the Air, Shirley Temple & Lionel

Barrymore in "The Little Colonel" and "David Copperfield" (Sunday nite when I came back) – all of which were splendid pictures – all, I think, too, on the approved list – & I know you'd enjoy them too. Did the wedding really materialize this time? I sincerely hope so – & that everyone concerned is happy. Doris & George didn't come to Oakley, so I didn't see them after all. Did you know that Sayde Yarabek & Bob Coon were married? They eloped about 3 or 4 weeks ago & went to Indiana & got married. I think that's all the big news I heard when I was home. I'm glad I went when I had a chance – Mrs Newton isn't going to let anyone go again this term or next term either. Just 4 more weeks tho, and I'll be home again. It's spring now – seems like it anyhow – but it was awfully slippery today & we have plenty of water around too. Spring can't come a bit too soon to suit me. When it's summer the miles aren't as long, either, are they? After the show Sunday nite, we had 5 of our pals in for a spread – toasted cheese sandwiches, tea, cake & apples – & a good time was had by all. Tuesday nite we have a play given by the M.P. Little Theatre group as a number on the lecture course & I think with that I can be content & be willing to abstain from shows, etc., etc. during Lent. I must read "Christabel" now, so I'll give you my Love, dear, from Daisy

xx & Good-nite, Pal

Mar 10, 1935   CSTC

Dearest Pal – (Sun nite 11) If lots of water & mud & robins prove that it's spring, then spring really is here to stay this time. I do hope so. About 5 this afternoon, a flock of a dozen robins arrived & sang in the tree by our window – first ones I've seen this year. I'm lonesome, Ellis, for you. Do you suppose the roads will be dried up in a couple of weeks & it will be nice weather? If you are located so that you can, & don't have anything more pressing to do, would you like to come up & see me? I wish you could. There are three more weeks in this term & two weekends – this coming one & the next. I could have late permission until 1 Saturday nite & there wouldn't be a big party to spoil everyone's good disposition, etc. It's just a suggestion & you might not seem to be able to come, but if you can, I'd love to have you, you know. And you could bring Bill along for company if you could get in touch with him. Anyway, I hope you can come, but if you don't I'll love you just as much. It's Lent now & it seems such a long time until Easter. We went to 7:30 mass this morning & oh, it was slippery & Helen fell down once, but we had a ride back. So we decided we wouldn't go down to eat this evening, but just stay home & starve. Then Marvel & Vonnie came back from home & invited us down to the dine-a-nite & we had homemade buns & scrambled eggs & cake & enjoyed it so much. About an hour & a half later Buena came down & asked us for a spread. We had sandwiches of fried tenderloin (home-butchered) & apples. Helen just said that she feels a little sick – I wonder why. We went downtown at 4:00 yesterday to go to confession but the priest didn't come so we went down again at 7:30 & it was such a lovely evening to walk. I felt so turbulent & restless & wanted to do something but we couldn't on account of Lent so went to bed at 9:30 & slept it off. Must have been spring fever. I think I shall retire now, so good-nite, my Dear. Love, Daisy x

---

Mar 13, 1935   CSTC

Dearest Ellis – (Wed nite 11:15) Waded thru the snow to church again tonite to get preached at – getting almost as bad – or as good – as the mission. Isn't it just awful? I'm afraid you'd get marooned in a snowbank if you come up this weekend. I've just given up looking for spring – robins don't mean a thing. I'm glad you could go home & had such a nice weekend. I had a letter from my mother & she said Uncle Phil is sick in bed again & the Dr says he'll never get up & Aunt Stacia is in the hospital – but I don't know which one. I imagine she has pneumonia – she has it nearly every year. I hope she comes thru it as well as she has before. My roommate is writing a short story – about hell – and oh, the horrors she has in her hell. I think I'll be good. So you're going to Kalamazoo. I hope you'll like it there – but gee, it seems you get farther & farther away – I hope you won't get so far away that we can't see each other sometimes. Once in a while I get lonesome. I'm glad you're not going to trade off the little Ford – I like it a lot & I hope it'll bring you up to see me again soon maybe. Gee, this sounds silly, but I'm awfully sleepy & tired. Just a creampuff, I guess – can't take it if I don't get my 8 hours every night. I had more to tell you but I can't remember now – I'll write again. So good-nite now, Dearest Dear. Love, Daisy x

---

Mar 17, 1935   CSTC

Dearest Ellis – (Sun 12:45 AM) You're my inspiration & you're sitting on the radio right now in front of me & the sweetest, most romantic music you're bringing. It's raining tonite & I was lying on my bed reading Keats's poetry & listening to the rain & remembering so many rainy nights that were lovely, & a white wooly sweater so soft & sweet-smelling & clean rain-washed air – and a girl sang, "Just a Year Ago Tonite" – & then I remembered last St Patrick's & was thinking of the things I'd write to you. Then I went to sleep & dreamed of Christmas tree lights & campfires in Cathedral Woods & I guess I'm not awake yet. I intended to study a lot tonite & I did study but I still have a lot to do. Today was high school day here for girls' basketball *teams from all over this section of the state. They played basketball this morning – & after our cafeteria dinner hour was over, we came over to the dorm & fed them – about 250 of them. Then we saw the exhibition game in the gym between Central's phys ed majors (girls) & University of Michigan's. We won 20-22. It was a good game – first girls' game I've seen since a year ago when they were here for the same thing. At 4 I went to the science building to study topographic maps for Geography, but I couldn't get much out them so I proof-read a girl's short story for her & went to work at 5 & when I came home at 7 it was raining – & still is. This afternoon my mother sent me a stool she made me from a wooden candy pail. It's padded & covered with rust, yellow & green plaid & lined inside & it's so nice to sit on – we have it in front of our radio – I'm sitting on it now. Yesterday was Conservation Day – sponsored by the Ag Dept & there were speeches & programs & movies from 3 until 10 at nite. There was a banquet for the people – 250 – at 6:30 & they went thru the line & we fed them in about 20 mins. But we didn't leave 'til after 7:30, so we didn't go to church (heathens!) but went & saw the movies in the auditorium instead – nature, wild life (wild animal life). Went to visit Harriet Abbey (steno) & downtown for a soda & came home at 11:30 so I didn't do any studying yesterday either. The orchestra just played a St Patrick's Day medley – "My Wild Irish Rose," "When Irish Eyes Are Smiling," "Where the River Shannon Flows," etc. – and now they've degenerated to some modern jazz. We (Mercier Club) are having a bridge party Tuesday nite (for the purpose of making $10 to pay for our Chippewa picture) & we expect to have about 12 tables. Hope this one turns out better than our pancake supper (which we didn't have). I received your card this morning from Benton Harbor, saying you weren't coming this weekend & it looked so much like a storm (weather) that I was glad you weren't coming (not glad, but I thought it was better). Anyway, after I wrote you before, I received you letter saying you'd be going to your grandmother's. If or when you come up next weekend, I hope it'll still be balmy spring weather with neither rain nor snow. If next weekend won't be as convenient for you as another, or if you'd planned anything else, just let me know & I'll understand. I'm always glad to see you tho, you know, don't you? Gee, 3 stations have signed off already & I've just had to fill my pen & maybe I'd best sign off too or you'll probably be sending clippings of this letter back to me for an explanation – you'll excuse any slips tho, won't you, on account of I'm so sleepy. So Good-Nite, Dearest. Love, Daisy X*

(Sun 10 AM) Dearest Ellis – The ground is all white with snow this morning – the hard, slippery, sleety kind – & the wind is o-so cold. We went to 7:30 mass & we were there before the sermon started, believe it or not. We had a ride home & ate breakfast in the cafeteria with the good old "Breakfast Club" singing "When Irish Eyes Are Smiling," etc. How I love those old Irish

songs. Fr Mulvey's sermon was about St Patrick this morning. The sun is shining now but it isn't so "hot." I hope you're at your grandmother's all stretched out for a snooze on the parlor sofa. Wouldn't mind being there myself – lie to snooze somewhere anyway. How are Bud & Kate getting along – happy as ever? Hope so. Must do more mathematics for Agriculture – senseless stuff & I go to work at 11 today. So, bye now. Love, Daisy

(Mon morning 12:15 AM) Dearest Dear – Don't let me get in wrong again by writing this in installments, will you? I like to write often & then I don't get so lonesome. Rather – when I do get lonesome, I get over it quicker. Again I'm sleepy, but I just want to say Good-Nite. I wouldn't feel right if I didn't, with you right here by me. (Wish you really were.) Are you going to be in GR this week? Hope you had a nice weekend. I studied in the library all afternoon & in the room here all evening. Have a test tomorrow & Tuesday in Comp Lit. I won't have much to do next weekend. I'm so sleepy, so Good-nite, Sweetheart-Pal. Love, Daisy xx

---

Mar 19, 1935   CSTC

Dearest Ellis – (Tue nite 1:00 AM Wed) Now I really think that 2 letters in the same mail call for an acknowledgement. So here it is – not that this is a duty letter – never! Your letters were sweet, Ellis, as sweet as you are. The weather reports for this weekend as prophesied by the roommate is wonderful – with a nite as lovely as tonite – & tonite is a night of nights – with a beautiful moon & soft breezes & everything that makes you feel you don't want to be alone. It's going to be a grand weekend, Ellis, I know – & there's not going to be anything going on here – our schedule is empty & all we'd have to do is be on time & we really can. If you can surmount all your difficulties & come, I'll be so glad – & if you can bring Bill along, you'll be making another little girl happy. It won't matter if it's late when you get here – we can have 'til 1 o'clock & you

Ronan Round Table Week
at Chrystal Lake.
Helen & Daisy

can stay over & sleep late Sunday morning. Gee, I hope you can come – & I'm praying awfully hard. I'm glad you had such a nice weekend & that you're going to get a new truck. Is this one going to be red too? I hope you can get your flour unloaded early too. "How're ya doin'? Not bad, big boy, not bad." Critchell said she was wondering why you went to Carson City so often. I'd say you're doing fine. But really I think you should drop down next weekend & see your namesake too – another reason. We had our bridge party tonite & everyone said it was awfully nice. We took in $12 – enough to pay for our Chippewa pictures. Helen & I went downtown at 10 & bought the groceries for the party & made sandwiches, etc. all afternoon. I really quite enjoyed playing bridge tonite – first time in a couple years. We had some sandwiches left & brought them to the dorm & sold 'em to the kids & got 75c for them. So we think we're not a bad team of managers. In the morning at 7 I've gotta go over & help clean up the place too. O, by the way, I'm not going to shows either in Lent, so that's all right, but what was your other resolution? I hope it wasn't to abstain from coming to Mt Pleasant. Ronan Round Table is sponsoring a tea Thursday afternoon & I just got thru typing invitations to faculty & I must take those over in the morning too. "Am eating no more sandwiches with nobody tonite." G'nite. Love, Daisy xxxxx

Dad's friends in Carson City, Mick & Mary Churchill, had named their newest baby Ellis. (They had two older boys, Larry & Don.) Hence the remark about visiting his "namesake" there.

Mar 27, 1935   CSTC

Dearest Ellis — (Wed nite 8:45) I thought maybe you'd rather get a letter with a borrowed stamp on it than none at all - none - letter, I mean - not a stamp. You seem to be doing a lot of traveling this week, but I'm taking a chance that you'll be back in Grand Rapids Friday nite. It has been raining like hell here since 7 this evening. It rains every Wednesday & Friday night when we go to church. So we just don our boots, slickers & beret & enjoy it thoroughly. I hope it's not raining tomorrow – I love the sunshine. But the rain brings happy memories too. I went to 7:30 mass last Sunday & it was a grand day. I had sleeping sickness most of the day but woke up long enough to play a half-hour's tennis about 5, & at 7 we had a spread in Margaret Emery's room after which I promptly went to sleep again & finally got up & retired. Had my final in Eng Lit at 8 this morning – left me feeling rather weak in the knees. How I fared I'll know Friday. I have a test in Geography tomorrow & one in Ag Friday. George Burns & Gracie Allen are on now – crazy but can't help laughing. The number of people we're going to feed Saturday has swelled to 1800 – I'm looking forward with dread anticipation to the event. I'm afraid the Newtons will be so wrought up about it by Saturday that they'll forget to cook the potatoes or some such momentous thing. I think, however, that I'll live through & be that much gladder to get home. Helen appreciated the M.W. joke very much, & although she doesn't have one on hand right at present to return, after vacation she might have a few. I have a final in Comparative Lit Friday too, but I don't have to study for it & that makes me very happy. Nevertheless I should do some reviewing for Ag now. But Jan Garber is on – what else can I do? O, Ellis, I'd just love to spend a weekend in Carson spring term when Crystal is open & I think it's awfully nice of Mrs Mick to want me to. So I "hope so" too. Have you your new truck yet? I'll just bet you won't get it now 'cause you didn't stay & go after it when you were supposed to. Seriously, I think it was grand of Mick's to name their new son after you. Guess it shows who rates, doesn't it? I'm sleep now, so G-nite. Love, Daisy xxxxx

---

Apr 3, 1935   Oakley

Dearest Ellis – (Wed nite 10:00) Vacation is half over & I'm just getting into the "home frame-of-mind" in time to go back again. I'm so contented & sleepy here on the davenport now that I don't care if I ever move again. The temptation is almost too great. But when I drop asleep the noise of the Frigidaire (we have a new one) soon wakes me. I trust you enjoyed your drive from Detroit to Kazoo Sunday (at 20 per) – at any rate, you must have got a good look at the scenery. How's the new truck? I came home Saturday night about 5 with Lucille Copernall, desiring nothing more than a place to lay my weary body. We went to Owosso & to the show (broke a resolution but what could I do?). Anyway it was more penance than pleasure. I went to sleep in the

middle of a very thrilling western & don't remember what any of it was about. We fed 800 farmers chop suey, etc. Expectations ran as high as 1800 at one time, & 1200 were planned for so we had enough food left over for a couple of meals each for all the people in Oakley. Worked from 8:30 to 2:30

Saturday – served from 11:30-1. My report came today with 4 B's. Do I still suit? I didn't expect a B from Calkins but I liked him & maybe that counted for something. I earned a B in Ag from Mr Cobb but I didn't think I'd get it because he doesn't like the girls. I think he made allowances tho, 'cause I stayed over to feed his farmer friends. Fr Grinzinger from Chesaning held services here tonight & he has such a soothing voice that I had to summon all my faculties to keep awake. He really is a good speaker though. I was over this afternoon to see Steph & her "family.' The baby is fat & pudgy & good-natured, & looks just like Pete. Pete has a couple of young hounds tied up in the chicken-park & they're serenading us most of the time – sound like half a dozen. The newest Clark is a bouncing boy now & better looking every time I see him. There was quite some excitement in town the first part of the week over elections. The republicans won tho, & last night the dems celebrated in the hall. Only one democrat was elected – John Thiel – road commissioner. Joe is still managing his elevator but I guess his business isn't ever too rushing. Mrs Gower hasn't been able to walk downtown this winter on account of her rheumatism, & that, I believe, is the extent of the local news – no scandal that I've heard as yet – I haven't been to see Aunt Flory & Uncle Phil yet. When I do, I'll get the low-down on everyone. Dorothy & Alfred & 2 kids were here all Sunday afternoon, & Helen & Rosalie & Jimmy were here Monday PM. Tuesday PM we went shopping & the rest of my time I've spent sewing. I suppose I'll discover all the things I've been doing wrong when I sew. I suppose you've your room all selected & settled in Kazoo now. Hope you'll like it as well as Grand Rapids. You'll be farther away from home again tho, won't you? And 50 miles farther from me too. O, dear, s'pose I'll be seein' ya often enough so I won't forget what you look like? But I couldn't do that. Wish I'd be seein' you this weekend. But – ... Wish you could be her now too – just for a Good-Night. Love, Daisy xxxxxx

---

Apr 7, 1935 (Back at CSTC again)

Dearest Ellis – (Sun nite 10:30) It's cold COLD – I hope it's a lot warmer where you are when you get this – down south in Kazoo, I supposed. We had some heat here for a few hours but it seems to have evaporated (?). Otherwise everything's okay & it seems kinda nice to be all settled here again. It's always so restful to have nothing to do the first two nights of the term. Helen & I arrived at the same time (4:45) this afternoon so neither of us had a chance to get lonesome. I bet Helen wishes now that she would have about a half hour in which to get lonesome. She's writing to Bill & I keep saying something to her & disturb her "train of thought" – not intentionally of course. The Weems Orchestra is on now. Our radio maybe isn't quite as powerful & selective as our radio at home – but

I don't know what we'd do without it now. The folks brought me back. Lucille Coppernall came with me & between the two of us we had a load. "The Lullaby of Broadway" they're singing now. I like the song a lot. It's so catchy. The folks are coming up to see me Easter Sunday. I'll be so glad when Lent's over. But do you know what I did when I was home? I went to 5 shows (2 double features) & ate candy too – but I didn't dance. Thursday nite I saw Janet Gaynor & Warner Baxter in "One More Spring" – it was different. I liked it. Sat nite I saw 2 that were just grand for entertainment. One was a British picture – filmed by an English motion picture company I mean, with English stars n' all – "Jack Ahoy." The other one was an animal story, "Trailing the Killer," & it was a lot more exciting than it sounds even. It was awfully wearing on me – and on the seat too, I'm afraid. Now she's singing "When the Moon Turns Green" – supposed to be the most popular song of the week in the west. Did you ever see the moon turn green? Neither did i. I haven't even had a good look at the moon in such a long time. Just think – in a few weeks it will be really summer with no more snow & cold winds. I'll be so glad. Gee, you know last Saturday night when I was all "cleaned up" I felt so good & O, how I wished you were coming & then I thought of the long, long miles & sometimes I wish that Central were where Western is – but I'll bet you're glad it isn't too. I'd like to have you here for just a wee small while to say Good-nite, but the best I can do is send just loads & loads o' Love & Kisses for Ellis from Daisy xxxxxx

---

Apr 8, 1935   CSTC

Dearest Ellis — (Mon nite 11) You don't know how good it made me feel to get a letter from you this morning & one this afternoon too. I was writing to you last nite at the same time you were writing to me, but you probably won't get my letter right away because I sent it to GR, not knowing you Kazoo address. I'm glad you like your new location & hope you'll continue to like it. Bill's coming over to see you soon too. I didn't enroll until 9:30 this morning, but it only took me an hour. I'm taking 3 English courses – 8, 9 & 1 – and Home Ec, sewing 3-5. I think I like my schedule. I'll know very soon anyway, for classes start tomorrow & it's back to work again for Daisy. I'm so tired tonight tho, just from doing nothing. We went downtown this afternoon & O, it was cold. I guess the heating plant engineer thinks that because it's spring term we don't need any heat. Anyway, we haven't enough to keep a fly warm. Hope it's warmer tomorrow. It's nice that you had company to go with you to Detroit & that you had such a nice (?) party too. But really, I'm glad you enjoyed yourself. We're hearing a duet – but the men are singing different songs. We can get two stations at a time on our radio - pretty darn good, what? Not all radios are like that. I'm so sorry you were lonesome last nite. I was lonesome too, & I wish I could have been there with you to "do" - wonderfully (?). How is the new truck? Does it still do 20? My dad is getting his new car this week or next, so I suppose he'll have it when he comes up Easter. So the Carson City oil well is bigger than the Mt Pleasant oil wells - but - we've still got more of 'em. And you can't beat us in numbers very soon. Quite a number of new girls in the dorm this term & some of the old ones have left. I'm sleepy now too, & guess I'll have to go to bed to keep warm - so please consider yourself thoroughly kissed. xxxxxx Love, Daisy

P.S. I seem to have a choice between 883 & 833, & since 833 appears twice & 883 once, I'll try that first. He's - "tight again." Love, D.

Apr 14, 1935   CSTC

Dearest Ellis – (Sun nite 8:30 PM) Your letter was so sweet & I'm ashamed of myself for not having written you before because I probably haven't been any more tired than you were at night. I'm glad that the Wheaties sales have improved. Hurrah for Shirley Temple! I wish all the other products would get a boost like that. A typewriter is a handy little thing to have around sometimes, isn't it? But I can read your "stuff" with no difficulty at all & I like much better your own handwriting (if you don't mind). I saw some new Royal portables at Gover's today that are probably like yours. I think they're pretty keen myself. I'd be lost without mine now if Helen didn't have one I can use. I left it at home for my Dad to use & he's going to bring it up to me Easter when he comes. I've been reading "The Life of Benvenuto Cellini" & it isn't particularly uplifting. However, it is supposed to be the world's most famous autobiography & the reading of it is required for out Italian unit in Comparative Lit. Today & yesterday have been just grand. Such weather makes me lonesome. Last night was opening night at Crystal & most of the kids went "by hook or by crook" & I was feeling so down, so I went down to Margaret Emery's room & we talked & talked, & thrashed out all the problems of life. But after all we had to come back to the present. I came home & couldn't study & I didn't want to depress anyone with a letter so I went to bed. We went to church bright & early this morning at 7:30 & weren't late. It was such a gorgeous day & O, how I wished you were coming up. I studied hard for a couple of hours this afternoon, then we took a book down to Mrs Maybee & went for a nice walk and had a sandwich at the Downtown and a sundae at the Olympia (giving 'em all a break). Then we just had to come home & go to work & I've been studying hard ever since. Yesterday at 1 we served at a dinner for the AAUW (American Ass'n of University Women) until 3:00. Doris & Vonnie & Helen & I served. Thursday nite Helen & I served a group of Mt Pleasant club women & they said that our "service was so soothing." Wednesday was Vonnie's birthday & we gave her a party & was she surprised. Dick & Pauline Houseman took her to the show & we were all in her room when she came home. I really don't think she was as surprised as she seemed to be tho. We gave her a silver clip for a bookmark with a Central seal on it because she reads so much. Margaret has a birthday this week or next too. The birthday business is going strong now. O, gee, I'm so sleepy. My roommate has retired. The mob will soon be coming home from the show & raising hell. Must write to my folks too. You know, Ellis, I've never seen one of the ice cream freezers you describe & I wish you could come up in a couple of weeks & tell me more about it. I'd love to hear. Would you be having a sales-meeting or anything then, do you think? I wish you could come up sometime pretty soon. I get so lonesome for you. Wish you were here now, to say Good-nite, Pal, 'cause ILoveu, Daisy

Shirley Temple did indeed endorse Wheaties in 1935 and went on to do the same for Bisquick and Gold Medal Flour, and her image appeared on Wheaties boxes nearly a dozen times over the next year. And Crystal Lake, just thirty miles south of Mt Pleasant, near Carson City, was a very popular night spot and vacation destination, with dining and dancing at the Crystal Palladium and other pavilions. Most of these places were to close in the next decade.

Apr 17, 1935 CSTC

(Wed morning) O, Ellis, it's just grand this morning so I can drag out the white shoes again. Had a grand sleep & a shower for an eye-opener & hope you'll be feeling as good when you get this as I do when I'm sending it.

Dearest Ellis — (Wed nite 10) I have only two classes tomorrow so tonight I'm taking a vacation from now on & going to bed early. But first I must say "Hello" to you, & how are the sales coming n' everything, including Kalamazoo? I'm in a pretty good humor myself, always am when I have the prospect of a long night's sleep ahead of me. This afternoon I went to sleep in the commons at 2 & didn't wake up until nearly 3 – hungry, so I had a nut roll & a glass of milk in the cafeteria & maybe that's what gave me pep for the rest of the day – or should I have had Wheaties? I was elected president of the Ronan Round Table last night & my troubles are beginning – or should I say worries? Every year the women's literary societies & the men's societies go to Crystal for a weekend house party & this year we can't get cottages so Thursday the presidents are having a meeting to decide where we can go. Memorial weekend we're going this year. In the course of this writing no less than 4 people have been in here to visit so it's now after 10:30 & the eyes are beginning to droop. Most of the kids are going home this weekend on account of school closes at noon Friday – but the cafeteria stays open & we stay with it. Tomorrow I must settle down & concentrate on a paper for English, the theme of which is to be: "a standard of values which will ultimately contribute a desirable American type effecting the establishment of an ideal American commonwealth" – & I don't like to think! Lovely weather we've been having yesterday & today, yes? No, 1,000 times NO! I don't like winter in-season, but out-of-season it's hateful, yes? Now I will close because I'm sleepy & say, Good-nite, Pal o' Mine. Love, Daisy

---

Apr 18, 1935   CSTC

Dearest Ellis – (Thurs nite 11) It's such a grand nite, Ellis, & I can't go to bed without saying a word to you – "Hello, Ellis! How're you?" We went to the show tonite – on Holy Thursday, & I know we should have gone to church, but wait until I tell you what it was – "Sequoia" & it was just ____! You supply the word. It was just the kind of show that makes you pound the arm of your seat & forget where you are – an animal picture, story of a deer & a puma raised to be pals. And O, Ellis, the most gorgeous moon – silver & so round – when we were coming home, I mean, a real moon, & Ellis, if you don't come to see me pretty soon, I just won't be able to stand it. I mean I hope nothing will stop you from coming & I hope Bill can come too. I must go to bed now, so Good-nite. Love, Daisy x

---

Apr 19, 1935   CSTC

Dearest Ellis – (Dorm, Fri nite 9) My dear, how did you guess that I was out of stationery? It was very thoughtful of you to include this in your letter. Don't tell me you were afraid I wouldn't write. Just try & keep me from it. It's kinda lonesome around here tonite. 'Most everyone has gone home for Easter. I'm glad that you can go home too. I've got plenty to do to keep me busy here this weekend. No trouble keeping busy so far anyway. Made salads from 10-12 today, served a luncheon 12-1:45 – to church at 2 & had to stand up for an hour. Downtown shopping with Helen for her hat until 4:30 – and then she didn't get any. Work 5-6:30 & home to wash clothes & clean up. Shirley came over this afternoon & she & June are gone to the show – they'll be back pretty soon & ready to do something – dunno what, but we'll stir up something – I'd like nothing better than a bed – but – such is life. But it's a grand life – or it will be next weekend if you come up as you suggested. And you'll be staying over Sunday too, won't you? I hope so. Doris will work for me Sunday so I won't have to if I should have a guest. Gee, it seems such a long time since I've seen you. And if Bill comes along, you'll be making four people happy. I'm glad you're going to have a vacation this year. It's been quite a while since you've had one, hasn't it? I'll be having my next one the last week in June too. So what? Gee, I'm sleepy, I suppose the kids will be coming back from the show pretty soon. Gonna play a game of tennis in the morning too if I don't oversleep. Signing off now. G'nite. Love, Daisy x

On stationery from the Occidental Hotel in Muskegon

Apr 29, 1935   CSTC

Dearest – (Mon nite 11) They're playing our theme song of Sunday – "When I Grow Too Old to Dream," & then I remembered that I should write you so you'll know I'm not "pouting" – as you call it. Everything considered, I've had a most successful day, even if I did sleep & dream over my studying last nite. Had 29 out of 30 in my 9:00 test, A- on my 1:00 theme & finished my "evening dress" in sewing class – so I feel quite at peace & quite sleepy now as usual. I'm supposed to tell you not to bring Bill with you when you come up in 4 weeks because Helen has asked a fellow here to the party that night & Bill will just have to stay home with his "Jumpin' Jenny Horsecollar," poor boy. I hope you haven't told him already that you're coming. If you'll just remember not to forget to bring yourself, however, I will be quite happy. Now I have quite exhausted my deep & ponderous thoughts – for the present anyhow – so Good-nite & 1,000 x's to Ellis from Daisy

P.S. Be good – I am – (?)

P.P.S. I'm so glad you came; it was so sweet of you. Love, Daisy x

---

May 2, 1935   CSTC

Dearest Pal – (Thurs nite 9:00) 'Twas a sweet letter you wrote me from "Blossom Town." It made me feel like a million dollars. I'd like to have seen the Blossom Festival too. Opal Jean Butts from Chesaning was "Miss Owosso." Clarence told me. He was up to see me today. I was so surprised when he came into the library at 11 where I was writing a theme. He has a week "off" & he's been in Midland the first part of the week trying to get into the Dow Chemical Co. & this afternoon he went to the Oil Refinery here, but didn't find anything. He intended to stay over 'til Saturday & we were going to the show tonite but he decided he'd rather go home tonite because there wasn't anything to stick around for, so we took Margaret

& Doris & Marvel down to the show & he left for home about 7:30. He has over 50,000 miles on the old Pontiac & it's still going strong. He ought to be home by this time. My dad got his new car last Saturday – a town sedan with a trunk on it – tan-colored. I think they'll all come up Sunday – hope so. We're having more fun tonite – we're staying with Margaret & Doris & rented our room to 2 County Normal girls (something after the fashion of your room-sharing with the "Blossom Beauties" – but we moved ourselves out to accommodate them). We're going to sleep on the floor tonite – it's supposed to be good for reducing the hips – we're a bit apprehensive tho – might not have any hips left in the morning. Today & tomorrow are County Normal days here & kids from 13 Co Normals round about are here – I think about 50 C.N girls are staying in the dorm. They surely did keep us busy at the cafeteria this noon & tonite – tomorrow too, I expect, they will. I surely hope Bill came out all rite on Monday, etc. – in his lessons & got his short story all OK. It rained here Sunday nite late too & it's been cold ever since. I'm glad you struck the nice weather Sunday – or did you order it? I was so contented & happy Sunday nite that I probably wouldn't have worried about a short story if I'd had one to write. I don't have any classes tomorrow PM, & that makes me feel quite "unambitious" tonite. Doris & Margaret have not yet returned from the show & we have quite thoroughly & comfortably installed ourselves in their room & I'm getting quite sleepy. Monday nite Helen & I were discussing our "during-&-after-dinner" conversation Sunday & became quite embarrassed – too late? We agreed that if it were not for the fact that all 4 of us are good Catholics, this might have been reason to be shocked. But being good Catholics we all understand that it's only meant to be funny. The lit societies sent a delegation to Chippewa Lake yesterday to look over the prospect of a house party there & it didn't seem to be so hot. I think we'll probably go to Wenona – at Bay City. Decoration Day is opening night there too. I'm looking forward more tho to the weekend before that. Hope everything works out OK. Have a good time this weekend, won't you – with Bud & Kate. Where are you going to be next week? Yesterday I worked for a luncheon at noon & dinner at nite – 120 U of M alumni at nite. No, that was Tuesday, guess I told you. Anyway I'm pretty sleepy, so Good-nite, My Pal, the "King." Your Loving Daisy xx

The "Blossomtime Festival" (begun circa 1906) is an annual event in the Benton Harbor – St Joseph area of southwest Michigan, obviously part of Dad's sales territory at the time. It's still going strong after more than a hundred years. Mom's brother Clarence was apparently out of work and searching hard for any kind of job, a rare, if oblique, reference on Mom's part to the Depression's hard times & rampant unemployment.

97

May 5, 1935 CSTC

Dearest Ellis – (Sun nite 8:45) How is my pal? Hope you're feeling as fine as I want you to. I'm so sleepy & I shouldn't be because I've still so much to do tonite. Thank you for the program. You were sweet (as usual) in sending it. Are you going to be in Benton Harbor this week too? I think it would be fun to be around & see the crowning of the Queen. I'd love to see the countryside all in blossom. All the trees were white here Friday PM – with snow. We had nearly a foot of it. It was a lot of fun sleeping on the floor Thursday nite – 5 of us in the room & we discussed the "really important things of life," you know, until nearly 2 in the morning, with yours truly contributing to the conversation between naps. I left the dorm Friday morning at 8 & didn't return 'til 7:30 at nite. I had no classes in the PM & I studied in the library – just catching up on back work. I've been spending about half of my waking hours working (café) all weekend. I got along quite successfully, however. Mrs Newton complimented me, & I felt quite proud of myself too. I know you must admire this fine penmanship. But please excuse it because I'm so comfortable here – half on my bed & half on the radiator, with pillows, blankets, etc. & getting sleepy-er every minute. We went to 7:30 mass this morning – late – as usual & sat way upstairs by the organ. My folks came up this afternoon. Mr & Mrs Thomas were with them. They had come to Crystal to see the oil wells & so came up to see me. & O, I went for a ride in the new car – pretty ritzy – 700 miles on it – a week old. Mr & Mrs Thomas got quite a kick out of looking the college over & seeing the oil refinery & former Indian School & our church & oil wells & the rest of our sights. Quite an adventure for them. I don't recall much local news except that Frank Hart is dead – last week he died. & the annual chicken dinner will be June 16. "Cardinal Richelieu" is down here tonite but we didn't go. Might go tomorrow nite. Margaret & Doris & Marvel were back when I came back from my ride, so with Vonnie & I we all had a most enjoyable lunch. Then afterwards we talked about everything & everybody under the sun for an hour or two. Then Doris & I took some junk over to Pauline Houseman that her mother had sent. It's still cold out. I don't like the weather like this. I like it the way it was last Sunday. Wish I could turn back the calendar – or ahead. But – yesterday, today or tomorrow, Ellis, I love you (more than anything in the world). Good-nite, Pal. Daisy

May 8, 1935 CSTC

Dearest Ellis – (Wed nite 1 AM) A test at 8 & a test at 9 tomorrow, that's why I'm still up & expect to be up for some time yet. So I thought that if I could talk with you for a while the night might pass a little less slowly. We had a social meeting tonite (RRT) at Jean Benford's home here. We had dinner at 6 & played bridge until 8:45. I really quite enjoyed myself. We entertained a few new girls & tomorrow nite we'll vote some of them into the society. I don't feel so bad tho, on account of for three nights past I've had lots of sleep. Sunday nite I went to sleep at 9:30 directly after I'd finished your letter so when Helen woke me up at 10 I went to bed & got up at 6 &, very inspired, wrote a paper for English on the supposed accomplishments of a 3rd political party, liberal in its views & progressive in its policies, if it should come into power. & I got an A on it. Early morning inspirations seem to be my best. Our instructor, Harry Miller, was knocked down by a car last Saturday morning & was pretty badly shaken up so he won't be back 'til next week. Miss McClinchy has been meeting with us this week. Ellis, I haven't yet asked Mrs Porterfield permission for the weekend (May 25) but I will as soon as I can see her & I'll write you (Yes, I hope). Helen & I are going to be in the 40th Anniversary Pageant commencement weekend. There are 12 of us (the rest phys-ed majors) in a dance club & we're going to work on the dance designs & train the dancers. I think it will be fun. That will mean staying over commencement weekend. I'm getting my credits checked tomorrow & I may not come to summer school, not that I would have needed to anyway. I met with the committee chairman today & got them started working on the Junior Reception. O, I am a very busy woman, I am. But never too busy to write to you. You don't believe that, do you? O dear, I'm getting so sleepy now. I think I'll get up early in the morning & study some more. I'm going to get a lot of sleep this weekend & next weekend – & the next? And please try not to break any more speed records before then. Have a nice weekend. Love, Daisy x

---

May 10, 1935   CSTC

Dearest Ellis – (Fri 7 AM) Just a line. I asked Mrs Porterfield yesterday for permission to spend the weekend at Carson & she very graciously said "yes" (after asking me if my folks knew I was going & where I was going, etc.). So - Love, Daisy

P.S. I'll write you tonite when maybe I'll feel better I hope. I love u. Daisy

---

May 11, 1935   CSTC

Dearest Ellis – (Sat 1:40 PM) I'm in the library, supposed to be studying, but somehow I don't seem to be able to apply myself. It's a grand day – we had rain a couple of nites past & everything is now so green & growing like everything. I do hope it will be like this two weeks from today. Ida May (from Flint(came up last nite & is spending the weekend with us.

She came with Marshall. I'm so glad they're together again. She's going to the party tonite, but neither Helen nor I am going. But Helen heard from Bill this morning & he might come up anyway. I went to the show last night with Doris & Margaret – "Go into Your Dance," Ruby Keeler & Al Jolson. O, it was just grand – I love to see Ruby dance. It was quite long tho, & I got so tired of sitting. "Stars Are Gonna Twinkle & Shine" was one of the songs & everyone is singing it today. Bed at 1:30 & up at 9 today. Worked from 11-11:30 – a lot of extensioners as usual & a banquet too. I've so much reading & writing to do – I wish the weekend could be stretched out a couple of days. I'm sorry I wrote you such a short letter Friday, Ellis. I was so down & disgusted with the world. Thursday nite I had a meeting of Ronan to vote in new members & decide about the house party & these kids agree just about like cats & dogs. And that made me feel very amiable indeed. We decided to go to Wenona Beach for our house party. I'm glad you can be home on Mother's Day. Wish I could. I had only one class yesterday – at 8. I listened to HS glee clubs 2 hours in the afternoon – Carson City, Vassar, Remus, Clare – & 6 others. Carson City had a girls' quartet, a trio & mixed chorus. I enjoyed it a lot. I ran out of ink a couple of minutes ago & filled my pen with water. How's it work? Can you read it? There's a Sister sitting right across from me. She's in two of my classes – studying so diligently now. They're always so industrious. I wonder if they ever get discontented. They're all so sweet. We have quite a few of them in school this term. Your letter was so nice, Ellis – as nice as you are. I was so happy yesterday. We went to the last few events of the track meet – mile run & 440 yard dash, pole-vaulting, etc. – Central Frosh, MP HS, Midland & Clare HS. This afternoon we have a meet with Kalamazoo College. It's so quiet & peaceful here. I could go to sleep. There are only 5 people in the library besides myself. Everyone is getting ready for the party, I guess. I'm going downtown at 3, so I think I shall go home & (?) – sleep probably. I'll dream about you. Love, your Pal, Daisy

---

May 12, 1935   CSTC

Dearest Pal – (Sun nite 11:20) Nearly everyone had her boyfriend up this weekend & I've been consoling myself with the thought of 2 weeks from now. I think it will be worth the waiting. Do you? Bill walked in quite unexpectedly last nite & caused quite a commotion. Helen had to break a date & I had to go down & do the explaining. Fun (?) Mrs Renwick came up to visit her mother-in-law & brought Bill along. He left quite early this afternoon. Ida May left tonite about 8:30. She had a grand weekend. I'm so glad she did. She & Marshall were driving back to Flint tonite. I haven't accomplished much of anything this weekend in the way of studying. Sat afternoon we went downtown & to the track meet & at nite after all the kids had gone I felt rather blue & went to bed & read awhile. We went to 9:00 mass this morning – worked 11-1 & read 5 essays for Eng 203. We went downtown with Doris & Marg at 5:30 & back at 7:30. Then Helen & I just talked & discussed our lack of ambition until 9 & washed our hair. Gee, I don't know what I'd do if I didn't have someone to talk with most of the time. I'll bet you get rather lonesome sometimes in hotels every nite with no one you know. Don't you? O dear, I'm nearly going to sleep. I've so much studying to do. I think I'll get up early & do it. Helen has decided she'll be sick tomorrow so she's peacefully sleeping. The Holland Tulip Festival started today. Will you be there to see it? I'd like to. I love you, Dearest Ellis. Good-nite, Daisy xxxxx

---

May 14, 1935   CSTC to 833 Clinton St, Kalamazoo

Dearest Ellis – (Tue nite 11) How time does fly! It's been two whole days since I've written you, but I'm not "pouting." My roommate has been popping corn & our room is all full of smoke but with a cool breeze flowing through it will soon clear out. Tonite our dance club met for the first time to work on the pageant dances. We did a lot of exercise to get limbered up & some crazy Egyptian dances. I feel quite weak & shaky after an hour and a half of it – haven't had the stuff for a year. I think I'll take a pillow to classes with me tomorrow – a la Harry Miller. I don't have an 8 o'clock tomorrow & I'm going to sleep- the most pleasant thing I can think of now (except you x). Have you received any of the Prosperity Club chain letters yet? I received my third one today. Shall I send you one so you can share in the prosperity? A girl near home has received $60 in dimes from those letters. Got one of them from my mother today. They expect to get their Travel-o Coach this week or next. Then I expect they'll be up again to see me. Last nite at house meeting (dorm) we had a style show & I modeled my white sailor pajamas (the ones that once were grass-stained). Gee, it was fun, parading in front of the people. Yesterday it rained in the morning & was a gray day. Today was nicer but not very warm either. I am very sleepy, so I will say Good-nite, Pal. Love, Daisy xx

---

May 15, 1935   CSTC

Dearest Dear – (Wed nite) It's late & I'm sleepy, but I think that a letter like that deserves a reply. X How about it? I know you'll probably be feeling lots better by today, so I won't hand you the Pollyanna line of "turn the dark clouds inside out" & "look on the sunny side," etc. (Hooey!) I've been there myself, brother, & I know that stuff doesn't improve matters one "heck of a lot." But about the rainbow. I really think that might be true. I'd like to come & see you tonite & try it. Gee, 'm so sorry that your mother's sick. I hope she's lots better now. I used to have asthma & I know it's not a nice thing to have. Feel rather stiff & strained tonite from my workout last nite, but I wouldn't mind doing it every nite after I got used to it. I should be studying now but I'm going to get up at 6 – write a paper on "The Changing Mind of America" for Karolena Fox & one on "the type of patriotism young men & young women should have to establish an ideal American commonwealth." It's terrible the way I've been letting things go this term. I don't guess I remember what I started to say. Too sleepy. I'm so sorry that the "job weather" hasn't been so good for you lately. Wish I could help. But I guess the only way to do is show them you can "take it" – & "dish it out" too (?). Hope I can do that well tomorrow. Good-nite, Dearest Pal, Daisy

My grandmother, Mary "Mamie" Bazzett, suffered from asthma her whole life, but I never knew my mom had ever had it.

May 16, 1935   CSTC

Dearest — (Thurs nite 11) You wouldn't let a pal down & deprive me of one-fifth of my chances of winning $1,562.50, would you? Here's a chance for you to make use of your typewriter in a big way. It would be grand if it would work, wouldn't it? I wonder who had the brilliant idea of starting these crazy letters. I've had two of them, so I'm hoping to get 5 dimes back & I'll be satisfied. A girl near home has $60 in dimes from these already. I've been very industrious tonite & think I deserve some recreation now. Library 6:30-8, revised & typed paper for Harry Miller tomorrow, did 5 cards for Doc Beck's English & prepared 10 of these letters for sending (but not all like this)). It's been a grand day although nothing unusual has happened – except my extraordinary industriousness. I still feel as if I'm walking on a couple of sticks instead of my legs. Tomorrow at 4 we have another session with the ancient Egyptians. I hope the sunshine today has helped to revive your spirits. But if you still feel like sobbing, I wish you were here to sob on my shoulder. Maybe together we could find a rainbow – or a couple of 'em. xx Nothing's doing this weekend & I'm going to study (?) & get all caught up. Are your plans still the same for next weekend? Must retire now. Good-nite, Pal. Daisy xx

The chain letter, enormously popular during the Depression (except with Post Office employees), has a list of six names and addresses at the top, four from Spokane, Washington, and the bottom two being Mom & her roommate, Helen, promises this: "This chain was started in the hope of bringing prosperity to you. Within three days, make a copy of this letter, leaving off the top name and address and adding your name and address at the bottom this list, and mail (or deliver) to five of your friends to whom you wish prosperity to come. In omitting the top name, send that person 10c (ten cents) wrapped in paper as a prosperity donation. In turn, as your name leaves the top, you will receive 15,625 letters with donations amounting to $1,562.50. NOW!! IS THIS WORTH A DIME TO YOU? HAVE THE FAITH YOUR FRIEND HAS HAD AND THIS CHAIN WILL NOT BE BROKEN." These chain letters were basically a pyramid scheme and very few participants, if any, every made any money on them. (First-class postage at the time was 3 cents.)

May 19, 1935   CSTC to the Post Tavern in Battle Creek

Dearest — (Sun nite 10:30) Please let me weep on your shoulder. I'm now badly in need of someone's shoulder & I wish you were here. I was feeling so good because it has been a nice day & my folks were up, but I guess that made me homesick & now everything is going wrong – nobody will cooperate with me & it's hell being president of a bunch of catty women. I could cry. I'd like to quit school & drop everything right now. I wish I could have gone home with my folks today & never come back – never. I get so sick of it all & my head aches & I've got a theme to write yet tonite. Just can't take it anymore. I'm a "kissie," a "pansy" – a what have you, but I don't care. This isn't a very nice letter at all to greet a tired man, is it? I'm sorry, Ellis, so sorry, but I just have to tell someone what I think of everyone in general (but you & my folks & my roommate). It has been just grand out this weekend – I hope the good weather continues (& my good disposition?) ...

(Mon morn 7:20) Dearest Pal - That's where I went under last nite, so now I've been up since 6 & have my theme all written & typed. Wish that I could take care of all my troubles that easily. It's a grand morning, sun shining in our window, birds singing, etc., etc. & now I think I'll take a shower & get started off on a new week. Wonder how it'll end. Good morning, Ellis. Love, Daisy xx

The Post Tavern in Battle Creek was actually a six-story hotel, later enlarged and renamed the Post Tavern Motor Inn. It was demolished in 1970.

May 20, 1935   CSTC

Dearest Pal — (Mon nite 12:30) I don't feel bad at all tonite. Your letter was very welcome. I'm so glad your mother is better & that you had an enjoyable weekend. I pretty well straightened myself & my affairs out today.

Served at a dinner tonite until 7:25 & had a meeting at 7:30 of the chairmen of committees for the Junior Reception & got everything underway. Came home & went to a street dance in front of the dorm. Tomorrow we have elections for student council & Ralph Dawe was doing some campaigning so he set up his broadcasting system in front of the training school & we had a good old-fashioned Central political rally with campaign speeches n' everything. We danced in the street until 10 & it was fun but the floor wax was not distributed very evenly & so it was rather tiring. There's a young robin squawking just outside our window. Guess he thinks it's daylight. I couldn't concentrate on anything more difficult than sewing tonite so I did some Italian hemstitches across the end of a towel. We started it in sewing class today & I like to do it. I thought I had best write to you tonite & tell you that in case you don't hear from me again this week, I'm not "pouting" at all. I'm just saving up my "letter content" for Saturday nite. 'Til then, Love, your Pal, Daisy xx

---

May 22, 1935   CSTC

Dearest Ellis – (Wed nite 12m) Ben Bernie's Orchestra is on now and the music is grand but I remember nights when the orchestra wasn't nearly as famous & sounded twice as grand & I'm looking forward with high hopes for another such evening – soon – & I'm so happy just thinking about it. I hope that your job was smooth sailing this week with no "roughness" – really I do. O, I have the funniest feeling – I just remembered that I must have a theme done for Harry tomorrow. I was thinking of retiring right off with "nary a care." Had a Ronan meeting tonight & that drove practically everything else out of my mind. We're going to Wenona over Decoration Day – finally got together on it. My folks got their Travel-o Coach today, I expect – it was due today. I wouldn't mind going home & taking a trip in it over Decoration, but – I'll start having my vacation this weekend. So good-nite, Sweetheart. Daisy xx

P.S. Just a reminder. Helen is quite worried for fear Bill will come up with you – & if he did it would quite complicate matters. So – D.

Ben Bernie, a jazz violinist & bandleader, was one of the most popular entertainers on radio throughout the 1930s. Known as "the Old Maestro," he was also the co-composer of "Sweet Georgia Brown," later famous as the theme song of the Harlem Globetrotters basketball team. Wenona Beach Amusement Park, situated on Saginaw Bay near Bay City, was a popular destination for vacationers. It closed in 1964.

May 28-29, 1935   CSTC

Dearest Ellis — (Tue nite 1:00) Aren't you glad I didn't write to you last nite? Tonite I am feeling just fine – sitting on top of the world – & last nite I wasn't quite so enthusiastic. For the past two days I've been occupied mainly with trying to keep myself awake in classes. But for 4 days beginning Thursday we can sleep most of the time if we want to – (& I want to!).

(Wed morn 7:30) Dearest Pal – I just couldn't take it so I went to bed last nite & didn't get up early either. I just can't depend on my capabilities of rising in the morning any more. We were celebrating last nite on account of Ronan getting into the news & my troubles seem to be temporarily suspended. With my little write-up in the Life about the Reception everything is straightened out for a while anyway. Attended the League Banquet last nite & everything went off just grand. Life got out this week's edition early so we had them after the banquet last nite. Had a short meeting of the girls going on the house party (12 of us) & we're going early Thursday morning (6:00) with the college bus. Kate Steed, an RRT girl, got the scholarship last nite & we're so proud of her. Had quite a majority of Ronan girls up for elections at house-meeting last nite too. So things are looking up for me. How're you? & how was the Detroit sales meeting? Hope you feel lots better after getting together & hashing over your troubles. It rained here Monday & Tuesday but last nite it cleared off about 7 for a gorgeous sunset & it's grand today & I want it to be just as grand for you this weekend as it's going to be for me. Love, your Pal, Daisy xx

P.S. There were a few more items in the Life besides the ones I'm sending.

Central State Life was the student newspaper. Enclosed were some clippings from Life about the annual Women's League banquet, scholarships awarded, and campus election results. A separate piece explained that an oil boom (eighty new wells) around Crystal Lake had created a housing shortage, which caused most CSTC clubs to cancel their spring outings. Ronan Round Table was the exception, having planned an alternative trip to Wenona Beach.

May 29, 1935   CSTC

Dearest Ellis — (Wed nite) 1:15 & in 5 hours we'll be on our way to Wenonah. Thank you for your good wishes. I'm sure we'll have a good time & the same to you. I thought you were going to Detroit this week, or is it next week? Have to go to 5:30 mass in the morning. Hope we don't forget to get up. It's been a grand day today – hope the rest of the week will be as nice. Had no 3:00 this afternoon. Went downtown & bought groceries.

We're going in the bus in the morning & coming back Sunday afternoon. I received another chain letter today – a 25c one – they're getting too large for my purse I fear. Looking forward to a long lazy weekend of sleeping & swimming. Looking backward to the best weekend I think that I can remember with you & I'm glad you have the same opinion. I think maybe we're getting better acquainted. Gee, my eyes just won't stay open any longer so good-nite, Sweetheart-Pal. Love, Daisy xx

---

June 2, 1935   CSTC

Dearest Pal – (Sun nite, Dorm 11:00) The house party is over & it was a grand success – weather, good time, swimming & everything. Lazy days, & lots of sleeping & eating & amusements. But this afternoon I did get a sunburn which I neither wanted nor anticipated. I only hope that it doesn't blister. We left here Thursday morning at 6:20 & arrived at the cottage about 8 – got back tonite at 5:30. We were very disappointed to find that the dance [pavilion] at Wenonah didn't open until June 7, but Paraleon was open & we went there & had lots of fun. My folks were in the State Park Thursday with their new Travel-o & it's a Jim-dandy. I went in swimming every day & twice today. The water was really nice. Helen & I went into Bay City Friday & did some shopping. Left the cottage at 12:30 & were back at 4. We had 2 meals a day – breakfast-lunch (brunch) at 10:30 & dinner at 5. Worked in shifts – 2 to get meals & 2 to do dishes – very satisfactory arrangement. Did you have a nice weekend playing golf & talking oil, etc.? Hope you enjoyed yourself as much as I did. I feel a chill on my sunburn. Afraid I'm catching a cold – so I shall retire. Nite, Pal. Love, Daisy

P.S. Dearest – I could write lots more but I'm so sleepy. I'll write more later. Love, D

June 4, 1935   CSTC

Dearest Dear – (Tue nite 11:30) it was an awfully little small letter that I wrote you on Sunday nite, wasn't it? I started to write a long one, but I go so sleepy I'm afraid it just dwindled off. But I'll tell you – I wrote you a real long letter when I was at the cottage & told you everything so it seemed as if I were telling you a second time. There were so many people around when I wrote it & I was interrupted so many times that it didn't even make sense so I tore it up. (I'm not fibbing as I did once, x my heart x.) These last three weeks are going to be the death of me – or very nearly so – I fear. Thursday nite is the last meeting of RRT & we're going to have a pot-luck dinner in the log-cabin. It'll be a relief to have that over. Tonite & every nite from now on we practice the dances for the Pageant. I'm in 3 for Miss Rogers & Miss Ryan - Egyptian, modern, & court dances, & a Grecian goddess I'll be for Harry Miller. That will last right up to the end of the term – Pageant Sat June 22. Friday night is the reception & I'll be so glad when that's off my mind. I conceived the brilliant idea of having an excerpt from the pageant as a number on the program & of course I would be one of the 6 chosen to give the dance. If I'd dreamed - x?x! - Hours more practice stuffed in this one little week. Saturday nite serve at the Senior Dinner - dance & from then on dinners & luncheons & even breakfasts practically every day. More fun! But anyway I'd still rather be alive & busy than dead & "resting" - 'cause when I'm dead, I'll be dead for a long, long time. How is the salesman's business coming? I wish it would boom like mine is. I got material for 2 dresses in Bay City. I'm making one in sewing class but GOK (God Only Knows) when I'll get the other one made. Tomorrow I have a breathing space tho, one class at 3, wish I didn't have to work at noon. I should use the time getting caught up on back work, but I feel myself weakening right now & fear I'll use it getting caught up on lost sleep. The radio's grand tonite. Wish I could turn back the calendar about 10 days & then jump it ahead about 3 weeks. O well, wishing my life away - if wishes were horses, etc. but I wouldn't mind living my life away like that. Good-nite, Sweetheart-Pal. Love, Daisy xx

---

Jun 9, 1935   CSTC

Dearest Dear – (Dorm Sun nite 9:00) if this doesn't sound quite as logical & connected as it should, I'll tell you why. I'm in Doris's room keeping her company until her roommate comes from the show & Vonnie is also here keeping her company & at frequent intervals Vonnie reads aloud especially choice passages from Walt Whitman's "Leaves of Grass" & Doris is looking at my Chippewa & making comments & asking questions. O, I forgot - we're here because Doris is ill - she has an attack of appendicitis & Dr Torres ordered her to stay in bed for a few days. I'm back home now in our own messy room. We're both working on wardrobe notebooks for Home Ec – cutting out pictures, etc. so we decided we'll leave things strung around until we get done. O gee, I'm so tired & I've got so much to do & we got up at 7 this morning & I worked 3 hours this noon. (11:30) I've been interrupted so many times & now I'm just so awfully sleepy I think I'll have to let things pile up as you suggested until I see you. Your letter was sweet, Ellis. I did wonder why you didn't write - thought maybe your weekend was too big for you. But really I know you're busy too. When are you coming to see me - 29th? Good-nite, Dear. I'll see you in my dreams. Love, Daisy

Apparently as late as the 1930s, a conservative approach to treating appendicitis often included a few days of bed rest & fasting before the appendectomy.

June 15-16, 1935   CSTC

Dearest Ellis — (Sat nite 2 AM-Sun) I haven't been very faithful in writing to you lately, have I? I'm sorry as can be & sometime I'll make it up to you if I can. I have been terribly rushed with pageant practices every day & banquets to serve every few days & lessons to catch up on besides a few other little things. I'm glad you enjoyed your weekend at the lake. Gee, today was just so grand & I wanted to go swimming but the shower was the best place I could find. I expected to get a lot done tonite, but didn't accomplish much – went to confession at 7, back at 8:15 & had company continuously until 12, but I'm not especially sleepy now. There's a reason – I went to sleep this afternoon at 2:30 & woke up at 5:10 just in time to get to work – 15 minutes late. Will go to 7:30 mass in the morning & see how much I can get done afterwards. Went to the show last nite – "Let 'Em Have It," and it was a lot better than I anticipated – a department of justice picture & really worth seeing, I thought. Today we practiced at 9 our dances & got our costume material – for 2 – & we have to have those made by Thursday nite for our dress rehearsal. Wednesday nite RRT are having a farewell banquet honoring our departing members – one is getting married, one is going into nurse training & 5 graduating – we're giving each one a gift. The folks are coming up Saturday nite to see the pageant & I'll be going home Sunday afternoon. I'm not coming back until Monday July 1 for summer term, I think. I wish you could come & see the pageant too. Are you taking your vacation this month or next? I'll be home the last week in June all except Friday nite, 28th. Thursday nite we had Senior Swingout & it was so impressive & solemn, made me glad that I'm not leaving this year, altho I suppose I'll be glad enough to leave next year. Right now tho, I'm leaving for bed. Good-nite, Sweetheart. Love, Daisy xx

(Sun nite 9:30) Dearest Dear – Sunday nite & I've been very ambitious all day. But now it's raining softly, quietly & steadily & I'm so terribly sleepy. I fell asleep reading a play about an hour ago & I've had such a time getting waked up again. I think I'll have to get up very early in the morning & study. I have to write synopses of about 6 or 8 plays & stories (4 yet to read) for Comparative Lit & altho they're all interesting it's just hell to keep awake doing it. One consolation tho, it'll soon be over & (I'll be seeing you?). Nite, Dear Pal. I love u. Daisy xx

Jun 18-19, 1935   CSTC

Dearest Pal — (Tue 12:55) I'm supposed to be writing a theme right now, but it's raining & the rain reminds me of so many times when we've been together – makes me rather lonesome. Gee, it's been such a long time since I've seen you – only 4 or 5 weeks really, I guess, but it seems like 10. Hope you had just a grand rest at home over the weekend. The annual parish chicken dinner in Oakley was Sunday.

(Tue eve 7:45) Dearest – Just started to go to dance practice at 8 & discovered my clock is 20 minutes fast. It's still raining, raining & it's so dreary & damp & dull. Wish you were here just for tonite. I'd throw up all my work & I wouldn't care if it never got done. Gee, I hope the sun comes out tomorrow – for you too. As I was saying – about the chicken dinner – Mama was going to send you a bill about it, but didn't know where to send it. Jimmie is better again now & is just learning to walk all over again. The roses are all out now. Maybe they'll still be in blossom when I'm home.

(Wed 2 AM) Ellis Dear – Just came up from the dining room where I've been writing & typing since 10 & I'm not nearly thru but I just couldn't think or hit the right keys any longer. I think it has stopped raining now. How I'd love to see the sun shining in my window in a few hours. No 8 o'clock tomorrow but – "there's no rest for the wicked." I must be terribly wicked. No dance practice at all tomorrow. Dress rehearsal Thursday nite. Tomorrow nite our RRT dinner-formal. Fri nite, Sat morn, noon, nite, Sunday morn, noon – dinners & luncheons & breakfasts to serve. One might think that the people are coming back for the 40th Anniversary only for the purpose of eating. Which reminds me – we were so hungry tonite at about 11 that we nearly passed out & couldn't find a thing to eat in the dorm. O, for the good old days when we could raid the kitchen. But it'll soon be breakfast time. So – Good-nite, Sweetheart. Wish u were here. Love, Daisy xx

Jun 25, 1935   Oakley

Dearest Sweetheart — (Tue nite 11) How are you this week? I hope you made it back to Carson in time for mass Sunday. We did get in a couple of hours sleep before 7:30 mass (& a few snatches during mass). I'm afraid I looked rather tough serving the senior girls' breakfast at 9, but with a nap between 11 & 12 I pulled through the day pretty well. Worked from 12 to 2:30 serving a dinner. Ralph did too, but he looked pretty worn out – couldn't take it – not used to it, I guess. Left for home at 5 & I slept most of the way. Boy, did it ever seem good to get here – just to think there was nothing to worry about. I went to see Grandma & then had supper & Julia (Agnetta) came over – she just came home Sunday too, for a 3-week vacation, & Harold & Helen & the kids came down. Then Julia & I went for a walk & talked & talked & took in the show (medicine show – in town for a week). First time I've seen Julia to have a real visit with her in 2 years. She's in training for a nurse at the Hurley Hospital in Flint – graduates a year from September. I went to bed at 11 Sun nite & slept the clock around + ½ hour – had dinner – went to sleep at 2 & up at 2 for supper. Bed at 10:30 last nite & I was up at 7:30 this AM feeling quite refreshed (really!). I've been ironing & sewing all day today, making a dress – white sport dress. Tonite Julia & I went for a walk & ended up at Mrs Gower's. We were there for over an hour & had a real nice visit. Mr Gower went to Chicago today to visit Ethel – he's coming back Monday. Mrs Gower was rather lonesome, I think, and more than a little afraid to stay alone. Isn't this ink a horrible color? I hope you can stand it long enough to read this, although it isn't so very important. Did you definitely decide not to come up this weekend, Ellis? Gee, I wish you were coming now. It seems sort of lonesome around here. How many miles have you on your car now? It's surely [3-4M]. Did I tell you how much I enjoyed Saturday nite (& Sunday morning)? I did, immensely. Dear, I'm so sleepy now. Must be from thinking about the weekend. It has been grand today & yesterday. Tonite we had a few passing showers. Julia & I are going to Chesaning tomorrow to bum around a little. We'll probably go to Saginaw Thursday to see Clarence. He works from 4 AM until noon – on the [1M]. Good-nite, Darling. I'll see you in my dreams – sweet dreams. Love, Daisy xxxx

---

Jun 29, 1935   Oakley

Ellis Dear – I received your lovely gift today – and equally lovely letter – and thank you so much. It was sweet of you to remember. You know how I love nice things (you included) and now I'll smell nice for you – will it be the 4th? I do hope so! However soon you can come up won't be a mite too soon for me. We don't have Friday 5th off, so of course I'll have to stay over the 4th and nothing to do. So I'm sending you my very most special invitation to come as soon as you can – & stay as long as you can. Rosalie & Jimmie were with us all day today – & Wednesday too. This afternoon we went to Saginaw & saw "Mutts" – sleeping as usual, and quite contented. He has a '31 Chevy coupe now – did I tell you? Yesterday Julia and I spent the afternoon in Chesaning calling on our friends. I found it quite strenuous & retired at 8 – lacked an hour of sleeping the clock around again. I haven't had a nap this afternoon so I feel pretty sleepy now. Wednesday afternoon I slept for 2 hours. We were going to Chesaning Wednesday nite, but we had a couple hours of "the Deluge" about 6 & a baby flood – so we didn't get there. I received my marks today too. Ellis, I'm slipping. Can't take it, I guess. 2 C's, a B & an A – and I'm quite ashamed of myself, but if you'll still come & see me anyway, perhaps I'll recover. I have my dress nearly done – have been working on it off & on &, with good luck, I'll finish it tomorrow in an hour or two. I'm glad you're "getting in" with your landlord & family. Maybe it won't be so lonesome for you. I'll be seeing you soon, won't I? I can hardly wait! Au revoir, Sweetheart. Love, Daisy xx

---

Jun 30, 1935 CSTC

Dearest Pal – (Sun nite, Dorm, 10 PM) Summer school! It hasn't begun yet, but doesn't promise to be very exciting. Dorm practically occupied by old maid school teachers coming back – just for a thrill, you know, & to recover that school-girl feeling too, I suppose. Went downtown tonite – just for the walk, & ate enough chocolate-covered peanuts coming home to make me just a little sick. O dear, I'm so tired & sleepy. I thought I was all caught up on my sleep, but it seems that just the atmosphere of the place gives me the old feeling. Helen came at 4. We left such a mess at the end of last term, but it's all straightened up now & it seems so good. O, Ellis, I hope you can come the 4th & stay all weekend – & I wish you could stay all summer. Clarence came home yesterday afternoon & we went down to see my old pal, Marjorie Devereaux, who's home on a 2-week vacation & had a good old "chin-chin" with her. 7:30 mass this morning & it dragged on until 9 – seemed like 2 hours. The parish cleared $170 total on the chicken dinner. Harold & Helen & the kids were down for dinner & came back with the folks to "deliver" me. I got a bouquet of just beautiful rose-pink tea roses in the Oak Grove cemetery where they grow all over, but they all drooped & died before we arrived & then I was sorry I picked them. I hope you had a nice time at home this weekend, Ellis, but of course you always do. Marg Denno is here for summer school too – you remember – the St Pat's dinner party. She taught in Dansville last year & she bought herself a seal coat & has acquired a diamond & seems quite successful. Not many of the old kids are back. We bought a box of candy for sale in our room all the time for Ronan. O gee, I'm yawning all over the place. So I'll say, Good-nite, Sweetheart, 'til we meet. Love, Daisy xx

---

Jul 1, 1935 CSTC

Dearest Dear – (Mon nite 9:45) How are you, Pal? I'm lonesome as the dickens tonite – nothing to do – that is – nothing I want to do. I can see right now that it's going to be very dead around here. But I'm not sorry I came. I'll tell you what I'm taking – 7-9 Commerce 101 (Beginning Bookkeeping),

& 1-3 English Teaching Methods from Dr Beck. I work from 10 to 1, so I'm through for the day at 3. Ain't that swell? I don't think it will be so bad when I get started. It was rather messy in the cafeteria today – everybody new & green – so I worked noon & nite too, but tomorrow I'll go on my regular hours. It seems rather quiet around here without Doris & Vonnie & the kids. We had a letter from Peg today. She left her tennis racket here & wants us to send it to her. That's why she was so prompt about writing. O gee, I'm sleepy again. I guess I always will be. I'll have to sign in now & go to bed. So, Good-nite. I Love u. Daisy

---

Jul 2, 1935   CSTC

Ellis Dearest – (Tue nite) It's 9:30 & I have to be in bed at 10 to get my 8 hours in – but here's to you – xx. I received your letter this afternoon – it was just grand, but O, I do hope you can come up the 4th or pretty soon anyway & when are you going to take your vacation? I thought it was this week. I like bookkeeping just awfully well. It's just loads of fun now, but I suppose I'll get tangled up soon enough with my post-closing trial balances, etc. I worked on it from 3 to 5 this afternoon & the time went like lightning. Gee, it seemed good to eat with Helen tonite out in the dining room. We went for a walk afterward to celebrate the occasion & we ended up at the Maybee's. They have just the most beautiful rose garden & Mrs Maybee gave us just a gorgeous bouquet of American Beauties. I wish you could see them. We have them on our little table by the radio. 10:00, time's up, but I'm ready for Love & you, Ellis. 'Nite, Daisy

---

Jul 7, 1935   CSTC

Dearest Ellis – (Sun nite 12m) I've written 5 letters tonite & I've just washed the greater part of the black & red & maroon & violet ink smudges off my fingers so I could have a fresh start for you. My folks didn't come today & I was so disappointed. Helen & Ralph went out to Coldwater today on a picnic & swimming, etc. Ralph came last night as per schedule. He leaves for Annapolis the 17th. He took us to 7:30 mass this morning – his folks' car is just like yours, but it hasn't any radio in it. I worked on bookkeeping this morning for an hour & worked 11-11:30 – read a novel & slept for 2 hours & worked on bookkeeping for another hour and then wrote letters. I felt so blue & so lonesome when I woke at 6:15 & my folks hadn't come yet & I knew they wouldn't come then. So I just had a good cry & got it all out of me & then I felt better. I'm so glad that I have all my bookkeeping done for tomorrow anyway. I worked on it for 1 ½ hours Sat afternoon too. I haven't done any English at all yet, but I'm not worrying.

I'll get it done sometime. I wrote to Shirley & I think she'll be coming up the 4th weekend, & to Doris & Vonnie & Peg, & they'll be coming up the 5th weekend maybe. Gee, Ellis, it seems the oftener you come, the oftener I want you to come. I was so lonesome this weekend, but next Sat will come soon – & don't forget your bathing suit. I wrote you a letter last nite – a funny little letter – there wasn't anything in it, so I won't send it. How do you like this ink? Since you don't care for my brown, I'll use this on approval. Tell me. I also have black, red & maroon. This is called violet, but it looks quite blue to me. How's business this week? Really, Ellis, you know that I didn't mean to make fun of your business affairs the 4th, don't you? I wouldn't for the world. I enjoyed your visit so – every minute of it, and I don't want to leave any wrong impressions. I hope next weekend will be as enjoyable, and the next, and then I wish it could be the next & the next & the next on & on. I'm awfully sleepy now, even if I did have my nap today. So Good-nite, Darling. What wouldn't I give for just one x from the best Sweetheart in the world. Love, Daisy xx

---

Jul 10, 1935   CSTC

Dearest Dear – (Wed nite) The heat is almost unbearable, but I'm looking forward to the weekend & with 3 or 4 showers a day, I'll manage to survive, I know. Your letter was doubly welcome. I didn't get it until 1 (the roommate brought it to class for me) & then I had to wait an hour to read it. But it was worth it – & I got the point about "Friday nite" too. After dinner tonite I stayed in the Ad & worked on bookkeeping until 8:30. It's so interesting now. We opened our sets this morning. Then we went for a walk & a Coke & puttered around & now, believe it or not, I'm going to bed at 10:30. I'm glad you had such a good sales day. More power to you. Went to the faculty reception last nite & had an awfully good time. My mother says I may go to Carson if I'll behave myself & be a good girl and "keep my clothes clean" & oh, it's a pretty big order, but I'll try if you'll help me. Be seeing ya soon. Love, Daisy

---

Jul 15, 1935   CSTC

Dearest Ellis – (Mon 3 PM) Just a line, 'cuz I'm in a big hurry. I wanted to ask you, if you haven't anything to do tonite (when you get this – Tue or Wed), would you like to come up & see me? I have something to tell you – just a plan – maybe it'll work – maybe not – Tue nite if you get this Tue, or Wed nite if you get this Wed. Anyway, come when you can – I'll be here – 3:00 on. Love, Daisy

I don't know what Mom's "plan" was, but I suspect it had something to do with spending maximum time with Dad during his vacation, which he may have spent at least part of in Carson City with his friends, the Churchills.

Jul 25, 1935   CSTC

Dearest Sweetheart Ellis [ringed in x's] – (Thurs nite 10:50) Your vacation is over now & here is my sincerest wish that you have survived the last week as well as I did my half of the first week. I hope you're all rested up & ready to go back to work and have the orders come rolling in. I fear I haven't been studying nearly as much as I should, but if I skim through, the vacation will be worth it. Tonite a traveling company presented a play, "The Rivals," in the auditorium. It was awfully silly, but so funny that I laughed until I was weak, and Helen too. We always enjoy such things so. Afterwards we had an ice cream cone & went flowering - 7 lovely nasturtiums - for Helen's luncheon in her foods class tomorrow. Helen heard from Ralph & he has passed all his tests is now installed in the Naval Academy and in very rigid training. Yesterday afternoon was the school picnic at Wilson State Park on Budd Lake at Harrison & we had a grand time. The water was swell, the eats were fine - the cafeteria moved up there (but I didn't have to work) - we had free ice cream & lemonade - and dancing from 8 until 10:30. I danced the last three with a professor and I was afraid of creating a scandal so I didn't let him bring me home but came with the girl we went with - Harriet Bennet from Corunna - she has a tan V-8 coupe. We stopped at Harry's & had a hamburg & were in on the dot at 11:30. Then we went down to June's & had Swedish bread and pickled bologna & Swedish crackers and chocolates. But it didn't seem to disturb my rest. Speaking of rest, I'll bet you enjoyed your stay at your grandmother's. I'd like to have been with you. I might spend a week with Aunt Stacia, so I'm writing to my fella to keep on good terms with him & maybe I'll have a date in GR too. The rest of the summer does look long to me - until 6 weeks is over anyway. Gover's were having a sale today on books & I got a few - couldn't resist the bargain. "Tanglewood Tales" - book of myths for children that I will perhaps find useful in my Latin teaching - "ahem." "Heidi," a book about a little girl in the Italian Alps, that I've known & loved ever since I can remember (just like u), & "Sorrell and Son," a novel by Warwick Deeping that was a popular movie a few years ago, and I'm just starting to read it.

The last page of the above letter seems to be missing.

Jul 31, 1935 CSTC

Ellis Dearest – (Wed 9:20 AM) I was very sorry to hear that your mother was sick, and I hope she is lots better now. I'm glad that you enjoyed yourself in the first part of your vacation. Those were happy days for me too, Ellis. Just a week from day after tomorrow I'm going home, & Helen with me, I think. Home a week – 3 weeks trip – then maybe I'll see Ellis again (?), I had my 7:00 off this morning, but I went over and worked on my bkp – lost 10c last night & can't find it anywhere. Haven't seen it, have you? Sunday PM Helen & I went to Cathedral Woods and had a picnic. We took our lunch and blanket and books and had a nice lazy 2 hours. If you had been there, it would have been perfect. I must go and meet a lady at 9:45 whose term paper I'm going to type. The days are dragging now and I'll be so glad when school is over. Then I'll soon see my Pal again. Love, Daisy xx

Dearest – I think I walked on air all day Monday, not realizing, or caring much, what was going on at all. And all the time I was hearing again just a few words you said before we came back to the dorm, and you were so near and so dear, and I didn't ever want to let you go. I love you, Ellis, I love you so. Always your adoring Pal, Daisy

Enclosed with the two letters above is a clipping from the student newspaper headlined, "Central Student Becomes a Middy – Ralph Rawson Receives Appointment to Naval Academy." Minimal research revealed that Rawson, a native of Cass City and USNA class of 1939, served in WWII as a naval aviator and was awarded the DFC. While still in the Navy, he attended MIT, earning a Master's degree in Aeronautics. He retired as a Rear Admiral in 1955 and went on to enjoy a successful business career. He died in 1991.

Aug 4, 1935 CSTC

Dearest Dear – (Sun nite 11:30) This is the third attempt & I have hopes that you may get this. The music is lovely – coming from the "Moonlight Gardens" (of Coney Island) – but the "chap" just came in & said, "Turn it off, please." O, Ellis, this is a crazy letter, but it's just the way I feel. It was such a grand evening with just a sliver of a moon and a handful of stars & we played (at) tennis until dark, then just wandered around & swang until we both felt rather upset & on & on. I slept all afternoon. I was so all-fired ambitious all week that I practically wore myself out. But it'll soon be over. And what do you think! Clarence's marriage license was in the paper Thursday. Ellen Graham told me today. I wasn't awfully surprised tho. O dear, it seems as if a lot of things have happened that I was going to tell you, but I can't remember

anything now except I love you x. I hope you had a good time at home this weekend & that your mother is lots better again. I'd like to see Benton Harbor at fruit harvest time. My mother says she's heard Yellowstone until she'd like to jump in the lake. I wish you were here. Good-nite, Dearest. Love, Daisy xx

---

Aug 7, 1935   CSTC

Ellis, Dearest Sweetheart – (Wed nite 11:15) I wonder where you are now – safe in bed sleeping & enjoying every minute of it, I'll bet. I'd like to have you here for a few minutes – it seems so long since I said good-nite to you. I'll probably be up the greater part of the night – but it's rather fun – makes it seem more like the end of the term – and I'll have a week to recuperate too. We're going to have a wedding at our house next week, did you know? I don't know any of the details except that I'll be in on it too. We're starting west on the 17th. Mother says she has removed everything from the buffet top & devoted it to maps, books, etc. "In a Little Gypsy Tea Room" – it carries me back to Crystal – and you x. Seems like ages. It isn't a bit hard to stay awake – all the lights on & the radio is outdoing its little self for our entertainment. Helen is working on a notebook (scrapbook) for Home Ec and has her papers scattered all over our two beds so I can't go to bed if I want to. I'm on the last long lap of my bookkeeping. I have the entries all done for my set & have to do my trial balance & close my books. I also have 2 ledger-closing exercises to do but I added everything on the adding machine, so I just have to get my numbers straight & go ahead. We saw 2 one-act plays tonite – given by Mr Beddow's dramatics class in the auditorium & enjoyed them a lot. "The Neighbors" and "The Mouse-Trap" – some of our friends were in them. Have you been in Battle Creek this week? – if my figuring is correct. How's business? Fine, I hope. Dear, I'm getting sleepy. What shall I do? I can't do that. I've been pounding the typewriter for the past 3 days getting my card pack in shape for English. Finished it last night – handed it in today – no more English class. We're going home Friday afternoon – at 3. Tomorrow night we're going out & celebrate (in our own simple way) – a movie – "Curly Top" – Shirley Temple – and then?? To bed probably – best way to celebrate. Jan Garber's Orchestra – "East of the Sun, West of the Moon" – O, it's so nice. Good-nite, Darling. Love, your Daisy xx

---

Aug 12, 1935   Oakley

Dearest Ellis – (Mon morn 8:30) Did you enjoy the game yesterday, Ellis? I heard it, but I didn't hear you. Gee, it's so nice to be home. We're not starting until Friday afternoon. Your letter Saturday was so nice, Ellis. But Clarence isn't getting married this week after all. I got the wrong impression from my mother's letter. Gertrude is taking instructions now & the wedding will be the 14th of September & they want you for best man & I do hope you can. That will be on a Saturday & O, I hope you can. I told Clarence he should write to you but he said he was too busy, you know. But that you should write to him – at Oakley. (And I hope you get this in time to write to me before we go too.) It was such a grand night last night & every night, Ellis, makes me wish you were still in Oakley. We were down to Gertrude's folks last night until 11. I like it down there – such a nice farm & a big house & big lawn & we watched the moon get big & bright & ate big yellow apples like the moon. O, Helen & I went to the dance Friday night & had a lot of fun – there was a big crowd & they had a saxophone added to the orchestra & it sounded swell. We went to a couple shows Sat nite & they were good too. I'm seeing that Helen gets her sleep (& Daisy too). I'll be so glad if you'll come for the wedding, 'cause Clarence & Gertrude want you (but I want you too). Love, Daisy xx

---

Aug 15, 1935   Oakley

Dearest Dear – (Thurs nite 9:30) I've been busy all day long, haven't even had a nap, went to church this morning & don't feel a bit sleepy now. And do you know the secret of it all? None other than "Wheaties" for my breakfast! More power to 'em. Especially when the flour business isn't so hot. Except for a few little pick-ups we're already to leave as soon as the "mail-man" gets back tomorrow. And Ellis, you can write to me. I mean, if you want to – c/o Mammoth Lodge, Yellowstone National Park, Wyoming. I'd be so happy to find a letter from my Pal waiting for me there. O, Ellis Dear, I do so hope you'll be here the 14th – & the 13th (night before). Clarence & Gertrude were up tonite. We went swimming Monday nite (Helen & I) at the rec-park in Chesaning – remember? Where we went in a couple of years ago – but the diving board is gone so I didn't break my back showing off. The water was so warm – & nice too, when there wasn't a weed around our necks. The moon has been full for ever so long, Ellis. Do you suppose it will be again? Maybe there'll be a harvest moon next time I see you. We saw the best show Tuesday night, "The Farmer Takes a Wife" – Janet Gaynor & Henry Fonda – a story of the Erie Canal days before the railroads. I'm so sorry that your mother isn't well yet, Ellis. But I hope that your brother & you enjoyed the weekend in Detroit. I've read your letter over & over, Ellis, it was so different, but still so like you. I know I don't deserve the love of one half as fine and square as you are, Ellis, but I do love you so. Daisy xx

She went to church because it was a Holy Day, the Feast of the Assumption.

Aug 18, 1935   St Paul, Minnesota

Ellis Dearest – (Sun nite 8:10) I'm out here under the open sky – no stars because there is a storm coming up, but under an electric light where the pesky mosquitos nearly drive me mad. Just came from swimming at Phalen Beach a couple of miles from the camp, right in the suburbs & the water was just swell. Gee, Ellis, it seems so mean for me to be way out here when you shared 'most all of your vacation with me – but O, if wishing could bring you, you'd be here. We've been driving through hills all day – by the nicest farms – great, large barns and what look like apartment houses. They raise mostly corn & hay & small grains – wheat – & their grain is stacked so neatly & compactly – from 4-12 stacks to a farm. Last night we camped at Ocanto, Wis. – on Green Bay. We stopped at Menominee – that's just a resorters town – most snobbish people – not even a meat market – 1 grocery store – the tourist camp wasn't so nice, so we didn't stay & it was dark when we did stop. The moons over the water at night, Ellis! O, they've been just gorgeous. But tonight – no moon – no stars – storm in the offing. We forgot about the hour's change in time this morning & so were up at 5:30 – actually 6:30 our time – & drove 50 miles before we finally came to a church where mass was "on" – at Shawano – a high mass in a pretty little church with altars all gold & white. There are Catholic churches in every little town & where mass was going on, the crowd was half out in the streets. O dear, I don't like this lightning. We'll be in the Black Hills tomorrow night probably & in Yellowstone by Wednesday anyway, I think. We're coming back by way of Salt Lake City. Darn the mosquitos. I didn't tell you any of the local gossip, did I? Sayde Coon (Yarabek) has a young son (bzz-bzz). That's all I can think of now – and the Harvest Festival is Aug 29 (I think). O, did I tell you – Papa went down to Saginaw & joined the AAA Club & got all the literature, maps, books, etc. & the insurance, just as you said he would. They have the most attractive window displays in the groceries that I've noticed around here, Ellis – Wheaties – Bisquick – Softasilk, etc. – & all the stores seem to stock these products. But then why shouldn't they, when Minneapolis is their home city. And I do hope business is as good with you, Ellis, as it seems to be with them here. It was so nice to get your letter Friday for a send-off, Ellis. I'm sorry you were lonesome. I wish there were something I could do about it. But there doesn't seem to be – not for a few weeks anyway. I hope the supervisor has had a good breakfast when you ask him for the Saturday off. Did you know that Clarence & Gertrude have been engaged since last Thanksgiving? I'm supposed to have discovered it last New Year's but I can't remember exactly. It's beginning to sprinkle. Maybe this letter will look better in the daylight than it does now but I have my doubts. But no matter – I'm sending you my most sincere Love. Daisy xx

Mom's dad (our 'Grandpa Whalen') always did like to travel, or just to get out & drive. When we were kids there were two things we loved to do with him when he came for a visit: play cards and 'go for a ride.' As a card player, he played fast & loose with the rules, i.e. he cheated (but we didn't care). As a vacationer, he obviously most liked to cover ground, i.e. see how many miles he could travel in a day – or a week. Moving was the thing. Resting was beside the point.

Sep 3, 1935   Oakley

Dearest Dear in the World — (Tue nite) Forgive me, Ellis, please, for not having written you before. I received your two lovely letters in Yellowstone & they were just grand, dearest. Made me wish more than ever that I could be sharing my vacation with you as you did yours with me. I'm back at home now in my own four-poster – where it isn't so far to the floor if Helen starts shoving (or vice-versa). I've had so many things to tell you, Ellis, but it seems every new one crowded out the rest & now I can't remember anything. I'm sorry the flour business isn't so good, dearest, but we did our best about the Wheaties – used 3 boxes on our trip & will bake bread tomorrow – don't know what kind of flour tho! Arrived in Oakley at 5:30 this evening – to learn that Grandma had died the Wednesday after we left & the police & broadcasting stations had been trying to locate us but we hadn't heard a thing. We were up to Harold's tonite to see the family. Rosalie started school today & is quite excited about it. Margaret came over tonite with the report that the new teacher is "meaner n' the dickens." We camped at St Joe last nite and O, Ellis, today if you were in Kalamazoo around 2 PM, driving your Wheaties truck – I was within half a block of you walking down the street & you turned the corner & didn't even see me! But then maybe it wasn't you. Anyway, good-nite now, dearest, and really I'll try to write real soon now that I'm home – If you'll write to – Daisy, who loves you so dearly. Xx

---

Sep 8, 1935   Oakley

Dearest — (Sun nite 10) O, how I wish your picture could talk, Ellis. It seems ages & ages since I've seen you – & it has been nearly that long. But "maybe" next Friday nite, dearest, & I'll be "waiting for you on needles & pins." I did get your letter Saturday morning, thanks to your hustling. You're just the dearest dear, Ellis. I wish you were here right now. It's so quiet here tonite. I don't know what I'll do without Helen for two whole weeks. Don & Elsie came for her today & were here for dinner, and Clarence & Gertrude too. Harold & Helen & the kids were down too. Jimmy & Rosalie surely can keep things lively. Had the best chicken dinner I've had in a long time. I do hope you didn't get lonesome today if you were in Kalamazoo all day. I'd like to have been there too. We're giving a shower for Gertrude Thursday nite & I've just written 20 of the invitations. Thought I'd best write to you before I get writer's cramp. I'll do the rest tomorrow. Friday I'm going down to Kairot's to help in the preparations. Oh dear, I'm getting so sleepy. We were in Saginaw all afternoon Friday. Thursday afternoon Helen & I visited Chesaning High. There are 5 Central kids teaching there – Wattrick, Central's football, basketball, etc. star, is coach there. Friday nite we saw none other than Howdy Loomis – our campus crooner – up at the dance – & he was as surprised as we were. I'd dearly love to give you this x tonite – but I'll save it for next Friday nite. Good-nite, Sweetheart. Love, Daisy

I'm not sure if Mom's college roommate, Helen Critchell, went with them on their camping trip to Yellowstone, but from the context of this letter, it sounds like perhaps she did.

Undated, prob Sep, 1935   Oakley

Dearest — (Wed nite) I've wanted to write you every nite but my common sense said perhaps you had enough of me to do for a while without having to read my letters too, but tonite I weakened, Ellis, & here I am, loving you as much as ever and I just can't leave you alone. These past three nights I haven't been able to sleep for thinking of you. For a week before you came I couldn't sleep for dreaming of you. O, Ellis, what can I do? I couldn't stop loving you if I tried – and I'll never try. Perhaps I'll be in the sleeping habit again before school starts – but Ellis, after that you'll have to come soon & often so the effects won't be so (bad?). And to lend me moral courage & support too – for 2 things – RRT & Latin teaching. I'll be so glad when school will be all through. When old-maid school-teachers are no longer in demand, I think I'll turn my hand to sewing – preferably plain-sewing – by the day. I cut out a dress tonite & hope to get it done Friday – and I won't have time to stop & bake any pies. The days are too short now & there aren't enough of them. I wish there were a whole summer vacation ahead of me again – one just for you. I want to tell you that I'm sorry, Ellis, for the things I said (to myself) about you Friday nite. I took them all back before I went to sleep. I can't stay angry with you any more than an hour when you're away – and not even that many minutes when you're with me. And I really don't mind your teasing, Ellis. I wouldn't have you stop it for anything. I'd rather have your teasing than someone else's love-making anyway. Goodness me! This sounds like a "True Confessions" letter. I think I'd best stop before this becomes too "sentimental." And also before the bugs run me out of bed. And now I'll tell you my bedtime story. I love you, dearest heart. Good-nite. Daisy xx

1936

1936 Chippewa

Sep 23, 1935   CSTC to the Hotel Vincent in Benton Harbor

Dearest x – (Mon 12m) I wish you would come up with some nice fresh strawberries and take me home with you and we'd have strawberry shortcake. O, Ellis dearest, there've been so many people around all day but I've been lonesome. I wish the summer were beginning again. I'm glad it's the last time I'm coming back. I've been as restless as a freshman – couldn't sleep last nite & was bored to death with nothing to do today – freshman day. Tonite there was a mixer for the girls in the rec room downstairs & it was rather fun. I came back yesterday about 5:30. Clarence & Gertrude & Harold & Helen & the kids were at our house for dinner. It was our folks' 26th wedding anniversary – and Dorothy & Alfred's 8th – and Clarence & Gertrude 8 days. They still can't see anyone else. Rosalie & Jimmie both helped me pack & we got along famously. Aunt Stacia & Tom were out Friday all day at our house. Seemed so good to see them. They live at 58 Quigley Blvd [Grand Rapids] now – south of where they were – off Division, right in Burton Heights, I think. I hope there won't be any County Fairs in your line of action around Benton Harbor this week. When we were in Gillette, Wyoming, we thought we had at last struck into some real cowboy country when we saw cowboys roaming the streets in full regalia, but we discovered that the county fair & rodeo were in town & we were disillusioned again. Have to start out early in the morning & get enrolled – practice teaching in everything. Ooo, Ellis, I don't dare weaken now. Tell me when you're coming to see me. Love, Daisy xx

---

Sep 26, 1935   CSTC to 833 Clinton St in Kalamazoo

Dearest x — (Thurs nite 9:30) If you really mean what you said about coming up any Saturday (and I don't think you'd say it unless you do), I'll send this on the fastest train & pray that you'll get it Sat noon. And although I will confess that I slept pretty soundly last nite, I haven't ever been "kidding" you, dearest. I like all my courses this term. For the first time since I was a freshman, I have time to study as much as I should & still have time left for – anything. I'm just getting acquainted with my pupils now & observing. I won't be actually teaching for 20 3 weeks. It rained all day and looks as if it will continue. So if (or when) you come, you'd best bring your raincoat, and, for Helen's sake, bring Bill too, if you can. (Do you think you can?) Love, Daisy xx

P.S. I love u.

Oct 1, 1935   CSTC to the Hotel Vincent in Benton Harbor

Dearest Ellis — "How do I love thee? Let me count the ways. / I love thee to the depth & breadth & height / My soul can reach, when feeling out of sight / For the ends of being & ideal grace. / I love thee to the level of every day's / Most quiet need, by sun and candle-light. / I love thee freely, as men strive for right. / I love thee purely, as they turn from praise. / I love thee with the passion put to use / In my old griefs, and with my childhood's faith. / I love thee with a love I seemed to lose / With my lost saints. I love thee with the breath, / Smiles, tears of all my life; and if God choose, / I shall but love thee better after death." Daisy

Mom, obviously swept away by the words of Elizabeth Barrett Browning, wanted to channel her feelings directly to Dad, so she copied the famous poem in longhand.

Oct 2, 1935   CSTC

Dearest Sweetheart — (Wed nite 1:00) "Heaven! I'm in heaven!" croons the haunting tune – and it makes me remember now even more strongly than I have been every minute of every day since I was "in heaven" – with you, Ellis. I've been busy every minute this week. I've been studying, doing library work, reciting, visiting with people, transacting candy business, making plans for RRT dinner & homecoming; I was even "partying" tonite – dorm pajama party – but all the time there is an undercurrent in my mind & heart that sings – "I love Ellis so dearly , and he loves me, and some day we're going to be together always, and I'm going to cook for him things that he likes, and do everything I can to make him happy – and we'll share our thoughts and our happiness and our love" – and I've been so gloriously happy within me. O, Ellis, this doesn't make sense. It's just telling you over again how much I love you. I hope you sold everything out in Benton Harbor, and that the Wheaties, flour, etc. business is booming like our candy trade. We've sold 9 boxes since Saturday nite. Teaching is grand so far – I haven't taught yet. But I'm getting the "feel" of a teacher & am anxious to begin. We're having a dinner in the commons tomorrow nite in connection with the first Ronan Round meeting. Plans for homecoming are getting under way now. Homecoming is the 11th & 12th of this month. Thursday night is faculty reception. I'm going home Friday – and Sunday night when I come back – I'm going to see "Anna Karenina." If you go to Detroit & take your mother this weekend, I know you'll have a grand time – and if you go to your grandmother's, I'm sure you will too. Wherever you are, Ellis, my most loving thoughts go with you. Always yours, Daisy

Besotted with love for Dad as she was, Mom was still also the "candy czar" of Ronan Hall.

Oct 6, 1935   CSTC

Ellis Dearest – (Sun nite 11:30) I love you so & I wish you were here so I could tell you. I came back from home about 6 tonite & I am a bit homesick & lonesome now, tho heaven knows I shouldn't be. There's been enough things doing & people around. We saw "Anna Karenina" tonite & it left me so saddened. I'm so tired & weary, but I did get lots of sleep at home. Ellis, your letter was so sweet, & it came Thursday, just at a time when I needed a little reinforcement. Four weeks more & it's been a year already, dearest. You must have had a grand weekend in Detroit with your folks & all, Ellis. I must say good-nite now. I'll write more later, tomorrow night perhaps. Love, me/Daisy

---

Oct 8, 1935   CSTC

Dearest One – (Tue nite 10:45) This was a beautiful day, the kind that makes you forget winter is coming. On a day like today was, Ellis, I'd love to be with you – just to live & breathe together in the sunshine – and dream. But when I can't be with you, the next best thing is to write to you. I half-promised that I'd write you last nite, and I didn't. I'm sorry. You know, though, that we can't always do the things we said we will, can we? That wasn't quite fair, was it? I'm sorry. I'll tell you some of the Oakley news now – as much as I can remember. First & foremost, Joe & Agnes (Stasek) have a new baby – a daughter, Barbara, born last Thursday. Stella Basovsky & Frank Kunik (of

Albee) are going to be married. Their bans were proclaimed for the second time Sunday. It also might interest you to know that Mr & Mrs Neal Mormon are expecting an addition to the family in November – also Mr & Mrs Art Hill, if I remember correctly. Fr Grzybowski attended the Eucharistic Congress. Clarence & Gertrude spent the weekend with us, & Uncle Henry & Uncle Bert & another man came out from Detroit Sunday & were also at our house for dinner; & I made some awfully good fudge – wish you could have had some. I think that was about the extent of my weekend – except I slept a lot too. Guess what, Ellis – 3 guesses! Miss LaMore, my critic, lives in Jackson, & goes frequently on weekends to Jackson, Battle Creek & Kalamazoo, & she said that anytime I want to, I may ride down with her, & back on Sunday afternoon. If you don't say, "So what?" maybe we could figure something out – just maybe. I have my 8 o'clock off in the morning – but I won't sleep. I'm really ambitious this term – probably because I haven't so much to do anyway. This weekend is homecoming though, & there will be lots going on. We play Wayne University. We beat them last year. Aren't you glad that the Tigers came out on top? At the high school there was a radio in the auditorium where the kids could listen in their free periods & in classes you could hardly hold them down. The shop classes were suspended because the machinery interfered with the reception. Must say Good-nite now, Dearest Pal. I'll see you in my dreams. Love, Daisy xxxx

The Tigers did indeed win the World Series in 1935, defeating the Chicago Cubs 4 games to 2. It was Detroit's first World Series win in the club's history.

Oct 13, 1935   CSTC

Dearest — (Sun nite 11:15) It has been a grand weekend for homecoming, but it's thundering now and there are flashes of lightning and I fear we're going to have a storm. Today was simply beautiful, a perfect fall day – warm wind & clear blue sky & gorgeous reds & yellows all around in the trees. And O, how I wished you were here, but tonite when it started to thunder I was glad you weren't because now you'd be going home in the storm. I sincerely hope that you enjoyed today as much as I did. Ida May & I went to 10:30 mass together after a good nite's rest, & this afternoon we all went to Cathedral Woods on a "nature tour" – the woods usually so solemn & silent were a riot of color. We collected tiny spruce cones and acorns to use in making bookmarks – we helped Doris identify trees for biology – and all the time I was thinking of you, Ellis – and now I stop & think & think, & forget to write. If only I could write all the things that I want to tell you from time to time, my letters would come every day & be awfully long, but when I write, I can't remember many things. And now, too, I'm rather sleepy. You've probably already read how we entertained Wayne University (13-6) – but the fellows played a good game of ball & that's the thing that really counts. Friday nite we had a big pep meeting & bonfire & then we went to see "Annapolis Farewell" – Helen wouldn't give us any peace until we went with her. It really was a good show tho, & it made me cry a little. Ralph says that it idealizes life at the academy, but "Shipmates Forever," minus the feminine interest, is really representative. Ida May came Friday nite & stayed with us – she left for Flint (where she teaches) about 5 tonite. Saturday morning at 9 we had the all-literary-societies breakfast – which was quite an event & where each of us got a darling corsage of yellow & brown straw-flowers which everyone wore to the game too. At 12:30 we had the parade which ended at the field just before the game. Our fellows have new suits – yellow, satiny-looking pants & black sweaters with a yellow C. The stands were filled. Ida May & I went down for confession after the game & arrived just too late. We all took a 2-hour snooze before the dance – & I didn't get thoroughly waked up again until this morning. Bill Porter & his Orchestra were here from Lansing – Nate Fry Friday nite. Layman was here. I was talking with him. He's superintendent at Birch Run this year but he doesn't like it very well. Next Thursday & Friday is teacher's institute at Flint – no school at the [1M] – no practice teaching. We have a game with Alma, I think, next weekend – or the next, I don't know which. I think I'll go home again sometime soon. Bill (Bromer) went home this weekend. He had a chance for a civil service job – in the post office, I think. And his father wants him to quit school & take it. Don't know how he'll come out – but I do know that Helen doesn't like the idea at all & if he does take the job there's liable to be a "bust-up" there. The storm seems to be going over, I wish it could be like today when you come again. Hope it's like this when you go squirrel hunting I seem to have taken 4 pages in saying a little bit of everything & not much of anything, but it only takes 3 little words to tell you what counts most of all – to me. I love you, Ellis Dearest. Love, Daisy

---

Oct 16, 1935   CSTC

Dearest Pal — (Wed nite 11:30) Have a grand time this weekend at Detroit, won't you. I know you well, showing your mother & Bernard the town, & having Bud & Kate along too. I hope the sales meetings aren't too long and boring. You will miss out on your squirrel hunting though. How about pheasant? Is the season still open the next weekend? If it is, & you're not going to your grandmother's, I wonder if you'd like to go hunting around Oakley – Clarence or Harold ought to be interested. It's just a suggestion. I don't even know about where the hunting is best or if the season is still open then or not. You've probably made other plans, so tell me if you have. I'm not sure whether or not I'll be going home (not that it has anything to do with the hunting). I could go home this weekend (any weekend now), but I think I'll stay & do some work for Psychology. We have to make a notebook & write a term paper & I haven't started either. Thursday & Friday is teacher's institute in Flint so I don't have teaching – nothing in the afternoon. Only one class on Friday too. I start teaching Monday – have full charge of the class. I taught the first half of the hour & it was a total surprise to me until the minute class started. I'm glad I had to though (even if it did leave me rather weak), because I won't have any qualms about getting up in front of them Monday. They're really nice kids – the cream of the freshman class. I like them all & they like me – and that counts a lot in working together. Just like you & me, Pal. We had a reception tonite at the church – with an attendance of about 50 or more – played Pedro & "donkey" & had ice-cream (too much) & cookies. Met some darling freshman girls, but the boys don't seem to turn out for such things. We're planning a Mercier party for Tuesday nite. Had a meeting a week ago & (ahem!) I was elected treasurer (footnote: no opposing nominees). Have a RRT meeting tomorrow nite just because & I have no worries about it. Everything seems to be going along fine now – especially the things I worried about all summer. Saturday we play a homecoming game at Ypsi, & O, I do hope we beat 'em! But even if we don't win, I know we'll play a good game – and don't you worry, we'll be up n' coming at Western too, when they come at us. I saw a shooting star last nite, Ellis. (xx glorified kiss xx) Love, Daisy

Dad's brother Bernard would have been just 6 years old in 1935. Bud & Kate are, of course, the Brorbys.

1936 Mercier Club

Oct 21-22, 1935 CSTC

Ellis Dearest – (Mon 1:30 PM) I had such a guilty feeling when I came home today at 11 and found your card & letter, because I hadn't written. But I hope you've lived through my long period of silence. I'm glad your sales meeting came out all right & that you could be with your family too. My mother said in her letter today that my Dad has been hunting every day this last week & they spent this weekend at the Au Sable. I looked for them up here yesterday. I'm going home next weekend – 26th – I think. I won't be counting on you for any weekends before the 9th, but I do hope you can come then. I'm sorry Bill won't be able to come. I'll take Helen home with me this weekend if she'll go, & I think she will. We've had simply glorious weather here for the last two weeks but it's raining now. Good? omen for my first day of teaching. I'm not very nervous about it tho, & that scares me. Friday I taught the first half of the hour – a very sudden surprise to me – but I came through all right. Here's hoping I do today.

(Tue morn) Dearest – Am in class now, will write later. Love, Daisy

Oct 22-23, 1935 CSTC

Dearest Ellis – (Tue 3:30 PM) Business before pleasure – then more business. I just completed my teaching business for the day and at 4 I have critic meeting – so I'm using my time to sandwich in a little pleasure – for me. For you? There's such a hubbub in the halls that I can scarcely hear myself think – lockers slamming, feet running back & forth – combined with all kinds of voices at all levels. My teaching was much better today, I felt, & I hope it continues to improve. The first thing I have to do is overcome my nervousness – and I'm doing that. It was terrible yesterday though, it's like standing in front of a small group & giving a 45 minute speech – only worse – you have to be prepared for anything. One thing that I am thankful for is that I have no problems in regard to discipline. I keep them busy enough to keep them out of mischief. I was just weak yesterday afterwards. I am quite calm today but rather apprehensive about the critic meeting soon to come. Miss LaMore wasn't in the room at all yesterday & only a few minutes today. Well – enough of that – but I'm glad to get it off my mind. Right now my mind is blank except for a bedlam of Latin forms that are rushing through it. So while I'm still in the mood, I shall start to correct a whole slew of papers that I have. OxOxOx, Daisy

(Wed 9 AM) Dearest – Got my papers all corrected this morning & sent down to Miss LaMore. Load off my mind. Critic meeting not bad at all last nite. I enjoy them the same way you seem to like your sales-meetings. Had a Mercier party in the Den last nite. Played billiards & shuffle-board

& pool. More fun, but we didn't play for money so I came out even. I had to get up at 6:00 to correct my papers & it nearly floored me - but there was the most gorgeous sunrise - that saved the day - a grand day too. Must go to English now. Be seein' ya (in my mind & in my dreams). Love, Daisy xx

---

Oct 24, 1935 CSTC

Dearest Pal — (Thurs 2 PM) I haven't been writing you very nice letters lately, have I? And I'm terribly sorry and very penitent. This weekend I'm going home & Helen isn't going with me and I'm going to get all my lessons for Monday tomorrow because I have no classes except teaching so when I'm home I'll take an evening off & write you a letter as nice as ever I can. Mama said, "Is Ellis coming Sat nite?" and I wish he were - but. She probably thinks that's why I'm coming home. But it isn't at all - it's because I want Aunt Flory to teach me to knit so I can stay here with my "knittin'" on weekends - and think about what I'm missing. Love, Daisy

---

Oct 25, 1935 Oakley

Dearest — (Fri nite 9:00, "Hollywood Hotel" hour, in front of the radio) Harpo Marx is playing "Alone" - a harp solo, & it is beautiful. It's so peaceful and cozy here, Ellis - but there's some One lacking - guess who? You're right, Sweetheart. If you were here, it would be perfect. X my heart. I love to sit here & dream of you, Dearest. I don't want to come to earth and think about anything (but you). I "needs must," however. First I'll tell you about my teaching. Because it has been going so well. Today the lesson went like clockwork - with enough time left over to make up a reading lesson we didn't have time for yesterday - and enough informality & exchange of ideas during the hour to leave everyone in a good humor for the weekend. I didn't get my 3 sets of lesson plans, for next week, done today as I had planned, but it won't take long tomorrow. And then - the test I had at 9 yesterday that left me so weak - I got the highest mark! I'm not bragging (please), but it made me feel so good to know it. I may spend next weekend in GR if nothing happens. Miss LaMore is driving down to Kazoo Saturday morning & returning Sunday afternoon and she asked me if I'd like to go. I'm writing to Aunt Stacia to see if I may come. I hope she'll be home so I can. Do you? I'm getting wise, Ellis - O, don't be frightened. I'm cutting a wisdom tooth - and it isn't much fun. By the way, did you read in the paper about the man in Washington who cured more than 400 cases of sleeping sickness merely by saying 3 little words?

Stella Basovsky was married last Saturday. I think – quite an elaborate affair. Also Bob Coon killed Helen Cermak a couple of weeks ago and there's quite a lot of consternation around here about the way the jury let him off. I'll tell you more of the details when I see you. It wasn't a very nice affair. "Campbell's Tomato Soup" is going off the air now & I think I will too – before Dick Powell's "Moon Song" gets me. So Good-nite, Sweetheart. I love you so, Ellis. Daisy xx

P.S. The three words were: "Congress has adjourned."

P.P.S. I went to church tonite. Aren't I good? Love, Daisy

Oct 29, 1935   CSTC

Ellis Dearest – (Tue nite 12m) Nice work! Keep going! And that goes for me too, Ellis. I hope you're right at the top tomorrow when the contest is ended. But – if you're not – you know you're always at the "top" for me anyway. I can get to Kazoo Saturday morning, Ellis, by way of Lansing & so not hitting Grand Rapids. I'll be there by 11 – or perhaps earlier, maybe later. I'll wait for you at the YW (& go with you to GR, if I may). I'm "encouraging" you to be on hand Sat afternoon – as you suggested. If this arrangement isn't satisfactory or convenient for you – will you write or wire me, so I'll know if I shouldn't come? And did you know, Ellis, our frosh are playing GR Junior College Sat afternoon? My teaching is still going fine. At critic meeting tonite, Miss LaMore told me I was doing a "nice piece of work," and, coming from her, I can appreciate it. Your supervisor & my critic must have gotten together to make us both feel good at the same time. I hope it lasts – until the weekend is over anyway. And please, don't let it snow. Until Saturday – and always, I love you. Daisy xx

---

Nov 3, 1935   CSTC

Dearest Sweetheart – (Sun nite 10 PM) I am going to "bed now," but I want you to know that I got back all OK at 5 to 8. It was terrible driving – a regular cloudburst all the way & we couldn't see the road & kept running off the pavement – but here I am now. I slept most of the way in from Lansing. I'm so glad you weren't driving thru tonight. Thank you, Ellis, for a lovely, loving weekend. I had a perfectly grand time. Now when I think about it, it seems all too good to be true, especially you, whom I grow to love more & more every time I'm with you, dearest. Love, Daisy

P.S. Good luck to you n' the supervisor n' the sales business. D.

Nov 4, 1935   CSTC to the Hotel Vincent in Benton Harbor

Dearest Heart – (Dorm, Mon 12m) I'll begin by saying I love you more than I ever knew I would love anyone, because that's all I can think of for the present, Ellis. I saw "The Dark Angel" tonite, Ellis, & if you can see it, do. You must not miss it. And I walked home with the rain fresh and clean and pure on my face, and the memory of you still strong and sweet in my heart. It was dear of you to write so soon, Ellis, and I do appreciate it - I always do, Ellis. I was in Lansing at 5:30 when you wrote, dearest, just as you thought. As to my coming so far to see you, & giving up my weekend of rest, etc. - it was worth coming 10 times as far and when I think of how many, many times you've taken the same long, lonesome ride, it was the littlest thing I could do for you & I hope I can do it again. My regards to the supervisor, but to you, dearest pal, my whole-hearted Love, Daisy xx

---

Nov 6, 1935   CSTC

Ellis Dearest – (Wed morn 8:20) How was the ass't supervisor, but especially how are you? Hope the winter weather isn't getting you down. Got out of psike early today and as I read the paper (Central State Life) I had a brilliant idea, but I just thought of a catch to it. There's an all-college dance Saturday nite & I thought how much fun it would be if Bud & Kate could come up with you & go to the game (Ladies Day) & to the dance at nite. But I just now remembered that Kate probably wouldn't want to ride this far, nor dance after she did get here. Anyway, it would have been fun. How's Benton Harbor? I'll bet the wind off the lake sends chills thru you. Bud sent me the menu he "lifted" for me Saturday nite. Wasn't that nice of him? I'm going to see "Shipmates Forever" tonite - have to go to the second show because Helen has a Home Ec meeting at 7. Friday nite there's another number on the Lecture Course - Dalies Frantz - young pianist. But I'm going to get a lot of sleep (sometime), maybe Sat morn, so I'll be good-natured at least, I hope - and if you go to the game with me & yell for Western, you'll be mobbed & I'll help 'em. So on that lovin' note, I'll stop and say - Love, Daisy xx

Dalies Frantz (1908-1965) was a child prodigy pianist from Denver. He received a Julliard Foundation scholarship to the University of Michigan. He later traveled to Europe where he studied under Vladimir Horowitz. Upon his return he debuted with the NY Philharmonic and the Philadelphia Orchestra, and gave concerts nationwide. An extremely handsome man, he also had parts in a few films. He served briefly as an intelligence officer in WWII, and spent the latter part of his life teaching at the University of Texas in Austin.

Nov 10, 1935 CSTC

Ellis Darling – (Dorm, Sun nite 9:30) "Ring" kisses aren't very substantial when you're all alone, are they? O, my Dear, today has been so empty & lonesome without you. Perhaps it's best that I won't see you again soon. The oftener I see you the harder it is to get over leaving you, it seems. That's what I meant, Ellis, when I said last nite that it might not be so nice to have you in Middleton. When you were in my arms, Dearest, school and lesson plans and teaching were never further away and I wished – I can't tell you what I wished, Ellis. I didn't want you to ever go away again. And I wasn't really cross and tired that last hour, Darling; I knew you would be leaving me soon, and I couldn't bear to have you go – I didn't want you to know it. Love me, Ellis, and don't ever doubt me, please, even if my letters aren't always what they might be. I'll make it all up to you, Dearest. I love you, Ellis, so much I could cry, but that doesn't help a bit, I know. Instead, I'll dream of you – the sweetest dreams in the world are of you – for your Daisy. xx

---

Nov 11-12, 1935 CSTC

Dearest Sweetheart – (Mon nite 11:45) Everything is white with snow tonite and it's beautiful. But I hate it, because it keeps you away from me, Ellis. I wish it were summer again, but I don't want time to pass so quickly either. Life and Love are too brief for that. There has been so much talk today of war and death – O, Ellis, I pray God never to let anything take you away from me. Without you, there wouldn't be much of me left alive, darling. Tonite when I came home to everything so cozy and dim and warm and peaceful, I thought of how sweet it will be to have you come home at night to me – to warmth and comfort and Love. Dearest, I'll try so hard to make you happy. Because I Love You, Ellis, with all my heart, Daisy xx

(Tue morn 11:15) – Ellis, Dearest – Everything is so "all right" this morning, and I feel so good. I like mornings like this – even the snow doesn't matter so terribly now. For one reason – we got back our test papers in Evolution & I carried off the honors with the highest mark. Of course, it doesn't mean so much (an A for the term if I can keep it up – and I can) but it is an encouragement to keep on – about the way you feel, I imagine, when your supervisor tells you you're in the winning. Yesterday's half-holiday did its part too, in my getting everything straightened up for a fresh start. And now our room is so clean & quiet & secure. I wish I could keep this feeling for a long, long time, and give it to you too, Ellis. I planned to go home this weekend & Helen was going with me, but Miss Hogue has asked us to work at the Country Club Saturday night and we really should

see our last game of the season, so I think we'll stay here after all. Sunday nite, "Mutiny on the Bounty" is here and I have to go see it for our class in Literary Criticism – we all have to go & then we discuss it afterwards in class. Ellis, I really can't tell you how very much I loved having you here Saturday, but perhaps you know how I feel. Don't let us ever grow away from each other, Ellis – it's so easy to do & so hard to return. If we can always keep on loving and understanding each other as we do now – (& better perhaps) I know we'll be happy. Your pal, Daisy xx

---

Nov 16, 1935   Oakley

Ellis Darling — (Sat nite 12m) How I wish you were here! O, Ellis, it sounds terrible to say it, but there's even a kind of emptiness about coming home when you're not coming at all. And New Year's seems so very far away. When I see you again it will be the eve of 1936, and I wonder what that year will hold for us. I'm glad we can't know though, for if it's something unpleasant we'll be happier now not knowing it – and if it's pleasant, it's so much nicer as a surprise. Goodness, it must be the late hour that makes me sentimental – and maybe because I'm lonesome too. I hope you enjoyed yourself at the game today – I know you did – and we didn't bet on it after all, did we? I don't know yet how our game came out. Not very school-spirited, my coming home, was it? But I feel more obligated sometimes to show home-spirit. I really shouldn't have come home at all. I should have stayed with dear old Alma Mater & helped with the youth-adult conference as I was asked to do, but that would have interfered with my getting my schoolwork done anyway – so here I am. I took my first lesson in knitting this afternoon from Aunt Flory and am considering knitting a dress – for next summer. I think if I begin right away, I might finish it before the season is over. We saw "Diamond Jim" tonight – did you see it? It surely is good – same type as the Barnum picture. We were down to Kairot's last night & got filled up on sweet cider & apples. Clarence had an accident Wednesday – ran a tine of a beet-fork through his foot – nasty-looking hole, but it's healing now. We looked for them up tonite but they didn't come. They'll come tomorrow. I didn't write since I received your letter, did I? So I'll tell you now how sweet it was, Ellis. I hope I can't be called "sloppily sentimental" for reading it over & over and then keeping it under my pillow. It's so very precious when it's all I have of you, Dearest, really alive & talking. I must close now (mass at 8), but I'll talk to you after I go to bed – and in my dreams. Listen, Ellis, & you can hear me – tonite & every nite – always – I love you – Dearest Pal & Sweetheart in the world. Daisy xx

Nov 18, 1935 CSTC

Dearest Pal — (Mon nite 11:06) I'm so glad you were having such a good time at the game, Saturday. But you didn't lose, Ellis; you didn't bet, and you probably would have won one way or another anyway. I'll always count on you for a winner. But I do feel sorry for your Michigan team, Ellis. It's tragic when the defense can't hold the visiting team down to at least no more than 2 touchdowns. 'Nuf said about the subject of football. Season's over now. How are Wheaties sales coming? I listened to your Wheaties program tonite & just hearing it gave me the pep, moral courage, stamina, etc. to meet my critic face to face in my own room, and the soft-headedness to stay up half (or more) of the night working on lessons. Seems foolish now, but it will be time well spent tomorrow. I haven't even started yet. Have to wait until the chaperone goes off duty to do my typing. We're starting our kids on a contract plan next week – you know, so much work for a C, more for B, & still more for A. Making plans for it now. Our room is all dressed up in a new blue desk blotter & white chrysanthemums – in honor of our critic meeting here. And you sat on the dresser & watched it all, Ellis, & I wondered what your opinion of it all was, but you only continued to look slightly amused (& wholly lovable) & never said a word. I don't feel bad at all tonite. Last nite I was so down & lonesome & I was going to write to you but thought better of it. If you'd suddenly drop in sometime when I'm feeling that way, I wouldn't let you go away without me. I don't know what's the matter with me, Ellis; I must be losing the zest of youth or something. Let's go "haywire" together. My mood may have been partially brought on by "Mutiny on the Bounty" that we saw last nite. It was a wonderful film, but it was so nerve-wracking & positively painful. Clarence & Gertrude did come up Sunday. Mrs Youngs came back with us. She'll soon be leaving for Mancelona to spend the winter with her daughter there. Joe Stasek is working in Flint now, did you know? Can't think of any more Oakley news that would be of interest. Mama made her Thanksgiving fruitcakes a couple of weeks ago & she will save you a piece for New Year's, she says. Last week a girl from the dorm went home with diphtheria, and several girls have sore throats now. Mama sent me back with a kit of Vicks supplies. You'll take care of yourself won't you, Ellis. I know a girl who loves you more than anything else in the world and she'd want to die if anything ever happened to her sweetheart, and that girl is – Daisy x

Nov 20, 1935 CSTC

Darling Ellis — (Wed nite 11:06) I love you so, but Dearest, I really wasn't trying to break down your resistance – honest, x my heart, I was only trying to build up some. But if that is what has happened – ? And you really want to see Oakley – it's a grand town, Ellis, when you're there. And when do you want to be there? When I'm there? How nice! That will be Thanksgiving Day, Friday, Saturday & Sunday – you have your choice – one or all – that's what I think of you. If you plan to stay over Sunday, Ellis, you can leave directly for home if you'd rather, & my folks will bring me back. Truly, Ellis, the one & only reason I'd rather have you do this is because it would make such a terribly long & tiring drive for you. Today the sun shone here for the first time in 11 days – & I do hope it was shining for you too. It had stopped shining when I came home, but it burst out in a flood of warmth again – right out of the mailbox. I'm glad you enjoyed yourself so in Ann Arbor. And I'm waiting to hear the rest of it. O, dear, I'm getting so sleepy. But even when I'm sleepy, Sweetheart, I mean what I say 100% – if I don't remember what I said, just show me it, & I'll show you that I mean it, Ellis. Good-nite, Darling x "Parting is such sweet sorrow / That I'll say good-nite until tomorrow." – bit o' Shakespeare. I want to say so many things, dearest, but it all amounts to this – I love you, Pal. Daisy xx

---

Nov 23-24, 1935   CSTC

Ellis Dearest — (Sat nite 11:45) I'm awfully sorry, but I just want to tell you tonite that I love you and I want to be your pal & sweetheart & friend. Always, Daisy

(Sun morn 11:30) – Dearest Pal – Everything is grand this morning. It's a beautiful day & I hope it will be as nice & I'll feel as peppy as I do now – let me know when you're coming – when you come. We went to 9:00 mass – Helen & I. Then we ate breakfast in the cafeteria & sat for an hour talking & philosophizing. We do that so often – just drop what we're doing & talk for hours. Some kids think it's so funny when they come in & find us talking so interestedly, just the two of us. I guess they think that when 2 people have lived together for 4 years they should have run out of things to say. But it isn't that way – the longer we live together the more we have to talk about, & the better we understand each other. I think that's the way it should be when people are married. Marriage has to be built on a sound foundation of understanding if it's successful, and that understanding, like love, has to grow & grow through the years to include all the interests of both, the man & the woman. So many marriages go on the rocks because from the beginning one or both refuse to recognize & understand the needs of the other. I don't see how marriage can fail if love is true & understanding is complete & it really is a partnership. No, dearest, this isn't quoted from a book & I didn't read it anywhere, but I've seen so many kids get married & be terribly unhappy because they didn't understand each other – just love isn't enough. This didn't really start out to be a treatise on marriage.

(2:10) – Dearest – that lapse of time denoted dinner. I must finish soon though, or this will be an installment letter, a plan taboo-ed by you once, I think. I want to extend to you my deepest sympathy, Ellis, for I know you must feel badly after the rather "crushing" defeat of your favored team yesterday. But don't take it too hard, maybe next year you'll have a better team – maybe. I'm glad that you had such a nice visit with the supt Tuesday nite, & I appreciate your remembering me. Thank you for the souvenir – and I can keep it without a guilty conscience, can't I, because I know you didn't carry it off hidden under your coat. I'll keep it in memory of an 'honest' man. I went to bed at 9:15 Friday nite & got 11 hours sleep. (I'm saving for you, Dear, Everything.) And I studied all day yesterday & last nite I got out my knitting (no cracks, please) & I taught Helen how to knit & I learned how to purl, & Peg & Marvel came over & we all took turns, so I didn't get anything done last nite, but I'm going to study this PM. I have a stack of books a mile high. Tomorrow my kids start on their contracts too & I have to prepare for that. Miss LaMore will take the class for me on Wed so I can come home at noon. Isn't that sweet of her? She's really grand. O, Ellis, I can hardly wait until you come. I'm so glad now that you "resistance" broke down. Please don't get brave & build it up again. Tell me when you're coming – W-Th-F-S-S – I wish you had the whole weekend too. But I'll be there, anyway, when you come – ready, too, if I know what time it will be. So – until I see you – to tell you – I love you, Dearest Dear in the world. Daisy xx

"Love me, honey? / Course I do. / Kiss me, honey? / 'Fraid to. / Cold, honey? / 'Bout to freeze. / Want my coat, dear? / Just the sleeves."

Nov 25, 1935 CSTC

O, Ellis Darling – (Mon 11 AM) You sound almost insane, but if you are, I am too & isn't it a grand & glorious feeling? I'm afraid that I won't even remember how to explain the 3rd conjugation, etc., etc. this afternoon & I'll be telling my kids what a grand person you are & I think they're too young to understand. I can hardly wait until Wednesday now, Ellis. Of course you can plan to stay at our house & I'll tell Mother to set an extra place Wednesday nite. O, I'm so glad you can have your Thanksgiving at home with your folks & then with us too. Do try to contain yourself until Wednesday. And if you value my sanity, please don't write me another letter like that in the middle of a school-day – not this week anyway. Dearest Ellis, I Love You So. Daisy X

Dec 1, 1935 CSTC

Dearest Dear in the Whole Wide World — (Sun nite 10:30) That means you, Ellis. O, it was sweet of you to have a letter full of Love & you (& they mean the same to me) waiting here for me tonite. And it was especially nice because I didn't expect it at all. My "congrats" to you on the flour sales. I'm glad for you, Ellis, that you're "in the money." It's so nice that you're going to be godfather. Will it make you feel very old and important? I'm so glad that you enjoyed your visit at our house and I so loved having you, even if the time was all too short. I couldn't bear to see you go, Ellis; it left such a big empty place in my heart. I have a feeling that even "forever" with you would be all too short. But four weeks from Wednesday, it isn't so terribly long – this month yet – and how can I see you go away again, Dearest? The roads are so slippery, and you are so far away. Take care of yourself, my Lover, until the "sometime" when I can take care of you. Always, Daisy

---

Dec 3, 1935 CSTC

Dearest Heart — (Tue nite 11) Dec 3 – Dec 31, I wish the time would fly as quickly as I can write it. But it's only 4 weeks from tomorrow and we'll both be in Oakley again. It's the two weeks until Dec 18 that will get me down, so if my letters don't sound very cheerful or optimistic & are few & far between, blame it on the end-of-the-term strain, Dearest, and don't think my attitude toward you is changing – because if I know you now as well as I think I do, Ellis, it never will – unless for the better. I hope you aren't having too much difficulty in keeping your truck on the road, it's still slippery as hang around here. Did I tell you, Ellis, that I'm tatting now? Aunt Flory gave me a lesson in that art Friday along with my advanced knitting lesson. It's really fun. And what do you think I'm going to knit? A baby sweater! I'm afraid it's the baby who'll wear it that will need the sympathy. Can you answer this: When an automobile slides on the pavement, whose children are they? My kids are literally swamping me with papers now that their contract will soon be over. I have a whole slew of them to do in the morning – no 8 o'clock tomorrow. I went into a hot & cold sweat & had chills & fever yesterday when I heard Miss Barnard was coming to visit my class. At the end of the class period I was nearly exhausted from the strain & she comes trundling at a quarter of 4 (class over at 3:30), explaining that she was "unavoidably detained," but she'll be down Friday for sure. The kids are getting an hour-long written test Friday – I hope she enjoys it. {*theautomobile'skids*} Will you ask your brother, Kenneth, if he remembers Maxine Pierce? She tells me she had a crush on him when she was a freshman in HS – Martin, I think. She's working at the Blackstone & taking Latin to make up a half-credit so she can go into training at the Butterworth Hospital – an awfully sweet girl, full of pep too. She went* *to Western last winter. Rosemarie Brancato, mezzo soprano, was her last nite on the lecture course. She had a lovely voice & everyone liked her, but the "setting" became so unbearable that Helen & I came home at intermission & studied. You know Pete Troy? He & Dot McDaniel are getting married on New Year's Day & they're going to live in Flint where Pete is working. Yesterday was blue Monday for me – everything went wrong all day, but it hasn't been bad today – guess I'm all over the effects of the Thanksgiving "turkey" now. Music now is from the Aragon – Jan Garber – "Treasure Island" – wish you were here, Dearest Ellis to say Good-nite to you Pal & Sweetheart, Daisy xx*

Rosemarie Brancato (1911-1994) enjoyed a long career in opera, performing with the New York, Chicago, Detroit & Cincinnati opera companies as well as doing nationwide concert tours. The Aragon was one of the most famous ballrooms in Chicago, and often served as a venue for radio broadcasts by popular orchestras and big bands.

Dec 5, 1935   CSTC

Dearest Pal — (Thurs nite 10:45) The best part of having plenty of time to do a thing is the first part, said some wise man, and he was probably right, but does anyone ever follow the advice of wise men? A whole term would have been considered plenty of time to do 2 term papers & a notebook & it seems that now the best part of it is over. I've started none of them yet, but here I am, putting pleasure before business – and how does it all concern you? Just that you're getting a letter out of it. Firmly as I resolve to get my work done before I can write to you, it seems I always weaken. I like to write to you, Ellis. I can say anything and you always understand – at least I hope you do, because if you don't, I'm making a fool of myself half of the time. I write so many things to you that we never even talk about, but I think that's because we're never together long enough to even get started talking. Just once this summer, I remember we did get started in a real talk & then you had to go home & I had to come home too. But sometime we can talk – and talk – and talk. My kids finish their contracts tomorrow & have a test on Monday. I've been staying until 5:00 with them every night this week. Miss Barnard will visit my class tomorrow and she's going to see one grand scramble, with everyone wanting to do a different thing at the same time. Let 'er come. She can't bother me. Do you know what a "fuddy-duddy" is, Ellis? Doesn't that word just express the old-fashioned type of school teacher – prim & fussy & insisting on observance of details, etc., etc.? Don't ever let me be one. If you ever see me leaning in that direction, will you make me snap out of it? If you can – and I think you can. It's this weekend you're to become a godfather, isn't it? Don't drop her, Ellis. I'll bet she's cute. I'd like to see her. How's the flour business now? Are you thawed out yet from those few days of real winter? But hasn't it been grand out today, and it will be tomorrow too - I can feel it. Joe Bowditch died Friday afternoon after Thanksgiving. I don't remember if I told you. Helen is sleeping so peacefully & soon I will be too. A dozen term papers couldn't keep me from peaceful slumber & sweet dreams. I don't see how people can really live without being in love. Of course it's true that no one has lived fully until he has loved. But there's something about being in love that tempers and mellows everything you do. It keeps you from worrying about little things or taking them too seriously because you know that over & above all there's one thing that ranks higher than everything else together, and that's love. To love someone completely and have him return that love completely is, I think, the deepest and the highest happiness a human can know. Can it be love that has made me turn dreamer, philosopher (& essay writer)? I'm sure it is, Ellis, and I never, never want to lose it. And it's only you, Ellis, that I could ever love so deeply. I've given my heart to you. Keep it always, for Daisy

P.S. Will you forget me, Ellis, if I should go as far away as Big Rapids next year - to teach? D.

Dad had four younger brothers: Don, Ken, Vern and Bernard, in that order. I'm not certain, but I think he was godfather to Donna Jean, Don's first child, born November 24, 1935. Donna Jean [Abel] died in 2013.

Dec 8, 1935   CSTC

Ellis Darling Sweetheart — (Sun nite 12:15) It's late & I'm so sleepy but the orchestra is playing such sweet music that it makes me remember & remember - and all my memories are you. I'm head over heels in work, Ellis, but I must be head over heels in love too, or I'd be sleeping now. I wish you were here now, Dearest. I think it would be very near to heaven to fall asleep with my head on your shoulder. The weeks are going, Ellis, but oh so slowly, when I think of you. I wish the weeks & months would just fly by until - . O, my darling, I love you so. I shouldn't write these things to you, Ellis, but sometimes, like now, all I can feel or know is that I love you above everything else & I want to tell you. And for now, Dearest, this is the only way I can tell you. Good-nite, Sweet Heart. Daisy xx

---

Dec 9, 1935   CSTC

Ellis Dear — (Mon eve 6:30) I don't know why you're so insistent that I save all my love for you. I wouldn't want to think that you're selfish. But, if it will make you rest any easier, Ellis, I promise you that I'll save all my love for you, on my honor, until next year. I went to confession Saturday nite too, and to communion at 7:30 mass yesterday morning. Then I studied so hard all day.

From 4:30 to 7:30 though, I attended a birthday party – Horace's – my pal of 2 years ago, to whom Miss Barnard introduced me. Yesterday, Dec 8, was the 2000th anniversary of his birth. He was the Roman poet who wrote in lyric verse of the joys & pleasures of country life, and to live today, for tomorrow we die. It was a very enjoyable party, much more so than I expected. We had a program centered around the life & works of H., sang Latin songs, & had refreshments. I had my credits checked today and Mr Barnes was so encouraging that I'm afraid of being disappointed. I'll tell you what he said – "With your marks and such a combination as you have [English, Latin, History], you can't help getting a very good job." Or words to that effect. It made me feel so good and I hope he's right. I've only 3 more requireds to take – 2 teachings and a history methods – and 5 electives. I'm going to take 2 in Home Ec, 1 in English, & I haven't decided on the others yet, but I feel almost like a free white person again. O, don't take me too seriously; it isn't that bad. You shouldn't have expected a Baptism so early, Ellis. Your little niece was only 2 weeks old yesterday. She's still pretty tiny for a shower bath. Don't you think so? Only 7 more days of classes! O, Ellis! I could hug someone for joy – but you're not here – and I've given my word of honor. My kids had a test today so I have a neat little bunch of papers to correct tonite – that, and the thought that I'll be teaching every day up to & including Wed, Dec 18 – and I wanted a chance to observe again. Probably Miss LaMore's theory is that the practice will do more good than observation. (What do you think?) O, my dear, I'm getting sleepy and that will never do. So I must leave you, Pal, for the present, & get busy. Daisy

P.S. Did the all include letters too?

P.P.S. It's funny how my letters keep going to you like ticker-tape reports ever since I told you I'd be too busy to write. But I can't tell you why – 'cause "I promised."

P.P.P.S. This doesn't count as breaking my word because this comes before my promise. So I can say, I love you, Ellis. Daisy

[This last P.S. is written upside down at top of first page. Clever, huh?]

The Mr Barnes Mom consulted with on her credits and job prospects was undoubtedly Charles C. Barnes, the Registrar (and Dean of Men) at Central then. Barnes Hall, the first men's dormitory, was constructed in 1951. It was demolished in 2019. And now I'm going to throw in a "wild card" here – a letter to Dad from Mom's mother, Lettie, my "Grandma Whalen." It will throw some light on Dad's perfect Christmas gift to Mom. And it also gives a sense of the formal letter-writing style my grandmother used.

Dec 16, 1935 Oakley to Kalamazoo

Dear Friend – I will answer your letter right away so you will have time to get my name in to Santa. Daisy's gloves are size 7 and I think brown would be nice. You know her coat, hat and shoes are brown, but you suit yourself. You might see some other color that would go good with brown. You get anything, and she will be pleased with it I know. Clarence has a job and they are living in Saginaw at 370 South Fourth St. He is working at the Malleables pouring iron so he gets good wages and are they tickled. Am glad you had a good time Thanksgiving and hope you can come Xmas or New Years. Jan 1 is Clarence's birthday so we will celebrate. I will tell you when I see you what Will said about him learning to yodel. I remain as ever your friend. Mrs Wm Whalen

---

Dec 20, 1935 Oakley

Ellis Dearest – (Home, Fri nite 8:20) "Love, Ellis"? I can't remember when I began to really love you, Ellis, but it has been growing and growing until now it seems as if there never was a time when I didn't love you, as if my whole life was spent in preparing for you, Dearest. "Love, Ellis" – command or request – I could stop breathing more easily than I could stop loving you, Sweetheart. xxx And on the 12th night from tomorrow nite, Darling, I can break the bank where I've been saving all my love for you, or you can, perhaps. It's grand to be home again, not only for the pleasure of home-cooking, leisure, etc., etc., but for the joy of sleeping, O, heavenly sleep. For two nights I've slept the clock around & I'm beginning to feel quite myself again. Monday night I went to bed at 4:30 AM & up at 6:30; Tuesday night Helen & I typed all night in the kitchenette downstairs & took a nap from 7:30 until 8:15. But I finished both my tern papers & my notebook & resolved for probably the 10th time to finish term papers early the next time I have one assigned. But I can't have many more anyway. I'm taking only 3 subjects next term and 3 spring term, Ellis. It sounds lazy, doesn't it? I need only 5 to graduate though & there's not much more that I want. Next term I'm taking Home Ec 102 (Foods) 8-10, Journalism 10-11, Teaching 12th Grade English at the HS 1:15, & Phys Ed 4-5. Spring term I'll take 9th Grade English Teaching, History Methods, & Home Ec 304 (Home Management). Miss LaMore told me Wed that she was sending in a B grade & a fine recommendation to the appointment office for me, that I had overcome my one weak point – force in handling the class – and that I will make an A teacher. She probably tells them all that, but, O, Ellis, it made me feel so good & I was about ready to break down anyway. And to think how I made half my summer miserable worrying about practice teaching – & RRT – and everything's going fine with that too, 2/3 of my term over & now everyone is busy with plans for the rushing party Jan 22, which I'll tell you about. We went to Saginaw yesterday afternoon, to Clarence & Gertrude's, & shopping. They're living just a half-block from the church where they were married. It's nearly 3 miles from the Malleable's where Clarence works, but they're going to move when the month is up for which they rented their rooms. Helen & Rosalie were down last night & we suggested to Rosalie that she write a letter to Santa Claus. Remind me to show it to you, Ellis, it's a masterpiece. "In a Little Gypsy Tea-Room," "Treasure Island," "It's Dangerous to Love like This" – our songs, Dearest. And I hope they'll play them all for us on the last nite of the old year when we'll be together. Your last letter, Ellis – I'm so glad you mailed it instead of tearing it up. When you write another like it & want to tear it up, please don't, Ellis. Remember that I love you, & every letter helps me to understand & love you more. So please, Dearest. And now to you in reply to your very lovely Christmas greeting, May you have every year a merrier Christmas & a happier New Year than ever before. That is the sincerest wish of Your Sweetheart, Daisy x

Clarence had apparently landed a steady job at Saginaw Malleable Iron Co, a foundry which was a division of General Motors. The company was divided into different components, one of which became Saginaw Steering Gear, which was where, I believe, Clarence stayed until retirement.

Dec 24, 1935   Oakley

Ellis Dear — (Mon nite 11:25) It's refreshing to know that you've lost none of your natural wit & irony, as evidenced by your letter today. Contrary to your surmises, I hadn't mislaid your address, & I hope you received my letter tonite to restore your "lost faith" in me. The period of silence on my part seems to have called forth quite a volume of comment & – a little worry, perhaps? It really wasn't intentional, Ellis, & it wasn't forgetfulness either. Perhaps I can explain it better when I see you. We received your box today, Ellis, & everyone was very pleased and happy – the "yodel-er" is very satisfied, & Mama says she'll have something baked for her star-boarder when he comes. And the gloves for me – they're the nicest ones I've ever had, Ellis. Thank you so much. They're just a grand Christmas gift. Now I won't need anyone but you to keep my hands warm – even when you're not around. I 'specially like the wooly ones – & the other pair too. O, they're both so nice – and they just fit too. Had mass at 10:30 here Sunday – which meant 11 to 12:30 – with toes freezing for 2 hours. Clarence & Emil & Art came up & were here until 4, then we took the things Santa left here down to Jerry & Kenneth & spent the evening (Dorothy & Alfred's). We decorated our tree tonite & Santa has already piled a lot of things under it. Tomorrow nite Harold & Helen & the kids &

Clarence & Gertrude are coming here. Just Harold & Helen & Family will be here for Christmas – & Clarence & Gertrude, New Year's. Clarence likes his work a lot better now, & they're going to move as soon as they find rooms nearer to his work. I'm glad to know that you didn't wear out little brother's train, Ellis. We have one here for Jimmy, and, would you believe it? We haven't even had it set up. I wish I could have been with you on your lazy Sunday afternoon, Ellis, just to keep you company – and so you needn't have used your pen to talk to me. And I wish you were here now so I needn't use my pen – to thank you for your lovely gift – & to say I Love You, & Good-nite, Sweetheart. Love, Daisy xx

---

Dec 25, 1935   Oakley

Ellis Sweetheart – (Wed, Christmas night 9:15) All day I've been thinking thoughts for you & about you & trying to save them until now to tell you but somehow now I can think of only about half of them. It's like that when I'm with you, only more so, to the extent that my thoughts all dissolve into one that can be expressed perhaps rather inadequately, in three words. Then my mind seems to be stuck, like the broken record, and just keeps saying "I Love You" over and over again. So I guess I'll have to always write you a letter when I want to tell you something. Isn't it too bad that words come hardest to us when we are so terribly sincere and when we want them to mean so much? There's been such an aching emptiness in my heart today at Christmas, Ellis, but I'll be so happy and contented at New Year's. You make all the difference for me, Ellis, you fill the emptiness so perfectly. I hope I'll never regret letting you mean so much to me, Dearest. So many things can happen. If I could have just one prayer, it would be that nothing shall ever come between you and me, that we'll always love each other and be together. And that is a great deal to ask, isn't it, Ellis, in a world of uncertainties with another world war coming on. And Dearest, (I can say it now because I won't send this), I want you to come on Saturday – three more precious days together. I can be prudent, Darling, & remind you of the distance, etc., etc., but when you do come & I see you standing there in the doorway so young & brave & dear, my heart does flip-flops & I wish that you'd come eternities ago & could stay forever. Love, Daisy xx

Mom's reference to "another world war coming on," is the first indication that she was keeping abreast of world news. Indeed, by the end of 1935, Hitler and Mussolini had both seized power and the perils of fascism, Nazi doctrine and anti-Semitism were dominating the headlines.

Dec 28, 1935   Oakley

Dearest Ellis – (Saturday 10:15 AM) Just received your letter saying you hadn't yet had a reply concerning my visit to Grand Rapids. I sent out a letter (written Saturday) to you Monday morning at the same time I sent the box & I can't understand why you didn't get it. I addressed it as usual, but with no return address. I'm really sorry, Ellis. I was half-looking for you this afternoon or tonite. I told you in my letter that my folks weren't planning to go to GR this weekend, but if you would like to come out Sat (roads, weather, etc. permitting) that I'd love to go back with you. If you've already gone, this won't reach you today. But if you're still at home, it will probably be because you're not feeling well and I wish I could be there. I do want you to know that I didn't ignore your invitation & I wish you were coming tonight, but, of course, I don't want you to be out in this weather when you're ill. Mama says if you some "yodeling oil" it might help – but I don't think it's that funny. We'll be looking for you on Tuesday afternoon, Dec 31, & I hope you'll be all over your illness then. Sincerely. Love, Daisy xx

(By the Christmas tree, Sat nite 9:15) – Ellis Dearest – O, I do hope you got my letter today, Ellis. But I'm afraid you didn't & are thinking that I didn't answer you letter of last Friday at all & you asked for an answer by Tuesday nite. I sent it out Monday morning, thinking you'd get it Tuesday. I can't think of a thing that could have delayed it, unless I addressed it Grand Rapids instead of Kalamazoo, but I don't think I did. O, Ellis, it wouldn't be so bad if I hadn't said I'd answered a letter once before when I didn't, & now you won't believe me when my letter really does get lost. Please believe me, Dearest. Your letter today made me want to cry, Ellis, not because I was so disappointed, but it sounded so tired and hurt and so unhappy. I can appreciate how you must feel tonite & I hope you're not all alone in a rooming-house with no one to look after you. O, Ellis, I wish I could be with you, here or there. Take good care of yourself & I hope you're feeling fine again when you get this letter (Tues morn?) & will come early Tuesday & I wish you could stay all week. It's so cozy here, but so lonesome – just the Christmas tree lighted & a smooth dance orchestra – just a grand setting – for nothing tonite. There's a gal singing now – "Please Believe Me," & it's what I've been saying to you. I made some fudge tonite & I wish you'd been here to help me. I haven't eaten any of it yet, so I don't know if it's good, bad or otherwise. The folks just came home & now I'm upstairs going to bed & it's 10 below zero, so maybe it's a good thing you didn't come, Ellis. Good-nite, Dearest Sweetheart in the World, Ellis. Love, Daisy xx

P.S. Tuesday nite I hope I can say good-nite to you personally. Until then, please Love Daisy.

143

 PIECES OF A LIFE

(Sunday 3 PM) – Dearest Dear – I love you & I'm living for Tuesday afternoon or evening. Love, Daisy xx

> The U.S. mail was obviously a lot faster then, if one could mail a letter
> Monday morning and it would get to its destination by Tuesday night.

Jan 1, 1936   Oakley

Ellis Dear – (Wed, New Year's Day) when you go today, my heart goes with you and the sincere wish that the road back may not seem too long & cold – & the thought that before we know the time has gone, you'll not be alone again – ever. Love, Daisy

> The above short note was actually written at the bottom of the letter
> Mom wrote December 25, on Christmas night, but did not mail, and
> probably gave to Dad when he left.

Jan 3, 1936   Oakley

Dearest Dear in the World to me – (Fri nite 10:15) Here I am alone but for a photograph of your dear self and a ring still warm with remembered kisses. There are you – 150 miles away and alone too. Three nites ago you were here and a Dream come true. And now I've read your books and perhaps if I were not in love I could sympathize with the reasoning and logic in them. But my principles have not been changed by them. I may be a pagan, Ellis, but I am open to suggestion and if you are really convinced that these writers are right in their views, you'll have to do some missionary work on me. Dearest, I meant to write you a long letter, but will you mind terribly if I stop now & continue later? I'm half asleep and I wish that I might have a dream as sweet and tender and full of love as our Dream that began a New Year for us. Good-nite, Sweetheart. Love, Daisy xx

> I don't know what Mom meant by Dad's books and writers. In my
> memory, Dad seldom read any books at all. He did have a copy of Dale
> Carnegie's How to Win Friends and Influence People and possibly a
> book by Norman Vincent Peale and some bookkeeping textbooks he'd
> studied. But mostly he just read the newspapers and the Farm Journal.

Jan 5, 1936   CSTC

Dearest Heart – (Dorm, Sun nite 10:45) All ready now to retire for the nite so I can get up early & get enrolled so I can collect class dues all day. Seems rather nice to be back in the dorm again – just once more to

come back like this, but I won't be sorry. I'll have something ever so much nicer to look forward to (?) And now I'm looking forward to your coming again – I love weekends when you come to see me. Sat nite we went down to Clarence & Gertrude's to supper. O, their rooms are so cozy & nice, & Gertrude had a grand supper. Have you any faith in my culinary ability, Ellis? I think you'll need it. Mama says I'll have to stay home this summer & learn how to can tomato juice – (anything else you'd like me to learn?) I'm going to take cooking this term – and I knew we had to wear smocks so I made myself a very bright little number of yellow & brown plaid & learned tonite that Miss Hogue very much prefers plain colors – and dark ones too. O dear, watta life! In fact, what a life! What a grand life, when you're around, dearest! I know you had a grand time in Detroit, Ellis. How's business in 1936? I wrote 1936 half of last year & now it seems it should be '37. Wish it were – in a way. The kids were in tonite & now we have each other's vacations all settled, etc., etc. Nice orchestra on , but no one to enjoy it with, so guess I'll have to go to bed & dream – of the Dearest Sweetheart in the World. G'nite. Love, Daisy xx

---

Jan 6, 1936   CSTC

Dearest Ellis – (Mon nite 8:45) Your letter was so welcome today, Dearest. I came home for just a few minutes at noon & found it here. It's one of the nicest letters you've ever written me, Ellis. I'll have to think it over more before I answer most of it. Gee, I'm so tired & all I've done today is sit at a table & collect class dues 9-12 and 1-5. I was all enrolled at 8:45. Dr Beck talked me into taking chances (in case I ever want to work on my Master's degree, & he thinks I should – that's what he thinks), so now I have a pretty full schedule: 8-10 Home Ec, 10-11 Journalism, 1-2 Teaching Senior English at High School, 2-3 Chaucer, at the college (guess I'll fly to & from – college to HS), and 4-5 Tapping, & one day a week critic meeting at 4 at the HS. Nice? Maybe. I'll tell you later. When are you coming to see me, Ellis? My weekends are all free to you. I would suggest 18th, or 11th or 25th – as suits your convenience, my Dear. I love seeing you anytime. Dearest, the X came too late for Sunday nite. May I have it tonite, please? And – not be outdone – I'm sending one to you, as a good-nite X – for my Sweetheart. From your sweetheart, Daisy

This letter was the first time I'd heard that Mom had been advised to attend graduate school, a rare thing for women in that time. But then there was Dad – and love.

Jan 7, 1936 CSTC

Ellis Dearest – (Tue 6:15 PM) The music is "goin' round & round" very loudly in the hall just now, as it is most of the time around here – quite irritating at times (hmm!). I'm waiting to eat with Helen (she works until 6:30). Wish I were waiting for you, Ellis. I think I could make it cheaper for you – 25c x 2, instead of 45/2 – I guess it comes out about the same. Shall we compromise? It was just grand to find a letter from you tonite when I came home. Peps me up for another day. Makes me a little bit lonesome too, but I'd rather be that way than not get a letter because when I hope for a letter & don't get one it leaves such a forlorn feeling. (7:00) Just came back from the cafeteria & it's so clear & not very cold. I'd like to see you tonite, Ellis. But I have to study – Journalism & Home Ec & Chaucer. Had a meeting with Miss Stegenga – my critic – at 4 tonite & she very encouragingly & very tactfully began by saying not to be "scared" of our class, even if most of them are as old as we are, or older. I have 30 in my class & I'll be introduced to them tomorrow. I'll observe for at least a week & a half though before I do any real teaching. Helen is knitting very diligently on a sweater. I gave her your regards & she says she's "sleepier n' hell, but thanks anyway." Are you still planning to go to Mick's this month, Ellis? I wish we would have a basketball game when you come up, but we don't have any home games on Saturdays. Perhaps we can find something to do anyway (?) Lowell Thomas is on now. The kids across the hall have a radio now & they don't spend so much time here. I wear 'our' wooly gloves to school, Ellis, & they keep my hands so warm.

(10:45) Dearest Sweetheart x – I've had my bath & now I'm so sleepy but I can go to bed with a clear conscience because my studying is all done. But first I must say good-nite to you. I'll dream of you, Dearest. Love, Daisy xx

Lowell Thomas (1892-1981) was one of the preeminent radio personalities of his time, as well as a writer, actor, explorer and world traveler.

Jan 8, 1936 CSTC

Dearest x – (Wed nite 6 PM) O, it's getting so cold again. It's snowing like everything & the wind is howling & moaning around the corner of the dorm – a condition not very conducive to peace of mind when one is alone. Isn't it strange how just one person can make all the difference in the world in a situation? Just having you around makes everything seem so different. I met my English class today & they're not nearly as formidable as I had imagined them. And I ride back to the college in the bus so I make my 2:00 class here on time. In cooking class we're beginning our work with beverages, coffee first. When we study a product, we learn all we can about it – where it comes from, how it is grown, its preparation for market, etc. & finally its preparation for the table. So for tomorrow we find out all we can about coffee. I think I'll like the class a lot. I've shifted my tapping class from 4 to 5-6 o'clock so it won't interfere with my 4:00 critic meeting at the high school. I don't like my schedule at all. It's full from 8 in the morning to 6 at nite, & I thought I was going to have such a snap this term. I think I'll take only 2 subjects spring term. (Sob, sob, I'm abused!) O, & I'll like journalism too. There are 14 of us in the class & we act as reporters for the Life. The advanced class act as re-write people, editors, etc. My regular beat is the English Dept – mainly Dr Beck, & Mr Bush, who is working on the Copeland program. I have to start looking for news tomorrow.

(10:50 PM) Sweetheart Dearest – I'm sorry for the extra interruption. I had dinner at 6:30 & studied in the library until 8:30. Just had a hot bath & I'm all set for slumberland (x & a dream of you x). I'm so sleepy. Save a dream for me, Ellis. Good-nite, Dearest. Love, Daisy xx

---

Jan 11, 1936   CSTC

Dearest Sweetheart — (Sat nite 11:15) To tell you that you're still the Dearest Dear in the world – that you always will be for Daisy – that you always were even if I didn't know it. How else can I tell you, Ellis, that I Love You, Love You as dearly, more all the time. I can't tell you what I felt when I read your last two letters and the enclosed article. I think I understand your feelings when you read of Mark Twain's romance. It's saddening to think that a companionship so beautiful & understanding must come to an end. I cried & I'm not ashamed of it. I can't bear to think of our love ending, Ellis. I want it to be as lovely & tender as was the one we read about, and please, God, may it not end too soon. My heart is so full tonite, Ellis, but I can't write you all the love that is there for you. God keep you, for Daisy.

Jan 12, 1936   CSTC

Dearest Pal — (Sun nite 10:30) For once I can go to bed with a clear conscience. I've all my lessons, my clothes all in order (& myself all clean too). I hope I can have all that done next Saturday when you come, & have lots of sleep too, so I'll be good-natured for you, Dearest, & then if you can stay over until Sunday we can go to church together. I'm pretty sleepy right now, but it's a warm, satisfied sleepiness (just had a hot bath), &

I'm going to bed early. Ellis, I can't tell you just how perfectly grand your letters have been this week. I've read them over & over. It sounds funny to say it – but I think that we're just beginning to know each other better. I love you because of what you are, Ellis. And I love you more knowing that you "are what you are 'cause you are." I think I have a sound enough set of values to know genuineness & I know you're the "Real Thing," Ellis. There is everything grand about you that I could say but it's being genuine & true in all of it that counts the most – for me – and for everyone in the long run. I could tell you more, much more – but I won't tonite, Ellis. I can hardly wait for Saturday nite to come – and you. Did I tell you that the Mormon family has been increased by two? – twin boys – Gene & Dean, Jan 8 – 4 & 5 lbs. I hope business will be just booming this week. If not, save your troubles to tell me, Dearest. I Love You, Daisy xx

P.S. Dearest, I can't tell you how sorry I am & sympathetic for the lonesomeness of a hotel room. But before long, Sweetheart, I'll make it up to you over & over again. Until then, please, be patient. Love, Daisy xx

---

Jan 13, 1936   CSTC

Dearest – (Mon nite 12m) I'm so sleepy, Ellis, but I must tell my Sweetheart good-nite. I hope Benton Harbor is treating you well, Ellis. We beat Alma tonite 20-17 in a hard-fought & peppy game. I do wish you could come up to a game. I got the proofs of my pictures today & I don't like them at all, so I'm going to have more taken in the morning. I'm getting some for appointment pictures, but the ones I got today would never get me a job. (Maybe they look too much like me.) Mother sent me some fudge today, plain & peanut-butter kinds. Our room certainly was popular for a while – until it was gone. This is just the beginning of the second week of school & it seems ages & ages since vacation. O, Ellis, will spring ever come? But there's one thing I have to live for – you'll come before the spring, Dearest, and with it & after it. I love you so. Good-nite, Sweetheart. Sweet Dreams. Love, Daisy xx

---

Jan 17, 1936   CSTC

Ellis Dearest – (Friday nite) The orchestra's so grand & I'm going to be abed by 11:00 tonite – I'm trying to get enough so I'll be feeling good Saturday nite (tomorrow nite). But sleep is the hardest thing there is to get around here. I'm so glad your flour sales are going along well – more power to ya, kid! Here's hoping the roads won't be so slippery tomorrow. My thoughts will be with you all the way & I'll try not to let you find me in the tub when you arrive. We had our Ronan Round picture taken tonite & committee meetings for our rushing party Wednesday nite. Had a grand time last nite at the "Femme's Fling" (co-ed prom – Adamless Eden party), but today I've been just dragging myself around & trying to keep awake in classes. But I won't need to try in order to keep awake Saturday nite. I'll be seein' ya, Sweetheart. I love you, I love you so. Daisy

1936 Ronan Round Table Literary Society

Jan 23, 1936   CSTC

Dearest – (Thurs morn) Please forgive me for not having written to you this week. I couldn't, Ellis, and say what I wanted to. I've been thinking of you, & us, all the time, & dreaming about you when I did sleep. I enjoyed every minute of the weekend with you, Ellis, and I only pray that we'll always be as close to each other and never have any misunderstandings. I love you, Sweetheart & Pal, more than anything in the world. I hope I can prove it to you, Dearest. Love, Daisy xx

---

Jan 26, 1936   CSTC

Dearest Sweetheart – (Sun nite 12m) Ellis, I've been sitting here & thinking & thinking to you & I haven't written any of it. There are so many things I want to talk to you about, but I'm too tired now to go into it all. I want to tell you my opinion of sororities & fraternities in a democracy, about my teaching, about the J-Hop, about the show tonite – "Magnificent Obsession" – I wish you'd see it too, Ellis – about our rushing party, that I'm going home this weekend, about what has happened to me since I left you a week ago tonite – but none of it seems very important now, especially when I think of you, Dearest – and all the time I've been doing other things I've been thinking of you "under my breath." My Dear, I wish you were here for a nice long talk & then I'd like to go to sleep in your arms. It's the only heaven I ever want, Darling. Ellis tell me, please, how soon can you "afford me," as you put it? I don't want to sound too commercial. I haven't a very practical or business-like mind, I'm afraid, but I might not be so terribly expensive. If I come to you without having taught, Ellis, I won't have anything to bring you – except myself – nothing to contribute to what I believe should be a partnership, & that doesn't seem fair to me, Ellis. It isn't a very good-looking business proposition, to say the least. Please understand me, Dearest, when I said I wanted to teach, it wasn't for myself as much as I was thinking I could make you happier if we could get off to a better start (& I don't mean that I thought that you couldn't give me enough now to begin with). But I've always been taking – and never giving anything, & I hate to start right out taking everything from you & not contribute my share even in the beginning. But, Dearest, I'm wondering now if perhaps Love counts more than all these things. A year in a lifetime doesn't seem long, but a year lost can never be lived again – & so many things can happen – O, Ellis – I don't know. I do know that I love you more than anything in the world. Your love has been the most beautiful & wonderful thing that has ever happened to me & I just want to know that we're doing the right thing & the best thing for our love & for us. I hope you understand what I've said in a very inadequate way. Sincerely, Daisy

This letter is key to me, and to what Mom always told us about why she did have that one year of teaching at Remus before she married Dad, who obviously wanted to marry as soon as she graduated from Central. The family "story" about their long courtship (nearly four years) was that Dad wanted to feel secure enough in his job to "afford" to get married, to be able to support a wife & family. And Mom's part of the story was that she wanted to get married right away too, but that her mother convinced her that she should get her certificate and teach for at least a year, "just in case" something unforeseen should happen. It seems Mom & Dad had talked, perhaps even argued, about this key matter: "to teach or not to teach." And note the "Sincerely" this time, vs. the usual love and kisses closing.

Jan 29, 1936   CSTC

My Dearest Sweetheart – (Wed nite 8:00) You've been so quiet, Ellis, and I've been so quiet for the past week – both of us lost in our thoughts – and mine have been all of you, Dearest, even if you haven't heard them to date. I hope you haven't been lost in the snow-drifts – or frozen by the wintry winds. I wish you could come home to me when the nights are so cold (and even when they're warm) – I could keep your heart warm, Ellis. At least I've learned to make coffee, tea, hot chocolate & cocoa (alas, no Ovaltine!) in the line of beverages (as if I couldn't make them before), & the other day we made baking powder biscuits (much good that will do me as long as Bisquick is on the market) & today we made salads – I made tuna-fish – like it's so hard. That's the extent of our progress in Home Ec 102 – except for having planned, prepared & served (& eaten) a complete breakfast. I'm afraid that your faith in my culinary ability wouldn't leave you with a very satisfied feeling after a breakfast, lunch & dinner of tea, hot biscuits & salad. But you won't mind, will you, Pal? "You can eat when you're old." (Pardon, don't take me wrong.) I'm enclosing the rushing party write-up of the societies of which you so heartily disapprove. I agree with your principle that they are not democratic & cause a lot of grief to so many girls – we're having several instances of it now – so many girls rushed & not taken in by any – 2 especially sweet girls who were not taken in by either of the 3 they were rushed by because each thought one of the other societies would take them. But here they are, Ellis, & they're not going to be gone next year or the next, so why not take advantage of them while they're here? I've got what I wanted from them – more than I expected. I've got everything I hoped for out of college & more. I'll be satisfied to see it end this year before things begin to drag. But there's one thing I never want to see end, Dearest, and you know what it is. O, my Dear, I love you so, & I'm counting the minutes until Feb 8. Good-nite, Sweetheart Dearest. I wish I could tell you how much I love you, Ellis. Daisy

This letter too illustrates some of the sore points between the two. And one of them was what Dad saw as the snobbery and exclusiveness of the sorority system – or "literary societies" as they were called at Central then. But Mom loved her time in Ronan Round Table, and was not willing to dismiss her good times and shared experiences as part of that group. But here she is, trying her best to "smooth things over" with Dad, something she continued to do for the rest of their lives together.

Jan 31, 1936   CSTC

Dearest — (Fri noon) Evidently, I thought too much and didn't write enough. I'm sorry too. I wish you would bring that letter with you Ellis when you come again and if we go over it together, we may be able to figure out what it was all about. But maybe it isn't worth all that trouble, if not, you can just forget it. Ellis, to be perfectly clear, I'll tell you what I want to do. I want to spend the summer learning as much as I can about housekeeping in such a short time and marry you in the fall – this year. I can ask you, can't I, because it's leap year, but I'm not going to (ask you). That's what I'd like to do, Ellis, but it doesn't concern just me – it's you I'm thinking of – and my folks. I think I'm going home today – I am if my folks come, & Helen is going with me. I'm going to find out how my mother reacts to the idea of my not teaching at all. If she doesn't mind, I'm going to let you ask me (if you want to) what I could ask you - to marry me. O, my dear, that sounds terribly cold & practical, but I hope it's clear. I wish you could come tomorrow nite, but I'm not sure I'm going home, & you won't get this in time anyway. I do wish though, Ellis, that you will plan on staying over the J-Hop weekend so we can talk - otherwise I'm afraid it'll take us about 2 years to get straightened out and know where we're going. I Love u, Ellis. Daisy

Oh my. I think she has been pretty clear in this letter, although I can't help thinking she was probably more than a little pissed off when she wrote it, because she did love college, and probably wanted to teach too. Just sayin'.

Feb 2, 1936   CSTC

Ellis My Dearest – (Sun nite 11:30) I did go home in spite of snow, roads, etc., & had a nice, quiet weekend. Helen was with me. Friday nite we went to Harold's & saw the new baby - 7 ½ lbs and he looks just like his Daddy! Rosalie & Jimmie are very proud of him. Clarence & Gertrude came last nite & stayed, & Dorothy & Alfred & family were up this afternoon too. Saw the whole family, I guess. But it just isn't complete anymore without you, Ellis. I'll be so glad to see you Sat nite. Whenever I close my eyes I can see your face the way it looked the last nite I saw you & it makes me want to cry. I would cry myself to sleep tonite on the slightest excuse, & just for no reason at all – just the baby of the family yet, it seems. I'm so tired. I have a feeling that everything's going wrong tomorrow & I don't even care. This must be the way you felt when you wrote me Wednesday nite. I'm so sorry, Ellis, & I love you so dearly, my dearest. Love, Daisy xx

---

Feb 3, 1936   CSTC

Dearest Dear – (Mon morn) Morning kiss from me to you - X. It doesn't seem like such a bad old world this morning - and it's only 6 days more until I see you - xxx. Got up at 6 o'clock this morning & took a shower & I've been going strong ever since. Went to my 8 o'clock class & found I have an off-day today, & Wednesday too. This morning we got the lists of the girls we voted into our society. We have 8 out of the 10 we voted in. Our society got only 2 out of 5. The J-Hop bids were all gone by Saturday morning & there are a lot of girls who wanted to go and can't. Helen has asked Layman up but she hasn't heard from him yet so doesn't know whether he's coming. Peg & Marvel & Doris have their bids, but aren't sure whether they're going.

I've got just gobs of work to do this week & I want to get it all done before Saturday if I can, so if I don't write you again, you'll know I'm just saving all my Love for the Dearest Sweetheart in the World, Ellis. Daisy xx

---

Feb 10, 1936   CSTC

My Dearest – (Mon morn 9:00) I wish I could know now whether you arrived at Kalamazoo last night still intact. Believe me, I was with you all the way, in spirit if not in body. O, Ellis, if anything happened to you, I'll never forgive myself. I couldn't think of anything else after you left. I knitted until I made myself sick & didn't recover until 11:00 – and then in a very ungraceful manner. Still feel rather shaky. There is school today at the high school – at least I've heard nothing to the contrary – I haven't any lesson plans made – but what are a few lesson plans. I so hate to think of you working in weather like this. It was 16 below here this morning. This is such a nightmare. I wish we would be snowed in together somewhere for a week – then maybe we'd have time to do the talking that we didn't have time to do yesterday. My dear, I wish I could be with you now – I feel guilty in making you wait for so long. I know it's worse for you than for me because you're alone all the time. But all my folks ask is that I teach for one year, & after all they've done for me, I can't refuse that to them. This is the only time I have to repay them, in the smallest measure, & if I don't do it now, I never can. They want me to prove (& incidentally also to a bunch of jealous relatives) that I'm worth their investment & capable of doing that for which I've spent 4 years in the training. They can't understand, Ellis, how much this 4 years has meant to me – in the social training I've acquired, in the broader outlook on life & a clearer understanding in personality development, in the overcoming of a decided fear of people – to an attitude of liking to meet people & mix with them socially, in a realization of what I can do, even if I never do it – all these things mean more to me than a year's teaching ever can. But to be a successful teacher is the only way I can show them that these 4 years have been profitably spent. They'll be so much more satisfied too, to know that I can earn a living for myself if I ever have to. Older people think of that more than we do, Ellis. We don't like to think of those things but it's probably better if we do. Still, if the choice were entirely up to me, Dearest, you know what I would do. I'd rather be with you than anywhere else in the world. God keep you for me, Ellis. I love you so dearly. Love, Daisy xx

So, the parents have now weighed in on the "to teach or not to teach" question, probably much to Dad's disappointment, and maybe – just maybe – to Mom's unspoken relief. And, by the way, Mom's mother – my "Grandma Whalen" – in 1936 was just 44 years old, and her dad was 46. "Older people"?

153

Feb 11, 1936 CSTC

Dearest Sweetheart – (Tue nite 12:30) The music is so soft & sweet, & even if only for a little while, I can forget about lessons, tests, what I must do, etc., & dream of the Dearest Sweetheart Man I know. O, Ellis, at times like this, I wonder if our dreams will ever really come true, if we'll ever be together, just you & I alone, to live our life together. It seems so terribly long & you're so far away, and we're hoping for so much. My Dear, I love you so. If only you were here, just for a little while, Ellis – and didn't have to plow back 150 miles through the snow. That was so mean to make you come 300 miles all full of trouble just for a party and for me. I'm sorry as can be, Ellis, but there's nothing to be done about it now. Only it seems I'm more trouble to you than I'm worth. I'm so glad you arrived home safely – give my regards to the supervisor – and I'm so sorry that you had to freeze your ears. I had visions of you freezing arms & legs while walking into town, or being overcome by monoxide in the car, etc., etc. I'm so glad you're safe, Dearest – xxxx. "Moon River" program is on now – makes me so lonesome – for just you – xxxx. It was awfully thoughtful of you to let me know so soon about where you were. I received your Lansing note Monday afternoon & your Monday morning card this morning. I must be getting sleepy. I've tried so hard to study. I have a 6-weeks exam tomorrow in Chaucer – but I just can't now. I think I'll get up real early and study. Don wrote to Kay, so I know she got back all right. Some kids that went home for the weekend haven't come back yet. Take good care of yourself, Ellis, for a girl who loves Ellis Bazzett above everything – and who is hoping for an early spring, & especially an early June. Love, Daisy xx

---

Feb 15-16, 1936 CSTC

Dearest Dear – (Dorm, Sat nite 12:3) The Old Maid's Knitting Circle has broken up for the evening & this old maid takes her pen in hand & lays aside her knitting needles. Knitting is very entertaining (for some) & it is fascinating to watch a sweater grow from a ball of yarn, but I'd die, Ellis, if I had to substitute that for a life with someone I love. And right now all I can do is dream of that Someone; no constructive thought is forthcoming. Perhaps tomorrow I can think more clearly. But now – thank you for the lovely Valentine box of chocolates. Everyone enjoys them & sends their thanks with mine. And now "to sleep – to sleep, perchance to dream" – ? Good-nite, Sweetheart. Love, Daisy xx

Dearest Sweetheart – (Sun 5:00) There's an air of quiet Sunday afternoon peace about the place – it's good for the soul, methinks. Me also thinks it would be good for two souls if you were here. There's a lovely orchestra on & a girl with a lovely voice singing "Because I Love You" & "With All My Heart."

DAISY WHALEN BAZZETT

Do you like quiet evenings at home, Ellis – and do you like poetry? I had a weakness for poetry once and made a practice of collecting all kinds of poems – with the result that I now have an enormous scrap-book full of it. Could you endure a quiet hour before the fire with a girl reading poetry to you – a girl who once even had the urge to write such things? That girl has grown much more sensible in the last few years, but once in a while she can't refrain from getting out the old scrap-book and spending a sentimental hour or two over it. "Moonlight Madonna" & "It's Dangerous to Love Like This" – the program is over, my roommate has awakened & is stirring into activity, company comes – and the Sunday afternoon spell is broken – but all good things must come to an end. Are you going to be in Kalamazoo this Friday nite, Ellis? If so, would you like to have me drop in for a visit? There's just a possibility that I might be able to. Dr Arnold Mulder of Kalamazoo College is going to be our assembly speaker Friday & I'd like to bum a ride home with him. Of course he might not be going back to Kalamazoo on Friday, or he may not even drive – but I'll find out. And then on Saturday our debaters are going to Kazoo & coming back at night. And all this suggested something to me (the brain ? got to working). Probably Helen would come with me & she would visit a girl friend of hers at Western. We'd stay at the YW Friday nite. And Peg (fellow plotter) just said that if the debaters would come back through Belding, we could stay at her house Sat nite & come back with her on Sunday. Some weekend, eh, kid? – but it'll probably all fall through. Anyway, you tell me if you want me to come, & if I do I'll phone you from the YW Friday nite. And don't expect me very hard.

Several extremely corny jokes omitted here.

And the spell is broken, all right, all right – with those samples of dormitory humor, & rather mild at that. Oboyoboyoboy! I wish you could have seen our games Friday nite & last nite – (Ypsi 24 – Central 27 and Central 28 – Alumni 26). Darn good games they were. Ypsi game – in the first few minutes 11-3 in favor of Ypsi, & then we started to play – score tied up twice, at 21 & at 22 – fast & furious playing – well-matched teams – nearly wore myself out just sitting on the bleachers. Last nite everyone had a grand time watching the alumni & present team. The score was tied up 4 or 5 times & was close all the way through. At one time the alumni had 6 men on the floor & no one noticed it for about 3 minutes. Anyway there were no hard feelings & everyone enjoyed watching the "Stars of Yesterday" compete with today's "stars." This Friday nite we play Wayne here, and Saturday nite the 29th we play Ferris here. I wish it could be summer so you could come up then. Damn the snow anyway. I'll be so damnably glad when it's summer again. We'll probably have another big storm this weekend. The weather-man says the "cold spell" will last through February & half-way through March – cheerful *thought! Yesterday I did journalism from 11:00 until 3:00 in the afternoon – having interviews & writing them up, etc. Spent most of my time in the president's office. Me & Prexy are getting quite chummy. Wish he'd use some of his pull to get me a job in Kalamazoo. No hope tho. I'll probably get stuck in the sticks somewhere at $40 a month. I spent 2 hours in the library this afternoon and felt quite virtuous but I didn't get much accomplished. Yet tonite I have to make out a test over "A Tale of Two Cities" to give on Thursday, & make a complete plan for a general discussion of the story on Wednesday. O, woe is me: I have my worries. You should see my sweater, Ellis – half of the back done & it looks awfully pretty – here's hoping it fits. I'm sending you one of my appointment office pictures. Do you think I'll ever get a job if a superintendent sees that first? And will you please send it back? Just wanted your opinion of – how are my chances? This writing is awful & my letter is degenerating into chatter, so I'll discontinue now – until later. Love, Daisy xx*

Several more very corny jokes omitted here.

You may wonder, Ellis, where all this so-called "humor" comes from – from a publication of the U.S. Naval Academy – that's what they think is funny. My Dear, it's past 11 & I haven't done my work yet. I guess I'll just have to hide my knitting until I'm thru studying. I've got 9 inches done on the back. Music is coming from the Aragon now & O, Ellis, it makes me so lonesome for you. And when I think of you alone in a hotel room – then I wish I were Aladdin – or had his lamp. I'd wish myself to you every nite, Dearest. Gee, I hope you haven't had to shovel snow all week. My Dad got in so deep in one road that he couldn't even get the car door open & had to wait for someone to shovel him out. I must say good-nite to you now, Dearest, but not in the way I'd like to. I love you so, Pal. Daisy xx

Should anyone be wondering about – or scoffing at – the very low scores in the college basketball games, I might remind them that the jump shot had not yet come into practice, and, of course, there were no 3-pointers either. It was a very different game from the one we have today.

Feb 19, 1936   CSTC

Dearest — (Wed nite 12:30) All the luck in the world to you in your sales campaign! You deserve it, I know. And I shouldn't say luck, because it won't be luck you'll win on. I'll bet on you to win every time, Ellis. And even if I don't see you Friday nite, Dearest, my wishes for you and my love are the sincerest. Helen may go home this weekend, & in that case, I wouldn't come alone. Anyway, I'm not sure the speaker will be returning to Kalamazoo. So don't look for me, but if I do come, I'll call. (9009, isn't it?) But whatever, Ellis, Please Believe me. I Love You Dearly. Daisy xx

Feb 22, 1936   CSTC

*Dearest Pal — (Dorm, Sat morn 7:00) As the horizon is reddening &
'twill soon be day. "Knit on, knit on, knit on and on," said I to myself
this morning at 6:30 as I tried hard to calm my nerves & not let my
disappointment get the better of me. Because – you didn't know it, Ellis,
but I planned to be on my way to you at 6:30 – and at 6:30, 20 below zero,
trip cancelled – (curses). If I'd known at 6, I would have dismissed it with
a sense of relief & been glad I didn't have to go out into the cold world
today. So at 6:30, instead of starting for Kalamazoo – I started for my
knitting. I have the back of my sweater nearly done. Maybe I can wear it
for you the next time I see you – it looks now like a long time away – and I
can't even go home. I had a letter from Mother yesterday, and conditions
are terrible there too – no coal in town – the road into Harold's has been
blocked 2 weeks & he's running out of coal, so I guess they're going to
dig out on a sled & come to our house. I have it pretty soft, I know, & I sit
here & moan. Your letter sounded so good, Ellis, especially your aiding
& abetting of my plans. I was going down with the debaters this morning
& call you & let you carry out your ideas – Marvel even drew me a map
of Belding so we could find Peg's house. Dr Mulder wasn't returning to
Kalamazoo until this morning, but I don't know where he's staying – and
there's the possibility of not getting back if I did go – and it wouldn't look
so hot either, I suppose, if I were to go with him alone. So that leaves me
in Mt Pleasant & you in Kazoo (or GR) 150 miles apart – with nothing
to be done about it. Worse things have happened though, & here's to us,
Ellis – may we live to see the spring together – and lots more springs too.
I got a big kick out of Bud's letter, Ellis. Thanks for sending it along. I'm
returning it though, as I suppose you'll want it. I'd like to read Ko-Inks
articles – that excited so much comment – couldn't let me in on it, could
you? Congratulations on consummating (?) your big deal, Ellis – and
here am I betting on you to win the prize – every time! The lazy sun is
just getting up now, but it's setting the snow on fire. Our basketball team
didn't start setting anything on fire until the last half in the game last
nite – and that wasn't soon enough – which was too bad. I'm not making
any excuses, you see, I merely want to tell you before you tell me about
it. We had a dance after the game again last night & I had a pretty good
time – considering everything – I was feeling pretty gay, thinking of today
(past – no good prose). Friday nite, 28th, is the All-Lit party & I do wish
you were coming. But you'll have a successful sales meeting, & I hope
you don't get snowed in at Detroit. Gee, I'm hungry as the dickens. I wish
Sheldon would hurry & get up so we can go to breakfast. Helen went home
yesterday, & Marvel & Peg went home Wednesday – to the Dr – Dr Torres
here thought it might be appendicitis. I surely hope it wasn't. Only 5 more*

weeks until spring vacation – that's my one consoling thought now. But at the moment my most absorbing thought is of getting breakfast – so – if you'll excuse me, Sweetheart, Love, Love, Love, LOVE, Daisy xxxx

P.S. And more power to the journalistic tendencies, in spite of one person's opinions to the contrary.

> February 1936 was indeed a cruel month, one of the coldest winter months on record at the time, hitting record low temps and spawning devastating storms & blizzards throughout the Midwest and the Plains states too. At least fifty deaths in Michigan that month were attributed to the weather.

Feb 23, 1936   CSTC

My Dearest – (Sun nite 11:00) How does the world treat my Sweetheart? Your pal was lonesome for you this weekend – had lots of time to be. But tonite we (Doris & I) broke loose & went to the show – "Ah, Wilderness" – a clever satire of 1906 family life – quite different & refreshing. I had my work all done so came home & took a hot bath & here I am, sleepy & contented. My spring fever & discontentment of today has dissolved in the lovely music of the Aragon orchestra. Helen didn't come back tonite. Peg isn't coming back until Wednesday. I'm still pretty much alone, but it has been a pretty satisfying weekend from one point of view - especially when I wasn't thinking where I could have been. I really have nothing to say, Ellis. I just wanted to tell you that I love you, Dearest, & Good-nite. Daisy xx

---

Feb 24, 1936   CSTC

My Dear – (Mon nite, sometime after 11) Do you remember the last time we were in London, when the fog was so thick we could have cut it with a knife – if we'd had a knife? Ah, tonite is just such a nite – a nite when anything can happen – even a nightmare – and methinks that very thing may occur – especially in view of the fact that your sleepless correspondent has just recently completed the consummation of several toasted peanut butter & jelly sandwiches at the ungodly hour of 10:30 – and by that act shattered the contemplated possibilities of an early retirement and a long-sought nocturnal rest.

(Tues morn) And the aforegone paragraph, Dear one, completely wore out the correspondent & she fell asleep – and awoke to the merry song of the robin & the spring breeze wafting sweet expectations to her. O, Ellis, that

must be how spring fever affects me. It's so grand to be able to stir out of a building without first donning ear-muffs, buttoning coats, etc. Don't you find it so? Or is the weather underfoot getting you down? Do you think June will come very soon, Dearest? That's all I'm waiting for. I'm going to Midland & Saginaw tomorrow at noon with our Journalism class to visit Midland & Saginaw Daily News buildings & find out how a newspaper is really made. Helen came back Monday morning at 8 after a grand visit at home. Joanne – Don's 3 yr-old daughter – has a new doll & she has named it Daisy after me. Poor doll. She says she's coming to Mt Pleasant some Saturday and Daisy & Helen are going to take care of her. I'll bet you had a good time at Bud & Kate's this weekend – they're such jolly kids. Have a good time in Detroit this weekend, Ellis. I'm going to stay here again, but it won't be so bad. Friday nite is our "Women's Literary Ball," & although I'll be with another, I'll still be true to you, Dearest. And Saturday nite is our last basketball game of the season – with Ferris – and I'll be there to cheer – oboyoboy! But next weekend I think I shall go home, if everyone is agreeable, & methinks they will be. And now, Sweetheart, I must ignore the spring breezes, the song of the robin, etc. & write lesson plans. How prosaic! Here's to your health & happiness, Dearest, & may the spring inspire you to bigger & better achievements. Love, Daisy xx

---

Feb 25, 1936   CSTC

Dearest Sweetheart – (Tue nite before Ash Wed) Tomorrow Lent begins – and then – 40 days – Easter! Spring! Dearest, I wish we might watch the spring come together – but there'll be more springs to come – and perhaps – who knows – O, my Dearest, could I enjoy a Sunday of the type you describe? Honestly, Ellis, I love a lazy day like that – and with you, it would be perfect. Congratulations on your flour sales! I guess you're doing your part for the Gold Medal Co, aren't you? More power to ya, kid, and don't get spring fever – it isn't good for your ambition (from one who knows). We're going to 6:15 mass in the morning to begin Lent. Tonite we wanted to go to confession & tried hard but the church was dark when we arrived – so we went to the show – our Mardi Gras celebration – Dolores Del Rio in "The Widow from Monte Carlo" – rather light & silly, but entertaining. I'm going with Bob Miller to the Lit party – bashful freshman – son of the Miller-Walser Produce in Chesaning. Is he approved, Ellis? He's really very harmless. I'm going to try to not eat any candy or peanuts during Lent except on Sundays. That's all so far. Remember a couple of years ago when I told you all the things I was giving up for lent – you weren't coming to see me until after Easter? I wouldn't want to scare you away again. There's one pleasure I won't deprive myself of though, Ellis – that's writing to you. That may impose extra trials

*on you, I'm afraid. But I don't want to do that – so if you are ever bothered –
tell me, because I Love You, Dearest. Daisy xx*

*P.S. Please excuse the writing & smears. I'm in bed & not practicing
penmanship. D.*

The Gold Medal Flour comment brought to mind a clown suit Mom
sewed years later out of cloth Gold Medal Flour bags. My three older
brothers and I all got a chance to wear that costume for Halloween. And
the no candy/peanuts during Lent except on Sundays? That Sunday
exception still held true when we were growing up. It was kind of a
running joke. My brothers and I would give up movies for Lent, except
Sundays (which was generally the only day we went anyway). And would
Dad have approved Bob Miller as Mom's date to the dance? Hell no! Dad
was always an extremely jealous guy when it came to Mom. The next
letter is proof of that.

Feb 27, 1936   CSTC

*Dearest Ellis – (Dorm, Thurs nite 1:00) I've told you again & again that I
love you. If you believe me, Ellis, how can you think that I would deliberately
try to hurt you? O, my Dear, I told you about the party & who I was taking
only because I thought you would rather know than be kept in the dark &
not know anything about it. The remark which you repeat sounds awfully
flippant & as if I were flaunting in your face the fact, but please believe
me, Ellis, I meant it in sincerity when I wrote it. But even at that, I can see
now that I shouldn't have mentioned it at all. I'm terribly sorry that I have
hurt you, Dearest. If you'll forgive me, we'll forget it. We went to Saginaw
yesterday & visited the Saginaw Daily News Bldg & followed the making of
the newspaper from the time the news came in until the paper came off the
press. It really was interesting. I visited Clarence & Gertrude for about a half
hour until the bus came back. When I walked in, I guess they thought I'd run
away from school. It seemed so good to see "home folks" again. I can hardly
wait until next weekend to go home – it has been 4 weeks since I've been
home. And Ellis, I'd love to have you come – and I'm sure the Whalens will
be glad to "keep" you – especially the mailman's daughter. She gets pretty
lonesome for you, more often than she says. I hope you get your car back
in time to go to Detroit, it would be so much more convenient than a train.
I haven't asked my folks yet if I can come home next weekend but I'm sure
I can & I hope there won't be any more snow or freezing. Everything is just
awful now. Clarence has been sick & so has Gertrude & Clarence was laid
off for 3 days & now he's back working again in the same company – but in
the chemistry lab & he likes it a lot better. I start teaching again on Monday
– a one-act play unit. Don't have to go down to the HS tomorrow. No classes*

– they're having a vocational conference. The students are putting on the assembly tomorrow – we had full dress rehearsal tonite – 8 skits – RRT has one – and some of them are clever – I think the kids will like them. The student assembly is always the most popular one of the year anyway. As to your suggestion of the Lenten resolution to not write letters – I think it would be a wise one for me to adopt – at least until I learn to use enough common sense in writing letters to you so that a few words won't change your Love & x's to 'as ever.' Dearest Pal, please don't read any "malice aforethought" into my letters. I assure there's never anything in them intended to hurt you, although they may be thoughtless & ill-considered. Please believe me – I Love You Truly, Sweetheart. Daisy xx

---

Mar 3, 1936   CSTC

Dearest – From my lips (as you requested) – I'd love to see you in Oakley (as you suggested) on Saturday, March 7 – at whatever time it may be convenient for you to arrive (probably before midnite). Whatever there is to say I'll say to you, Ellis – I'm terribly sleepy now - & letters can be so difficult. Good-nite, Dearest, until Saturday & always, I Love You. Daisy xx

---

Mar 5, 1936   CSTC

Dearest Sweetheart – (Thurs morn 9:30) Please don't think because I haven't written that I haven't been thinking of you. You've kept me pretty busy thinking of you for the past week. Thanks just loads, Dearest, for the photograph. I love it because I love you. I'll be so glad when tomorrow afternoon comes & I'll be on my way home – cuz then I'll soon be seeing the Dearest Pal I've ever known. Love, Daisy xx

---

Mar 9, 1936   CSTC

Dearest Sweetheart – (Mon morn 7:45) I love you, I love you. Was it late when you arrived in Lansing? I know it was, but I hope you got as much sleep as I did. My cake was half gone when I came in & there isn't much left of it now – no fatalities yet. It looks rather warm out this morning but I do wish the sun would shine. It shines for us when we're together anyway, doesn't it? I hope it always will. Dearest Dear in the World, I Love You. Daisy xx

---

Mar 9, 1936   CSTC

Dearest Dear – (Mon nite 11:30) I've been asleep in the tub for nearly an hour but now I'm really going to bed – and dream – of the Dearest

Sweetheart in the whole wide world – you. I've accomplished nothing today & will probably do less tomorrow – I'm so tired of school – maybe just lazy – or maybe I know something better (?). I took your advice last nite, Ellis – it was very good counsel – I'll let you advise me again sometime. We ate in tonite – from the basket – but we didn't have cake – it was all gone this afternoon. But dorm girls will eat almost anything – will you? – that's my problem. We cooked steaks this morning in Home Ec class – they weren't so hot. I napped 7-8:30 tonite too. At this rate I'm not getting anywhere – but – I Love You Dearly. Daisy xx

P.S. I hope there is a run on GM flour this week. (Sealed with a million kisses for you – C.O.D. 3/28/36.)

Mar 10, 1936   CSTC

Dearest Sweetheart — (dorm, Tue nite 9:00) You really shouldn't give me such advice – "spread your work thin" – I'm afraid that's what I'm actually doing – at this rate I'll be going steady nite & day for the last week. I dropped the Grand Rapids dance group tonite. Takes too much time but it was a lot of fun. I was just looking in my diary & noticed that Ellis Churchill's first birthday is tomorrow. I was called in today for an English-Latin $105 a month job at Whittemore but I'm not applying – look it up on the map if you don't know where it is. It's what I want but not where we want it. Mr Robbins was reading us some new headlines from the Toledo Blade this morning – the editor told his reporters that he wanted original & different "heads" & these are some of the results – Story on a nudist colony: A SNOOPER & A SNEAKER, HE'S A RURAL NUDIST PEEKER. A couple insured against twins had twins (accidents will happen): TWINSURANCE YIELDS $1000. Society note on nudist wedding: BRIDESMAID WEARS COAT OF TAN AS NUDIST GIRL WEDS NUDIST MAN. Announcing the winner of a drinking contest: I AM HAPPY TO ANNOUNSH THE WINNER OF THISH CONTESH IS HORGLE BORLEUMPY GLUB. Next week the cubs (we greenhorns) put out the paper – edit it & everything – but no such clever headlines will evolve, I'm sure. Ellis dearest, please when you think about me, don't think I'm better than I am – if you idealize me, I'm so afraid I can't live up to you – and to disappoint you would make me terribly unhappy, & you too. The only "wonderful" thing about me is a Love for the dearest, most thoughtful, gentle, and lovable sweetheart in the world. Yours always, Daisy xx

I'd never heard of Whittemore either, so looked it up. It's about twenty miles from East Tawas in Iosco County, and, at a population of 384, is currently listed as the fourth smallest town in Michigan.

Mar 10, 1936 CSTC

Ellis Dearest — (Wed nite 11:30) I don't know, but I'm dreaming & hoping & planning and every day now is one day nearer. Soon it will be spring vacation & I'm going home and my "best fella" is coming to see me. Then it will really be spring – for me. The 'fever' seems to have had everyone tonite. We just sat around & gossiped and knitted – and did no studying. I went to church tonite, so I feel very virtuous. "A Tale of Two Cities" is coming here Sunday and I'm going to spend two days discussing it with my class – one before & one after they see the movie. I made peanut butter bread today – 2 little 'play' loaves, and it was good but it tasted a lot like cookies. The Home Ec club is giving a St Patrick's Tea tomorrow & they're serving orange bread! I'm going to wear the greenest dress I have. Your letter today was so sweet, Ellis. When I think of you coming home at nite so tired and rather 'down' sometimes too, I wish I could be there. When you've had a poor day, try to think of a better one coming. We have to muddle thru somehow anyway. But I'm not so good at that myself so don't think I'm preaching, please. I can talk – I don't have an 8 o'clock in the morning so I can sleep. I love you, Dearest, I love you. O, Ellis, you're the dearest Sweetheart in the world. I'm afraid I won't be worth to you what you think I will be. I wish I could practice housekeeping for a year before I begin with you. You're taking a great risk – but I can reduce your income tax! Good-nite, Pal. I'll be with you in my dreams. Love, Daisy xx

1936 Chippewa Staff Members

1936 Publications Group

Mar 12, 1936   CSTC [This letter is typed]

Dear Bazzett — (dorm on a dismal afternoon with all the lights on and still no cheer) As one 'journalist' to another, could you kindly advise me as to what is the proper setting, atmosphere, situation or what-have-you to inspire one to scale the difficulties that arise when one takes the typewriter to desk with the supposedly unshakeable intention and resolution of banging out a story-what-is-a-story? The formula would be most sincerely appreciated by one D.C. Whalen, member of the '36 Chippewa staff. Although it could be of no assistance in the present situation as the story in question is due tomorrow, I'm sure it would help immensely when the same difficulty again arises. The aforementioned D.C. has been pondering and pacing and pounding intermittently for the last hour with no sustenance except several homemade cookies which are all gone now and still no inspirations. The problem under consideration is the extremely important matter of how-shall-I-write-up-the-account-of-the-Femmes-Fling about which all the facts are here accumulated and no clever ideas are assimilated. Perhaps the party of the first part needs some kindly interested person to tell her that no clever ideas can be forthcoming from a void where no clever ideas are in hiding. Howsomeever – your correspondent will very shortly be among the "dear departed" – she's departing to grace the Home Economics Club tea with her presence. (To be continued)

Goodness-gracious-dear-me-for-heaven's-sakes-and-so-on-and-on-indefinitely – these people who are never ready to go anywhere on time. It seems that we do not go to the tea for half an hour yet already. Dearest, there are people in the world who are slower than yours truly when it comes to the point that yours truly has to wait for someone. Methinks my sympathies should be with you when you and I are going somewhere together? Do you think that with you as a trainer I could learn to be prompt? I d o n ' t w a n t t o g e t t o o i n v o l v e d s o I t h i n k I h a d b e s t s t o p b e f o r e I g e t r o p e d i n t o s a y I ' l l t u r n o v e r a n e w l e a f a n d t r y t o b e o n t i m e. A n d I ' l l b e t y o u w o n d e r w h y I r a n t h a t l a s t l i n e t o g e t h e r. It has been fully 24 hours since I have heard from you, Ellis, and no letter in this mail! My Dear, you're slipping. If your silence is continued for too long an interval, I greatly fear that I will be forced to discontinue my esteemed (?) correspondence. And will you be sorry! Or will you? 'Tis sad, 'tis sad – to find that one's company can be so easily dispensed with – and so flattening to one's egotism. The country dance group seems to be progressing as merrily without me as it did with me. At the moment they are practicing in the rec room and the strains of the good old-fashioned hoedown are wafted up to me on the none-too-balmy breeze accompanied by snow flurries just as the weather man predicted. I wish there were services tonite. I feel just like going to church, an unaccountable, strange feeling and one not often experienced by me. At last!! We're off! But I'll be back.

And here I am, Little Merry Sunshine herself, back to chase your blues away, away, away. And before I progress any further into my nonsense I must tell you lest I forget (as if I ever could in the world), I LOVE YOU. Did I ever tell you that before? Anyway, I'm telling you now. This week is going so fast, Ellis, and I hope that the next two go faster yet. Time can't pass too quickly to suit me anymore. I want to hurry, hurry and get through with everything. You know what I'm going to do next term? I'm only going to take two subjects – Teaching Freshman English and History Methods – and I won't be president of Ronan Round anymore and I'm going to sew and knit and go home on weekends and maybe sometimes I'll be able to see my fella when I'm not as grouchy as an old bear. But – I'll probably get the thirst for knowledge again and come back and sign up for 4 subjects as always. Two will keep me busy though, I think, with all commencement activities, etc., etc. The regional tournament games are being played here tonite, Friday, and Saturday nites. Life is getting out an extra tonite but I'm not on the staff this time and I'm going over to the print shop at 10 o'clock and see them sweat. Big Rapids, Cass City, East Tawas, Ovid, Edmore, Remus, Academy and other district winners and runners-up are playing. I sent for some booklets today on "Better Buymanship," "Tips for Lazy Husbands" (I don't expect you'll need that though), "Marrying on a Small Income" (?) "Money Management for Households," etc. I don't know if all my household aids in the way of books are going to be of any value or not. It's going to be funny – when we're going to do or buy something, I'll have to get out all my books and see what is best.

165

I think I'll take all my cookbooks and boil them up together and see what I get. I Love You, Dearest Pal. Love, Daisy xx

(Thurs nite 1:00) [longhand] – Sweetheart Ellis – My heart is so full of love for you tonite that I feel it will burst unless I at least write it to you. My Dearest, I love you so, I wish I knew a million ways to say it. I never knew there was such love in the world until I knew you, Ellis. And you're worthy of all I can give you and more, Sweetheart. I want you with me always, Darling; I know we can be happy together. We've just got to be. If I weren't happy with you, Ellis, there would be no life left for me. We have such high hopes – and we will have disappointments – please, God – make our love grow always. Through eternity. Daisy

---

Mar 15, 1936　　　　　　　　　CSTC to the Hotel Vincent in Benton Harbor

Dearest Dear – (Sat nite 1:30) You've been so sweet & I've surely been glad to see every one of your letters, TWThF. I "second" your hope that everyone is out of flour in Benton Harbor. How is it on the lake at this time of year? I'd like to be there now (when you're there). When we came back from our trip this summer we camped in Benton Harbor. I walked down thru the sand to the beach & watched the sun go down into the water in a blaze of beauty – and dreamed about you & me – and wondered if we would ever live such times together. And it looks as if we will, doesn't it, Dearest? I'm so tired tonite & I can hardly keep awake. I was nearly sick all day yesterday and only ate one meal. About 8 last nite Ida May walked in - surprise! We didn't go to bed until 11:30. Today we've been walking & gadding all the time. Helen's 3 yr-old niece, Carol Joanne, spent the day with us too, & Vonnie Wilcox – who teaches near Greenville & came up with an extension student. We went downtown this PM & to confession & Ida May & I went to the finals of the regional tournament. D – Merrill beat Mecosta; C – Edmore won over Sacred Heart Academy; B – Alma pulled Big Rapids down. The class C game was the best – score tied at 32, 34 & at 36 when the game ended – 38-36 at the end of 3-min overtime period. The last game was rather slow & the score was low. I had to struggle to keep awake & sit up. A lot of kids, alumni, were here this weekend - some for the tournament and some came just because it was nice - as Ida May did, & Vonnie. We're going to 10:30 mass tomorrow. Proof-read & rewrite "Life" stories 2-5, & see "A Tale of Two Cities" at nite & I want to see it thru twice. Doesn't look as if I'll get anything done this weekend – not even sleep – but I don't mind – it's worth it for Ida May. I'll say good-nite, Sweetheart Dearest. I Love You, Ellis. Love, Daisy xx

Mar 16, 1936   CSTC

*Dearest — (Mon morn 9) It has been a hectic weekend. I feel in a much
better humor this morning since I went to bed at 7:30 last nite & didn't wake
up until 7 this morning. I'm going to need all my reserve strength & sleep
& everything this week too! Ellis, please don't bawl me out for not planning
my work better. Plans just don't work out. There's always something to
upset them. And wouldn't it be a dull world if there weren't such things?
Tonite is a "Tap Jubilee" - specialty numbers of our tap class. Then to the
Life offices to proof-read copy the rest of the nite. Tomorrow nite - Mercier
bridge party - Grrrr! Wednesday nite Home Ec Dinner to prepare for & cook
& eat & clean up after - and so on & on & on. And then I hope you'll come &
upset the whole weekend for me on Mar 28-29. And I'll Love it. Bye now - I
Love You. Love, Daisy xx*

Mar 18, 1936   CSTC

*Dear Heart — (dorm, Wed nite 11:30) I'd like to be here myself to greet
you but this is the next best way to tell you I Love You. You'll probably be
busy all evening anyway with your sales meeting & I have a Ronan Round
Dinner & meeting & election of officers for next year. But that happens at 6,
so probably by the time you get this I'll be back here again wishing I were
there (with you). There's nowhere I'd rather be, Sweetheart, than where you
are. My mother sent me your letter today with the last sentence underlined.
She couldn't figure it out & seemed a bit worried. But I'm not worried -
unless I don't see you on Mar 28. I'm so glad this term is nearly over - then
only one more - and one more year. Dearest, I love you so & I can't say it
nearly as well as Elizabeth Barrett Browning did - so I'm saying to you
again - "How Do I Love Thee?" Daisy xx*

*P.S. Good luck at your sales meeting. Tell Bud hello. How's Sue Ann? And
Kay? L, D.*

> A handwritten copy of the Barrett Browning poem – again – is included
> in this letter, the second time Mom sent it to Dad. I find it a pleasant
> coincidence that 30 years later I took a course in Robert Browning at
> Ferris State University, and we also read Sonnets from the Portuguese
> that term.

Mar 22, 1936   CSTC

*Dearest Pal — (dorm, Fr Coughlin's Hour) In spite of the eloquent lecturing of
the Rev Fr, my mind remains blank and no ideas are inspired. I feel just the
peace of a quiet Sunday afternoon - and somewhere there is a dream - of a*

quiet Sunday like this and a more complete Peace – with you, Dearest. May that dream never grow old. And may it come true as soon as ever it can. Perhaps a little part of it next week? Today is Helen's 23rd birthday & we're having a little party tonite for her. Her mother sent her a cake & we've carved it out until only the letters are left – HC, her initials. Clever? But not much cake left. The robins have come back, Ellis, and so has the rain. I'm going home early on Friday and I'm going to sleep and sleep and sleep – maybe you will come on Saturday – and wouldn't that be a grand awakening? I Love You, Dearest. Daisy xx

Father Charles Edward Coughlin (1891-1979) was a very popular Catholic priest whose weekly radio show reached an estimated 30 million listeners throughout most of the 1930s. By 1938, however, his 'sermons' became increasingly political and anti-Semitic, and even supportive of the fascist policies of Hitler & Mussolini. He was finally forced off the air by the Roosevelt administration when the United States entered the Second World War.

Mar 23, 1936   CSTC

Dearest Pal – (dorm, Mon nite 19:15) Here's to your week! Your sweetheart is hoping & praying that it will be the biggest one ever for you – and as successful as your most fervent hopes desire it to be. Congratulations on the Sturgis meeting and Wheaties order. I too wish I could have been with you Friday nite, Ellis, & Saturday nite when you were so tired and still remembered me with a letter, and Sunday when it was so grand out. I'm so glad that your work is going so well, Dearest, and no matter how "tired & ugly" you are Saturday when you come – it will seem like heaven just to be with you again. (And I haven't always been so good-natured myself.) And spring – I have to shut my eyes & ears to its sights & sounds this week & concentrate like fury – but I hold you in my thoughts, Dear, & in my Dreams, and in my Heart, Always. I Love You. Daisy xx

---

Mar 25, 1936   CSTC

Dearest Pal – (Wed nite 10:30) I sincerely hope that the week has been just as "big" and more "successful" than you had dared hope – and that this weekend won't be a "let-down" for you. I'm living in "dreams" of you, Dearest. Right now I've been reviewing for a final in Journalism and it makes me so sleepy. (Ho-hum!) Dearest Sweetheart, my only clear thought now in my mind is "I Love You." I Love You, Sweetheart. Until Saturday, Daisy xx

Apr 2, 1936   Oakley

Dearest Sweetheart Pal — (Thurs nite 11:00) Your letter today was "welcome as the flowers in May" – but I don't believe there will be any flowers in May of 1936 – except maybe snowdrops (so that makes it doubly welcome). I love you, Ellis, I have to tell you now before I get to the end of my letter. It won't keep – the words I mean – I am having a rest this week, thank you, Ellis – and that is my idea of a "grand time" once in a while – like the Irishman's dream of heaven. I haven't read a word this week – except the newspapers, although I brought home 3 books – and this is the first time I've tried to write (as you probably have already guessed). Monday – Owosso, Tuesday – Saginaw (Easter bonnet), Wednesday – sew & knit, Thursday – knit & sew – so – here I am – trying to think of some adequate words in which to tell my Sweetheart how much I love him. I'll have to wait until April 11 and tell him. I could easily revise my calendar, Ellis, and count time by the number of days since I've seen you or until I'll see you. I'm looking forward to going back to school Sunday – for one reason – that I always enjoy that first week of the term the most anyway (& this will be the last "first"). But mainly for the reason that at the end of the first week I'll have a date with my Pal. Thrill of Thrills (for me)!! Maybe we can go ice-skating on Crystal Lake – yes? There's about 10 inches of snow here – but it isn't awfully cold. You brought the spring with you when you came to Oakley – and took it away again. Do bring it with you Central, Ellis, on the 11th. Today is Harold & Helen's 4th wedding anniversary. I must say Good-nite and Sweet Dreams, Ellis. I hope that all your dreams of happiness & contentment will come true – and may I add my dream? – if we're not always very happy – may we always love each other – always – whatever life brings to us. I Love You, Dear. Love, Daisy xx

---

Apr 5, 1936   CSTC

Dearest Ellis — (dorm, Sun nite 9:30) It was sweet of you to have a letter waiting for me on my return today. It was a dismal homecoming at best but your message made a spot of brightness in the gloom. You're always dear & thoughtful but it's times like this when I appreciate it most. One more short week, Dearest. We'll go to communion on Easter Sunday, won't we? We had all the Palm Sunday services today – and everything that goes with it. If you'd been there, we might have had the stations too – for added graces, you know. As it was, we were in church only 3 hours (& 10 minutes). I felt as if I could take wing straight for heaven when it was all over (& no breakfast), but my "wings" would need even more strengthening, I fear. Mama baked me a cake today – yellow gold with lemon filling and white icing – dee-licious – ½ gone – wish you were here to have a piece now. (Wish you were here even if I didn't have any cake.) Harold broke his shoulder in

2 places Thursday – slipped & fell & hit his shoulder on a beam in a barn – so he isn't working now – but he has accident insurance. The kids were at our house Thursday afternoon & Saturday afternoon. One doesn't get much accomplished with them around but they're a lot of fun. My credits came on Thursday, did I tell you what I made? – A, A, B, B, C – good thing it didn't go any further – A's were Journalism and Chaucer. I haven't decided yet what I'll take this term. I don't like the idea of beginning spring term in the winter – it's snowing again tonite. Damn! Helen just came in – "Nice winter weather" – is the report. She & Bill didn't break up after all – I'll tell you about it if you want to know. Peg & Marvel have been here most of the evening. We discussed the ins & outs of the Hauptmann case and moralized on it to some length but came to no definite conclusion. O, Dear, I'm getting so sleepy – tomorrow enrollment day & tomorrow night I'll tell you about the momentous decision in regard to how many and what subjects this term. Until then, Dearest, & until it's LEGAL, I'll have to say Good-nite, Sweet Dreams. I Love You and only u, Sweetheart. Love, Daisy xx

Bruno Richard Hauptmann (1899-1936) had been much in the news for months as the alleged perpetrator of the "Crime of the Century." Tried and convicted of the abduction and murder of the 20 month-old son of famed aviator Charles Lindbergh and his wife, Anne Morrow Lindbergh, he was executed in the electric chair on April 3, 1936.

Apr 6, 1936 CSTC

Dearest Sweetheart – (dorm, Mon nite 10:00) I love you so and it seems like ages until April 11. I do hope we won't have a blizzard then. Sunny & cold here today. I enrolled before 9 and took class dues 9-12 & 1-5 and I can still see lines of people going by. And after all I took 4 subjects – the fever of enrollment day (or somethin'). Teaching – 8:30-9:15, History Methods – 10-11, American Folk Literature from Dr Beck – 2-3, Advanced Journalism – 3-4, Critic meeting 2 days a week – 4-5. Doris moved out of the dorm. She's staying at Newton's and working for her room & board both at the cafeteria. We surely miss her, but she was over tonite for a couple of hours. She misses the dorm too. Helen works 9-11 at night this term (& is real burned up!). Peg and Marvel just came from town, they've been there since 3:00 this afternoon and are quite worn out now. Tomorrow I have just my 10, 2 and 3 classes & go down to the high school at 4. I wanted to take Tennis so badly but couldn't fit it into my schedule. I know one thing that is going to fit – & that's sleep – where I'm going pretty soon. And someone who fits my schedule any time is none other than YOU – and maybe someday I'll even build my whole schedule around YOU, Dearest Pal in the World. My eyes won't stay open any longer. Good-nite, Sweetheart, Good-nite. Love, Daisy xx

Apr 7, 1936 CSTC

Dearest Pal — (dorm, Tue nite 10:15) How are ya? I surely hope your Grandmother is better - so you won't feel so blue. And how is the General Mills best salesman, EEB? And (question of the hour), where is that elusive maiden, Spring? Are you holding her captive in Kazoo? If so, I wish you'd send her post-haste to Mt Pleasant. Enough. I met my freshmen today - was introduced to each one individually - 2 of them were in my Latin class fall term. I studied hard tonite in the library 6-7:30 - waxing conscientious in my old (school) age. Van Lieu Minor - the most exacting prof on the campus - my inspiration - History Methods - but I like it. Had an interview today with Supt MacConnell of Beaverton - for English-Latin (minus music). It looks as if I can have it if I want it, $990. ??? But ____ Am reading "Stars Fell on Alabama" - a true story of Negroes & whites of Alabama - interesting. And "The Tudor Wench" - biography of Elizabeth of England from 6 years to Queen. Must say Good-nite, Dearest. I Love You. Love, Daisy xx

And that salary offer of $990? That is very probably for the whole school year.

Apr 7, 1936 CSTC

Ellis Dearest — (Tue nite 11:00) I'm really sorry about your grandmother's illness & I do hope it will not be serious. If it's desirable that you go there this weekend, don't feel that you're breaking a promise or disappointing me, will you, please? I don't want to be in the way when your folks need you, so I'll be prepared if you come or not - and I'll not be too disappointed if you don't (or if you do) come. Our spring sunshine turned into a snowstorm today and you should have seen the spring suits disappear & be replaced by "ye olde winter coat." We had high school critic meeting today at 4 and went downtown afterward & nearly froze coming home. Studied in the library until 7:30 - Mercier meeting & election of new officers. I was talking with Neil Dunworth at the meeting & he knew about your grandmother. He's on a year's leave of absence from his school 3 ½ miles from your grandparents' (farm? [smudged]). I hope your towns this week aren't as dead as Battle Creek was. If you don't come, you'll write to me, won't you, Dearest? I Love You So. Good-nite, Sweetheart, I'm lonesome for you tonite. I wish you were here just for a good-nite kiss. But I can close my eyes & remember the first quiet, sweet kiss a week ago. Love, Daisy xx

Apr 13-14, 1936   CSTC

Dearest Sweetheart — (dorm, Mon nite 12:15) How is Benton Harbor & Lake Michigan? But most importantly of all – how are you? I hope you are getting caught up on your sleep. I slept 2 hours today 12-1 & 4-5 – and I meant to go to bed early tonite – studied in library 6-8 – but people insisted on paying friendly calls & staying & talking on & on until – here I am – but I must say good-nite to the Dearest Sweetheart a girl could ever wish for & to tell you how much I enjoyed the weekend with you – and – I Love You Dearly. Love, Daisy xx.

Good morning, Dearest - It's an awful day, but, rain or shine, I Love You. Daisy

---

Apr 15, 1936   CSTC

Sweetheart Dearest — (dorm, Wed nite 12:15) Your letter was dear, like you, but you really needn't have offered any apologies for Sunday nite or feel bad about it. I thought that was all straightened out & understood now anyway – and it was my fault in the first place. I love you, Dearest, more all the time. I never dreamed that there actually was a person as loving and understanding and dear as I know you to be. I hope I'll always appreciate you, Pal, & I will as long as I have sense – and love you as long as I have a heart & mind. I'm sorry the Bancroft job didn't come up to your expectations – maybe a better one will come along soon – just what you want. I don't know yet what I'll do – I wish my thoughts could reach you without my having to write them down, Ellis – but just imagine, Dearest, what would a girl think of the best pal and most loving sweetheart in the world? Daisy xx (Sealed With A Kiss)

It is a given in our family that Dad never really liked his job as a traveling salesman for General Mills, though he stayed with the company for several years as he moved up into middle management. But this letter may be an indication that as early as 1936, he was actively looking for something else. What job prospects there might have been in tiny Bancroft, Michigan, I don't know, but it was located in Shiawassee County, not far from Oakley and Owosso.

Apr 18, 1936   CSTC

Dearest Dear — (dorm on a rather chill, dreary Saturday afternoon) Detroit-bound Sweetheart - to always remember not to forget your Pal. I'm so glad to hear that your grandmother is recovering. I hope your sales meeting & visit in Detroit will be pleasant & successful. Letter from Mother - quote - "You tell Ellis I said our star boarder is always welcome & he doesn't have to bring something to pay his way either." I start teaching Tuesday – must write lesson plans this weekend for a 2-weeks unit & am on my way to the library now. Reminding the nicest fellow a girl ever had of – Love, Daisy xx

---

Apr 19, 1936   CSTC

Dearest, Dearest Pal — (dorm, Sun nite 10:00) I'm running over with high spirits (not the liquid kind) & I must relay them to you before they die down. O, Ellis, it's going to be just gobs of fun to be married to you, I know it is. We'll go to the circus & feed peanuts to the elephants & we'll go to a wrestling match & we'll see a hockey game & baseball games – & we'll make love, Dearest, & I'll be enormously happy & contented with just you if we never do anything more than the last. I Love You, I Love You, & I hope none of it wears off for another year – it can't, can it – when it grows all the time? O, Ellis, I wish you were here tonite. No – I don't – I have to write my unit for teaching & it's due at 8:30 in the morning. I'm all pepped up & ready to go on it though – if I don't fly to pieces before I start. And I'm afraid I can't concentrate. I think of your arms & your lips – Dearest, how long is a year? A year ago doesn't seem very long though, does it? Time will pass & maybe I'll have some good news for you this weekend – maybe. But it may be a disappointment too so I won't tell you now. I went to the show tonite – you ask me why & I'll tell you. It's a long story, but it was a good show – "Wife vs. Secretary" – Clark Gable, Myrna Loy (wife), & Jean Harlow (secretary). They were happy with a million dollars, but we will be as happy with love & whatever else we have to live on. I can't think coherently or I'd tell you what I've been doing this week – now I can't remember. Nothing important. I'll see you – Saturday? Love, Daisy xx

---

Apr 20, 1936   CSTC

Dearest Sweetheart — (dorm, Mon nite 10:00) What do I want to say to you? Last nite there were so many things tumbling forth that I couldn't begin to tell you half of them. Tonite __? I love you, Dear. That seems to express everything so completely – I'm waiting, waiting – until I can tell you with my lips. Ellis, I love you. Daisy xx

---

Apr 27, 1936   CSTC

Dearest Pal — (dorm, Mon 1:45 PM) – On my word of honor – I said I'd write you, didn't I? But truly, Dear, there isn't anything left to say now. When I think of you (most all the time) I think largely in terms of "I love you," and they are awfully empty words, especially when you think of the people who have used them, not even ...

PIECES OF A LIFE

[The above letter ends abruptly, I suspect a page is missing.]

Apr 28-29, 1936 CSTC

Dearest — (Tues nite 12:30) "Lights Out Sweetheart" the orchestra plays & brings with it the sweetest dreams ever. Last weekend seems almost like a dream now.

(Wed morn 6:30) And I went to sleep dreaming, Ellis, and I didn't wake up except to turn off the radio & the light – and to wish you were here. I do hope business is as good in Battle Creek as Kalamazoo & that Grand Rapids will be even better if you go there. I'm not going to Newaygo, Ellis. They didn't want me there because I'm a Catholic. That's the third time it has happened. Makes me boil. But there's nothing to do about it. Are you sure that my "religious preference" will make no difference in the job you offered me? It isn't very bright out today, no sun – but no rain either – yet. It was grand yesterday. Dear me, I still have teaching plans to make before 8. Don't know yet if I'm going home this weekend. Ellis, you don't know how dear you are to me. Love, Daisy xx

Mom was denied consideration for a teaching job because she was Catholic? And not just once, but THREE TIMES! Shocking today, but probably not that unusual in the 1930s when the KKK was still a thriving organization – and Catholics were one of their prime hate targets, along with Blacks & Jews.

Apr 29-30, 1936 CSTC

Dearest Pal — (Wed nite 11:00) Tomorrow & then tomorrow I'm going home again – and how I wish you'd be there too. But "tomorrow & tomorrow & tomorrow creeps in this petty pace from day to day" – for a long time again before I'll see the dearest sweetheart I've known. Helen's going with me & we're going to Saginaw to get our formals for the Spring parties. And we're going to have pie plant pie! Mmm! Got a letter from my mother today & she sent me the clipping I've enclosed. The accident happened immediately after we left Oakley Sunday nite. Mama says to tell you that's what happens to the V-8's that are driven so fast. She doesn't at all approve of speed demons. After the sun drove the rain away this morning, it turned into a perfect summer day. I went downtown this afternoon with Helen & this evening we played tennis for an hour and a half. I have a premonition that I'm going to feel it tomorrow. I don't teach in the morning & I have my 10:00 History class off, so it feels rather like a vacation. I believe, however, that I should take the opportunity to accomplish something. Had a very voluble visit from my dear friend, June, last nite. She can have Newaygo if she wants it, it seems, but now that she knows I'm interested in Grant, she's trying with all her might to get that. I don't know why it is, but for 4 years she's always wanted everything that I get or want – and now – we can't both get it. O, well – I'm glad she doesn't want you, Ellis. I'm thinking she'd have a pretty hard fight for you now. I want May to fly until the 23rd & then stay there for a long time with you. Tomorrow nite I'm going to see the operetta "Little Snow White," given for visiting county normal students – and for us. Will say Good-nite, Sweetheart. Love forever, Your Daisy xx

(Thurs 8:00) – Good morning, Dearest – I'm still in love with you. D.

And she throws in a line from Shakespeare's Macbeth, no less. "Pie plant" is, of course, the old-fashioned name for rhubarb.

May 1, 1936   CSTC

Dearest — (Fri afternoon 3:00) It's a grand sunny day now, but O, it's hot! Yesterday & today are County Normal Day – county norm students are visiting here and special programs are being put on for them. 60 of them are in the dorm. I'm glad the sun's shining for them. I haven't heard anything from Lansing. My hopes aren't very high. How's Grand Rapids? I liked your newest hotel stationery. My freshman English class have been working on a school paper & they finished it this morning & distributed it to all the freshman classes – "Freshman Flash" they called it – 6 pages. They wrote all the news articles & had their own editors. I cut the stencils yesterday & they all helped to mimeograph them & are they proud of it! (But no more than I am.) It has excited quite a lot of comment among all the HS students & faculty. Just had your last nite's letter delivered to me, and – O, Ellis, please don't tempt me. I'm all ready to go home & waiting for my folks to come. Helen isn't feeling very well though. She was chairman of tea yesterday & ate too many cakes & she was sick last nite & all morning. We're (RRT) going to Crystal Decoration [Day] after all, Ellis, on our house party. We had voted to go where the other societies go, but they wanted Houghton, so we changed our vote last nite & will go to Crystal if we can get cottages. We saw the operetta "Little Snow White" last nite & it was really pretty. Played an hour's tennis beforehand – and not so stiff today. Ellis, I don't want you to have a figure like Guy Kibbee's & you won't have. I want you just like you are. We'll have to go in training together. You probably won't get fat on my cooking. Going home now. 'Bye. Love, Daisy xx

Guy Kibbee (1882-1956) was a rotund character actor of stage and screen who played numerous supporting roles in films over a nearly twenty-year period. He is perhaps best known for his role as the newspaper editor of Grover's Corners, in the 1940 film version of Thornton Wilder's Our Town.

May 3, 1936   CSTC

Dearest Ellis — (dorm, Sun nite 9:45) Back again to where I hurriedly left off on Friday – and now in receipt of your Oakley letter – with its "What about it?" Ellis, my heart says, "Yes, anything you want, because I want you too." My head says, "No, not yet." Heart & head just won't cooperate. But O, my Dear, how I wish my heart could win. You think I'm being rather silly, don't you, Ellis? But you can see why my head says not yet, even when I think of you all alone & lonesome & wanting me & I wanting you. It rained most of the weekend but we endured it & minded it not so much. Saginaw shopping Saturday afternoon & home in time for Owosso Saturday nite. Record time for mass this morning – High mass – 8-9:10. Back at 5 today. Helen is gone to the show. Peg is out with Judd, & Marvel came back from 3 days in Detroit tonite all tired out & she brought us each a darling little white fluff of a dog – 4 inches long. Just had a hot bath & rather sleepy. I'd like living in Grand Rapids, Ellis. Your letters set me to day-dreaming – not good for the mind – weakens it. Rugg (new RRT prexy) was at Crystal today & reserved us a cottage about 3 blocks from the pavilion – big enough for all of us. How is Bud, & family? You'll enjoy this week with Bud. Tell me where I can reach you next week. What are they going to do with their house? Or don't they own it? Good-nite, Sweetheart. "I Love You." Daisy xx

---

May 4, 1936   CSTC

Dearest Sweetheart — (Mon nite 12m) Last nite I wrote you at Grandville. Tonite it's still Kalamazoo? Or are you undecided yet? I wish you could go to Grand Rapids. And are you going to the Blossom Festival this weekend? I don't know if the folks are going to Holland this weekend. I'm staying here. My latest is Remus – 18 miles west of M.P. The supt now at Elk Rapids will be at Remus next year & is now hiring his staff. He was here Saturday – interviewing. Yours truly was in Saginaw (shopping in the rain). But Dr Beck boasted me sky-high & asked him not to hire anyone until he'd seen me. Nice? Maybe. It's straight English & I'd like it – and – they want a Catholic!! Feels strange to have the situation reversed. What do you think? (Don't say it, I know.) My head is still reeling. (Don't try to figure this out until you get my Sun letter.) But it's only 56 miles from Grand Rapids –

about 75 from Oakley, o dear! I'm so tired. Was downtown 3-5 & played tennis 6-7:30 – Life office editing until 8:45. Washed hair & bath & here I am. Early morning lesson plans again. The reception of the "Freshman Flash" was quite remarkable – and enthusiasm runs high in plans for the next issue – May 15. Tomorrow 1-4 the Times-News office downtown. When Life goes to press, proof-reading, etc. & critic meeting at 4. "Trail of the Lonesome Pine" at nite. Counts as a class hour for American Folk Lit class. Student council elections tomorrow. Show rush at 4 Wednesday afternoon. Tonite there was a pavement dance & politics rally but I didn't go (no care – no go). O, Ellis, I'm so tired & lonesome & sleepy & wish you were here – forever & ever – and ever. Dearest, I love you so. I love you so. Daisy xx

The Trail of the Lonesome Pine (1908) was a best-selling novel by John Fox, Jr., which was first adapted to the stage, and then to the screen three times. The 1936 version starred Henry Fonda, Sylvia Sidney and Fred MacMurray. Since 1964 the stage play has been performed annually at an outdoor theater in Big Stone Gap, Virginia, the author's hometown, and is considered the longest-running outdoor drama in the United States.

May 6, 1936   CSTC to the Hotel Vincent in Benton Harbor

Dearest – (9:30 PM) I can't say anything that will do any good, it seems. Ellis, you know, don't you, that there's nothing I'd like better than to say yes to anything you'd care to ask now. If you don't know it, please believe me – I'm telling you now – and that I love you, Dearest. Sometimes you wonder if I do love you as much as I say I do & can keep on saying no. I'm not sure I'm right. I'm doing what my folks want me to do – and I owe it to them. I've never done anything concrete to show them I'm worth the investment. But I know I'm not being fair to you, Ellis. I wish you could plead with my folks as you've pleaded with me. It's not so much a question of obedience, but of loyalty. O, I'm getting all tangled up in words now, I wish you were here. I'm glad you're going to Grand Rapids – it isn't far away & it is a nice town too & you won't be so lonesome. Your family will be closer. O, Ellis, I hope I'll be worth all your trouble & waiting & worrying. Dearest, I can't wish either, it doesn't seem to do any good. But, Dear Sweetheart, I do love you. I Love You. Daisy xx

Obviously Dad's last few letters have continued to pressure Mom to marry him immediately after her graduation, but she continues to use the "family loyalty" excuse, and that she needs to "prove" that her parents' "investment" in her college education was a wise one. I find myself aching in sympathy for both of them.

May 9, 1936   CSTC to Grandville, c/o Mr Bud Brorby [typed]

Dearest – (dorm, Sat morn 9:30) How were Benton Harbor and Blossom Festival and parades and Queens n' everything? You must have had and are having a fine time. You must be watching the parade about now. Am I right? It must be beautiful. And are you going to be in Grand Rapids this week? Nothing doing here this weekend. I'm working in the cafeteria this noon, tonite and tomorrow noon. Back at the old job for the weekend. Marvel and I had a 6:00 tennis game this morning, and it was just grand out. I took a header on the gravel court and pretty well banged myself up, rather sore – knees, hands, elbows, and a cut on my hip (front) but not bad. Makes me sore (both ways). Worked on the extension paper Wednesday, Thursday and Friday afternoons. It went to press yesterday and is all out for "Ye extension students" this morning. The folks didn't go to Holland this weekend as far as I know. I wish they would drive up tomorrow, but I don't expect them. Have quite a lot of typing to do for Folk Lit class that I haven't got started on yet. Will be through teaching at the end of next week, when the second issue of the Freshman Flash comes out. This is awfully choppy and dull and senseless, but I'll try to do better tonite, Pal, I really will. Love, Daisy

P.S. This was in this morning's paper – these boys from Carson City HS were killed & one injured in an auto accident. (Charles Jassen, 18, Middleton; Wayne Wilson, 17, Sheridan; Wilson Bell, 16, Carson City; Carol North, 15, Butternut – killed. Forrest Fox, 17, Carson City – critically injured.) D.

Mom's tennis mishap left her with a permanent scar on her hip.

May 10, 1936   CSTC

Dearest – (dorm, Sun nite) Received your note Saturday with the pressed blossoms. Thank you, Ellis. I would like to have seen the parade with you. You'll be riding with Bud this week, won't you? That'll be nice for both of you. I hope you enjoyed your visit home today. I looked for my folks but they didn't come. Hot today. Went to confession last nite & 7:30 mass & communion today. Marvel came back all tired out a little while ago. Peg is coming back in the morning. Two more weeks. 0 – Ellis, Bill can't come to this party. He's coming to the Senior Dinner-Dance June 6. Judd is coming (Marvel's brother) & going with Peg. They want to go with us. The fellows are wearing white flannels or light suits. Rather tired & "ache-y." I'll say good-nite, Sweetheart-Pal, & With All My Heart, I Love You. Daisy xx

May 12, 1936   CSTC

Dearest Pal — (Tues afternoon in the midst of a rumbling, thundering, crashing, streaking storm 1:30 PM) This is a "swell" storm. Wish you were here to enjoy it with me – "The lightning flashed & the thunder roared, / And grandpa he layed there & snored." – quoting the roommate. We have company now. Just a caller for a candy bar – and then she stays here & eats it. The storm is going away & it's getting light again & I won't have to walk to the Ad building in the rain after all. Critic meeting this afternoon at 4. I'll be thru teaching this weekend. Some students from the psychology classes here are going to visit my class Wed, Thurs & Fri of this week when the class will be working on the paper, & it probably will look like bedlam to the visitors. How is Grand Rapids again? And Bud & Kate? Isn't it the same territory that you had before when you were in GR? Senator Gerald P. Nye from North Dakota "lectured" (hmm) here last nite on the "Munitions Racket" & gave very eye-opening disclosures. Quite worthwhile. The doctor had my elbow all bandaged up yesterday, so it looked quite badly damaged & everyone said, "O, what did you do to your elbow?" And today he just put a small pad & tape on it & it looks as if I was just showing off yesterday – building up to an awful let-down (or something). Anyway, it feels lots better now. My lunatic roommate just left – for the high school. She starts teaching next week – biography of Disraeli – whoever he was. Such a nice rainy afternoon. I'd love to stay home – but – when duty calls. Even when duty calls – I Love You, Pal. Love, Daisy xx

P.S. Thanks for the copy of the Blossom paper. I enjoyed it a lot. Love, Daisy

Benjamin Disraeli (1804-1881) was, of course, twice Prime Minister of England and a very influential figure in the British Conservative Party for many years.

May 14, 1936   CSTC

Dearest Sweetheart — (Thurs nite 11:15) I love you, but I can't think of a way to tell you tonite. If I had your arms around me, Ellis, but you're so far away. Will you plan to stay over next weekend? The party won't last awfully long, Ellis, and I do want you to know that I appreciate your coming when you don't like it. I don't know why it means so much to me, but it will all be over soon, & you've been part of it for so long, & please God, you'll keep on being part of me, after my school life is ended. I love you, Dearest Dear, with all my heart. Daisy

May 16, 1936   CSTC to the Hotel Occidental in Muskegon

Dearest Sweetheart – (Sat eve 7:30) This the loveliest time of the evening and a week from tonite at this time I'll be waiting for you. It seems ages and ages since the last time we said "good-nite." Ellis, if you could, & would like to, come to Mt Pleasant earlier than the party-time (which won't be before 9:00), cross my heart I'll be ready for you at 5 or 6 or 7, or any time after that, if I can come back to the dorm and have a half hour to get my party dress on. I do hope it will be as nice as it is tonite. I just came in off the roof where we've been watching the family progress of a robin who has built her nest between a chimney & the brick wall, just where we can look down into it from the roof. So far there are 2 little scrawny, red, naked baby robins and 2 blue eggs in the nest. It's just grand out, a perfect early summer evening. Helen went home yesterday and she'll know for sure whether Bill is coming to the party by Sunday. Marvel and I played tennis for about an hour this morning and then spent the rest of the morning at the Regional track meet here. We saw a class D student break the state pole-vaulting record with an 11'1" vault. Chesaning has some boys here, but none that I know. Peg went home this afternoon (with Judd) and she is going to the Tulip Festival on Sunday with Judd & his folks. Marvel stayed here but she went somewhere to a French Club dinner tonite. My folks went to Holland this weekend too, and took Harold & Helen with them. Holland seems to be a popular place this weekend. Even the book I'm reading has its beginning setting in Holland, "The Exile," by Pearl Buck. You must be awfully busy this weekend and last, and next too, I suppose. Does Bud like the idea of Detroit? How does the Grand Rapids territory compare with the Kalamazoo district? I hope to know by next weekend whether I'll be going to Remus. The prospects look fairly good – second-best though, Ellis. And please don't think I'm just being stubborn about this idea of a job. My mother nearly cried when I asked her if she would care a great deal if I didn't teach at all, and she said, "Well, I think that you'd want to teach at least one year after we've sent you to school for 4 years." You'd do the same thing if you were in my place, Ellis. Our "Freshman Flash" finally was completed & distributed yesterday at 11:30, and 8-page paper this time, with a circulation of 400. I was down at the high school all forenoon. I went to sleep at 2:00 when Helen left and didn't wake up until 5:30 when Peg & Marvel came in to go to dinner. We went for a walk in the college woods where there are millions of blue & yellow violets and snowdrops (but we aren't allowed to pick any). I have a ridiculous little bouquet of dandelions & spirea on the desk and an apple blossom in a thin green glass on the dresser and they are really so pretty – and "brightening." I think I shall study tonite, go for a walk with Marvel when she comes back, and then sleep, and dream – of the Dearest arms and the Sweetest lips I will ever know. Your Daisy

Enclosed with the above is a May 15 typed letter to Miss Daisy Whalen from J.C. Young in Elk Rapids. Mr Young was apparently the Superintendent there who would be the new Superintendent in Remus in the fall.

Dear Miss Whalen: I was sorry to have missed you when I was in Mt Pleasant ten days ago. You are very well recommended and the appointment in Remus will not be made until I have had an opportunity to meet you. It is impossible for me to set a definite time for an interview unless you are able to come to Elk Rapids in which case please notify me. My plan is to be in Remus for several days between the fifth and tenth of June and perhaps it would be more convenient for you to have an interview at that time. Respectfully yours, J.C. Young

On the bottom of this letter, Mom has written –

Dr Beck tells me that there are some experienced teachers going after this job now too, so if the folks are willing, we may go to Elk Rapids Thursday & come back Friday of this week. D.

May 26, 1936 CSTC

Dearest Sweetheart – (Tue nite 9:30) Here I am – pen in hand – and there's nothing to say that hasn't been said already. I haven't been doing anything worthy of note since Sunday nite except sleep in all my spare moments and hours and I'll soon be in Slumberland again. Worked on the Razz edition of the Life all afternoon & evening Monday. It comes out tomorrow. Had critic meeting this afternoon and it rained. Mercier tonite and it still rained. Have been planning for house party – food, cooks, menu, etc. Going out Friday – to Crystal. News all told now. And that's all – except – I Love You, Ellis – in spite of your teasing & "mads" – because you're the best friend & swellest pal & dearest Sweetheart that a girl could have. Because You are You, Ellis, I love You. G'nite. Daisy

---

May 30, 1936 CSTC

Dearest 'Toni' – (Sun nite 10:30) Just a good-nite kiss for you x from a girl who loves you so much that a lifetime is going to be too short to tell you just how much. I'm a trifle sunburned & tired, but clean now & quite contented to look at my bed waiting for me – just one thing could make it look more inviting. Dearest, you must be just dead tonite after so much traveling around. But you won't get this until Wednesday & I hope by that time you will have had a rest & a pleasant time with Bud & a profitable one with W.C. Co. Bud told me a lot of things about you, Ellis, that I had thought were true but you were too modest to tell me. I'm afraid I haven't been fully appreciating you. I only hope I can live up to you, Ellis. And you're such a dear too. I hope we don't ever have a fight again. I'm afraid sometime we'd have one & both of us would be too stubborn to ever make it up, even if our hearts were breaking. (If hearts really do break.) We went to 10:00 mass in Carson this morning. Swimming & sunning & sleeping again today. Fun riding the waves. We'd have fun spending a weekend together at Crystal sometime, wouldn't we, Ellis? Or anywhere. Came home on the bus – arrived at 8:30 tonite. Now I'm living for next Saturday nite & Sunday. Need I tell you what was the highlight of this weekend? You know, don't you, Dearest. I Love You, Dear. Daisy xx

"Toni (or Tony)" was the nickname given Dad by Bud Brorby. No one knows why and it's too late now to ask.

Jun 1, 1936   CSTC

Dearest – (dorm, Mon nite 11:45) Mount Pleasant on the air again in its regular nightly broadcast to GR to EEB, station CSTC, radio announcer DCW, announcing that a new bit of info has just been brought to her attention concerning Senior Dinner-Dance, June 6, at Mount Pleasant Country Club. The time has been disclosed as 7:00 o'clock PM & I know the menu too, but we'll save that for a s'prise! How do you do, Toni? I'm still very much in love with you, but I'm rather sleepy now. Saw "Little Lord Fauntleroy" tonite. It rained but it was just grand out when we came back. I was awfully sleepy today but made all my classes OK & in pretty good shape. Helen is going home tomorrow. Don's driving up – & coming back tomorrow nite. Ellis, would you like to come to Oakley June 13 when I'm home? I'd love to have you. Good-nite, Dearest Man I Know. Daisy xx

---

Jun 3, 1936   CSTC

Dearest – (Wed 2 PM) When you put ½ and ½ together you'll get an invitation – a formal one. And here's another one – from me. I'm looking for you. I love you, Ellis. Love, Daisy xx

A printed invitation to the June 6th SENIOR DINNER-DANCE at the Mt. Pleasant Country Club is enclosed, stating: Dinner at 7:00 – Dancing 'til 12:00. $1.50 per couple. Semi-formal.

Jun 3, 1936 CSTC

Dearest Ellis – (Wed nite 11:00) 3 more nites & 3 more day & – it seems too good to be really true. Have your letter written at the same time mine was last nite. I hope you do bring Bud & Kate with you Sat nite, Ellis. It would be lots of fun. I think they'd enjoy it too. We elected dorm officers at house meeting tonite but haven't gotten the results yet. Peg was up for prexy & I think she'll get it. It's cold here tonite. Had a pavement dance & everyone froze out. Helen's going to Mecosta tomorrow to see about her job. I hope she gets it. Our "Razz" edition came out today after much censoring but there was still a spark of life in it. I'll be looking for you Sat nite, Ellis. Be sure & bring Bud & Kate. You're kinda nice, Pal. I kinda like ya. G'nite. Daisy C xx

Jun 8, 1936 CSTC

Ellis Dear – (Mon nite 10:30 or later) I wish everyone would go away ad leave me in peace just long enough for me to say good-nite to you. Peg & Marvel have been in parading in our formals & Coppernall has been pestering and Helen won't keep still for two minutes & every 5 minutes someone comes in to buy candy & we haven't any and that's all of my grouch tonite & I'll bet that you wish you had only little things like these to worry you. I really don't feel as bad as I sound. But I'll bet you were tired & sleepy today and was your new truck waiting for you? Dear Ellis, maybe sometime I'll be close enough to you so you won't have to be losing sleep over me. Some pep talk, eh, keed? But just gimme time to get into my stride. Maybe I won't tonite tho – I'm rather sleepy. I was talking with Fr Mulvey today & he said I was looking fine & well, etc. but a little tired. You know these last few weeks are busy ones tho. Wednesday is Senior Skip Day. No classes for us. Picnic at Crystal. But I don't want to go to Crystal again so soon. I'm going to "hibernate" in the dorm & work on my list of library books for next year – and sleep, maybe. I wish I'd get a letter from Mr Young tomorrow telling me to come to Remus Thursday. Then my folks could stay for swingout & we'd go home afterwards & I'd wait for Saturday nite to come when a friend from Grand Rapids is coming to see me – it's his birthday & we'll have a strawberry short – birthday – cake for him. He's a very special friend of mine – in fact, I've even gone so far as to fall in love with him. But you'd love him too if you could know him as I do. Once I wrote him a letter – "Dearest Man I Know." I don't remember if I sent it – but – he's still the "Dearest Man I Know." I love you, Dearest Man. Good-nite. Daisy xx

Strawberry shortcake for Dad's birthday (June 13, 1910) was a long-standing family tradition at our house, but I hadn't known it went back to even before Mom & Dad were married, when his future mother-in-law would make it for him. In fact, this seems a good place to

include one more letter to Dad from Lettie Whalen, just because I like the way she writes.

June 5, 1936   Oakley to Grand Rapids

Dear Friend — We received your letter and check yesterday and will do the very best I can but you have given me a pretty hard job buying for someone else, but I certainly appreciate what you have done and I know Daisy will too, but she can tell you that for herself when she knows about it. Daisy is coming home the 12th, one week from today and I wish you could come the 13th in time for supper and maybe we could have shortcake, if not for supper we could have it for dinner the next day. Everyone is fine around here and Harold has gone back to work and Clarence has been promoted. He is a molder now. I asked him if he made better money at that, he said no but there was more of it. They have bought them a lot and this fall will build a tile garage to live in until they can save money to build a house. They are two happy kids now. The weather has been rather cool here the last two weeks but we didn't get a frost. Well the stork hasn't been to Oakley lately but the old reaper was here last week and got Mr Marks. He had a cancer. Well I must get to work so good-bye until the 13th when we hope to see you. Mrs Wm Whalen

---

June 15, 1936   CSTC

Ellis Dearest — (Mon nite) 22 hours since I said good-nite to you. And 2 ½ hours since I started staying in to make up time for its having been 22 hours instead of 23 as it should have been. And my name was on the bulletin board for having had no latenesses. I guess I fooled 'em! 55 minutes late & 4 hours & 35 min to make up – 2 nites worth. Poor, dear Ellis, you must have been awfully sleepy this morning. A cold shower woke me up & started me going. Maybe next weekend you can really rest & sleep. Four weekends in a row! That's nearly a record for us, isn't it? It surely was grand of you, Ellis, to come to all my parties. I really do appreciate it. I want to thank you again for the cedar chest too, Dearest. I can't tell you in words how perfectly dear & sweet you've been to me. I'm going to try awfully hard to tell you in another way though. Are you going to be in Grand Rapids all this week? You didn't tell me (and I must keep track of you). Can't lose you now. I'm not doing very much this week. Double time for teaching tomorrow – 12:30-2:00 correcting test papers and I'll be going to the high school no more. And not much of anything else to do. Isn't that just swell for the last week? I'll sleep – and that's what I will do – beginning right soon now. I'm just making talk now. There's really nothing left to say, Dearest, after I love you. Daisy

And that's not true either, is it? Because, after "I love you," there's everything in the world to tell you, and all my thoughts & dreams to share with you. Please, God, just loosen our tongues; give us words for our dreams & thoughts; help us to understand each other always, so our love may be complete – is the prayer of Ellis and Daisy. Good-nite, Dearest Lover. Daisy

---

Jun 17, 1936   CSTC

Dearest Dear – (Wed nite 9:30) I'm sorry as can be about the neuralgia. Really I am, and I have a feeling that I am partly responsible for it too. You haven't been getting enough rest, and it was my fault. You haven't even had one weekend to rest for the last 5 weeks on account of me. Dearest, please spend as much time as you can, and then some more, sleeping. And even when you come to see me on the 4th, I'll do my best to let you rest and not bother you too much. You can come on Friday nite or Saturday morning and we'll have 2 days together. Won't that be grand? Most of our commencement activities are yet to come – Ronan Round dinner and commencement play tomorrow nite, class day exercises Friday, senior girls' breakfast Saturday morning, rehearsal & first alumni meeting Saturday afternoon, and lawn fete, commencement dinner Saturday evening, reception for parents and baccalaureate Sunday evening, commencement address Monday morning – and I'll be glad when it's all over. Somehow I don't get the thrill out of it that I thought I would. Nothing exciting or breath-taking – everything seems so flat and senseless. I seem to have lost my sentimentality over such things that made high school graduation such a thrill. It might be that I've found something else so far outstripping this sort of thing in thrills & sentiment and real feeling that this can't even approach it. Do you think so? I know this, Ellis. Every time I see you, I love you more than before, every time I think I can't possibly love you any more – and find that I can and do. Dearest Sweetheart, do take care of yourself, for you & for me – for us, Dear. Thank you for your good wishes – next year I'll want them for a much greater occasion. Until then, love me, Dearest, as I love you. Your Daisy xx

---

Jun 18, 1936   CSTC

Ellis Dear – (Wed nite 1:15 by my watch but the poor thing still doesn't run right) This has been such a long, long day, and nice things have happened, but it's all over now and I'm so tired. Ellis, do get lots of rest, no matter what happens to the job or anything. We can't have anything happen to you and you're worth more than any old job. And tell me how you are, Dearest. I love you so. We went to the commencement play tonite – Helen & her mother & Joanne & I. Poor little Joanne, she's so sweet – she was so tired – Helen took her home at the end of the first act. The play was really good. Hilda Millette and Frank Myers (Jerry's roommate) had the leads. This afternoon Helen gave me a surprise birthday party at her house with cake & candles and everything. It was so nice – Peg & Marvel & Doris & Helen & Joanne. She gave me a Central letter opener that I've wanted for a long time. The Ronan Rounders had a dinner tonite honoring us seniors – formal & everything just right (with a really good dinner too), & we each received a gift – a tiny stand-up framed dog picture with a mirror on reverse side – darling, "Darling." I'm thru with all my classes now. Had my 10 o'clock today. Ran around & saw everyone & got my senior treasurer books all closed. Gave a 15-min talk in Doc Beck's class. A long day. Doris is going home with me Monday afternoon & stay the rest of the week. She has to start work in Penney's as soon as she gets home so she won't have any other time to come & see me. Peg & Marvel are coming to spend a week with me later in the summer. Helen can't, I guess. Tomorrow we have to put our room on exhibition for Helen's family & Jerry. We're being serenaded now by the Thulians. Howdy Loomis is back with them this week. They must be touched by the romantic spirit tonite. Right under our window. Soothing – "Girl of My Dreams" now. So, Sweetheart of all MY dreams, Good-nite. I love you. Daisy xx

1936 Senior Class Officers: Daisy Whalen, Treasurer

I don't remember Mom's CSTC letter opener, but when I graduated from Central 33 years later, a dear friend gifted me with a CMU letter opener, which I still have. The birthday party for Mom was a bit early. She would turn 20 on June 25th that year. And look how easy, no-big-deal that 15-minute speech was for Mom by this time. No stage fright, no worry. A seasoned, experienced speaker & teacher. It seems strange to me, because I knew her only as a shy, retiring housewife & mother – although she was the president of the Rosary Altar Society at St Philip's parish here in Reed City for a term or two. The Thulians were, I believe, a men's chorus or glee club at Central, and "Howdy" Loomis (class of 1935) was a cheerleader, and is also remembered for having composed the CSTC fight song.

Daisy Whalen 1936 graduation Central State Teachers College

Jun 19-20, 1936   CSTC

Dearest – (Fri nite 12:40) I'm trying hard to stay awake until Helen & Marvel come in. Peg & I sewed their sheets together & want to see the fun. Marvel went with Jerry's brother, Karl, who came up from Detroit to take Jerry home. Expect they'll be in at 1:00. Peg & Doris & Marvel surprised us tonite with a pair of book-ends – love-birds in alabaster – for me, and a Brownie Kodak for Helen. I think Helen & Marvel went to Crystal. Peg & I talked all evening while Peg packed & I wrote in her Chippewa. No classes today. All over. It doesn't seem like the last weekend here. Dearest, I write one minute and think for nine and say nothing. How is business this week? And how are you, my Sweetheart? Write to me in Oakley now. From Central now I send my Dearest – Love, Daisy xx

(Sat morn 10:20) – Dearest – Just came back from the Senior Girls Breakfast that carried out the theme of the words we hear so much – "out in the field" – and it was darling. Best of all was to find your letter waiting for me. And what do you think? Helen just got a call from App't Office. She's going to Mecosta at $100 a month. Isn't that swell? I'm worried now. I may not get to Remus. Haven't heard from anyone about it. But Dearest, I love you. The senior walk-around is at 11. When I can beg, borrow or steal a stamp, I'll mail this. Love, Daisy

P.S. (Sat) The sewed-together sheets trick worked swell & nobody was mad. L, Daisy

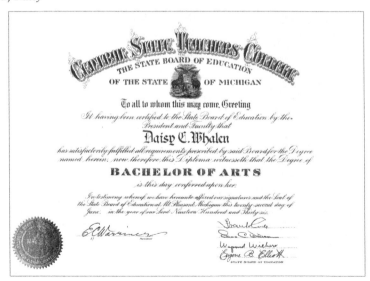

1936 Central State Teachers College diploma

Jun 20, 1936   CSTC

Dearest Sweetheart — (Sat nite 12m) For you certainly are the finest and dearest most thoughtful Sweetheart in the world, I've no doubt at all. Red roses, Ellis, the most beautiful flowers there are, must mean Love, the most beautiful thing in Life. And I look at them and look at them and read in them your Love, and love you so much that I want to cry because it hurts so. Darling, I can't say all I want to say - there aren't words for it. It's such lovely, thoughtful acts of yours like this that mean so much, Ellis, and make me really realize how dear you are. I love you, Ellis; I'd love you just as much if you hadn't sent me flowers today - but such "silent messages" make love a little sweeter. Always, Your Daisy

This was Mom's last letter from Central, not just a 'school' for her, because she was barely sixteen when she arrived there in the fall of 1932. She grew up at Central, physically, emotionally and intellectually. It was at Central that she discovered she was indeed a 'social creature,' and, first tentatively, and then wholeheartedly, learned to spread her wings and have some fun. She also made a circle of close friends, a few of whom she would stay in touch with for many years. So, no matter what she may have said or written to Dad, I suspect it must have been wrenchingly hard for her to leave the campus, her beloved Ronan Hall and all those friends.

Jun 23, 1936   Oakley

Ellis Dearest — (Tues nite 10:15) I did get your lovely & much appreciated letter on my Graduation Day and it was dear of you to think of me in that way. I'm all thru with school now, have my little degree all tucked away, and don't feel any different (wise or otherwise) than before it was conferred on me. Now - the Democrats are loudly campaigning in the downstairs region. Doris Sheldon is home with me - to spend the rest of this week. We've spent most of today sleeping. Went to Remus yesterday and talked with a school board member and he assured me that I will get my contract. We took Helen to Mecosta and she signed her contract and talked with the superintendent and is quite pleased with her prospects. I just love my - our - cedar chest, Ellis. I've really had a chance to admire it. Next year I'll see what I can do to fill it. The Owosso Centennial celebration is July 1-4, Ellis - Rodeo too. You'll come Friday nite, won't you - will you? (10 days) I love you, Dearest. Good-nite, Sweetheart. Daisy

Jun 25, 1936   Oakley

Dearest Dearest — (in the Travel-o, Thurs nite) 10 seconds before 11 o'clock (Bulova watch time). No other, that's you. This is Chubby's (Ordis) idea of a

good time – or a lark, or something. Here we are, sleeping in the top bunk of the trailer right in our own back yard – with my little radio working better than it ever has before – what fun! We went to Owosso to the show tonite – Strand. "Paddy O'Day" – Janie Withers, & "Dancing Feet" – Joan Marsh, Ben Lyon. Both good shows. I'm 20 years old now, honey. Next year at this time I'll be 21 and _____. Yesterday I was only 19 & there isn't much difference as far as I can see. We called on Aunt Flora today & didn't do much else. Clarence was up. He has a little vacation (inventory) until Wednesday – and he doesn't like it. Yesterday we had a croquet tournament. We're practicing up for you, Sweetheart. I'm so glad you're feeling better, Dearest. I love you. July 3? Daisy

It was Mom's birthday. Visited her aunt with Doris, then a double feature night at the movies in the evening. And now she & Doris are 'camping out' overnight in the back yard, with the radio playing. And I'm sure there was cake. Maybe not quite grown up.

Jun 28, 1936   Oakley

Dearest Heart — (Sun nite 10:15) In my 4-poster with the dearest face in the world on the dresser watching me. I'm so lonesome for you tonite. This week can't possibly fly too fast – until Friday. I want you so, Ellis. (10 mins) Dearest, forgive me for dropping from the sublime to the ridiculous, but I've just realized that this awfully empty feeling is because I'm hungry – but if I eat now, I couldn't sleep, so ___? (This isn't suggesting that you starve me to make me love you.) I haven't written you since Thursday nite, have I? Seems a long time. We took Doris home (to Greenville) Friday afternoon. Last nite to the Capitol to see H.G. Wells' "Things to Come" – very exaggerated, nightmarish, & frightening; & "The Girl from Mandalay" – jungle romance of a man with a family tree & a girl with a past. Today – 10:00 mass (7:30 next Sun). Parish netted $220 from chicken dinner. Rosalie had a birthday party this afternoon (10 little girls) & she was all excited – 6 years old June 22. Harold was 26 June 23. We played croquet tonite – supported by the "Invincible Agnettas" until it was too dark to see. I haven't yet felt any pangs about leaving school days behind. But I think I'd feel terrible, Ellis, if it weren't for you. You make me realize how trivial everything is but Love and Life. Dearest, I can't imagine how terribly vacant and meaningless my life might be if you'd never loved me and I'd never loved you. The saddest thing about it would be that I couldn't know what I'd missed. (Aside with the philosophizing for a moment, please, while I do away with a pestering moth.) Dearest Sweetheart, Good-nite. I love you more than anything in the whole wide world, says Your Daisy. And I'll try to tell you better. L., D.

The Agnetta family lived just across the street from the Whalens. And I can't help thinking that, without Dad, Mom might have gone on to earn an advanced degree, and ... But what am I saying? Then I wouldn't have been here. (Never mind.)

1936: Daisy and ELlis at Agnetta's house in Oakley

Jul 6, 1936   Oakley

Dearest Ellis – (Mon nite 11:00) How are you? I am well and hope you are the same – but I do worry about your "neurology." You take care of it and don't forget to rub some Hinkley's and Sloan's on it every nite. I always did say there's nothing like good old-fashioned liniment for taking the aches & pains out of a body. 'Specially after a 2-day Fourth celebration, such high livin' is apt to have some after-effect, so ___. So what? I guess that was enough of that. I trust the family all arrived safely in Grand Rapids. I can just see Tom pacing the floor in Owosso with his watch out every 2 minutes & wishing they'd taken the train – wondering why Ellis wasn't coming earlier. I wonder why? I know why. And I believe they didn't mind waiting as much as I would have minded your leaving without a nice long good-bye. No news here today. Washday. Hot. Caught 4 ground-moles. Croquet game tonite. Saw by the paper that we didn't reach our quota of 630 holiday dead. Better luck next year maybe. With all due apologies for not having written you on my "personal" stationery sooner, I am – Yours, Daisy

P.S. I love you. D.

Jul 8, 1936 Oakley

Dearest – (Wed 3:45 PM) 114 degrees in the sun. I say, nothing like this cool, invigorating climate to make one ambitious, aye, what? Dearest, I hope you don't get sunstruck or anything like it. (I'd like to see you moonstruck though.) I wish you could be working along the lake shore this week. Wouldn't it be kinda nice? How'd you like to spend a week with us (in our Travel-o) in the northern regions - Traverse, Straits, Sault, etc. - the first week in August - could you arrange it? If not, let me know. Perhaps we can arrange our schedule to suit yours. (Here's a) X (hot, sticky one). Ellis, if you've asked Aunt Stacia & Tom to come with you to the reunion & they've accepted, there's going to be a family feud - not the Martins & and the Coys, but between Bonnie Whalen & me - unless she gets an invitation to ride too. Ellis, this is a mess, & I didn't think of it until you'd gone Sunday. If you don't want to ask her, it's all right. She's about what I imagine your Mrs Hennessy's type in ambitious gossip. Just use your own good judgment. Harold & Helen were down for supper last nite and Vincent & I beat my dad & Margaret 3 games out of 5 - so we had to get out the rules - but we won fairly, it was finally decided. We're going down to Dorothy & Alfred's to dinner Sunday. It's Jerry's birthday - 7th. Be a good boy, Ellis, Dearest. Love, Daisy xx

---

Jul 10, 1936 Oakley

Ellis Dearest – (Fri nite 10:45) Show nite, 80 degrees F. This is Oakley's big nite and I wish you were here. We could have fun, couldn't we? One week is nearly gone, Dearest, and now only two more. Every time you go away, it seems longer until the next time. But just think of next year at this time. O, Ellis, I think about so many things and I wish we could be together and talk them over - and I can't write about them. There were two ideas I had today I'd like to ask you about but I will have forgotten them probably before I see you. If you can remember to ask em about - (1) lake, and (2) suit next time we talk, maybe I'll remember. We can see the northern lights tonite and I wonder if you can see them too. Do you ever look for them? It rained just a little here this afternoon and it's cooler tonite. I do hope our heat wave is over especially for your sake. Owosso was the hottest city in the U.S. Wednesday according to a national survey - and I think Oakley was next. We were down to Kairot's tonite. Gertrude doesn't seem to be feeling very well. Clarence was overcome with the heat yesterday and they put him on a new job today and closed down the line he was working on. The men couldn't stand the heat. He has another vacation week after next when they are putting in a new kiln (or something to that effect). Wednesday night we went to the show at the

Minter in Owosso and it was so cool – air-conditioned. Bruce Cabot & Ann Sothern in "Don't Gamble with Love," and "Dangerous Intrigue" with Ralph Bellamy & Gloria Shea – both fair shows. Haven't done much else in the last three days – except to try to sleep & eat a little and keep cool as much as possible. Had a letter from Helen today – has been on the job for a week and works quite a lot harder than she expected. She isn't going to stay as long as intended. I can't understand where you get cold sores, Ellis. Maybe I'm a "carrier" (?) – I've never had one. And I haven't told you before, have I, Ellis – it was awfully nice of you to take Aunt Stacia & Tom home Sunday nite last. Thanks – from me. x I love you, Dear, cold sores and all, and I'd like to have you here (if you had a dozen). G'nite, Darling. Daisy xx

It's not surprising that Mom would dwell on the hot weather in these last two letters. That week in July of 1936 was one of the hottest on record, with temperatures reaching triple digits every day between the 8th and 14th of that month. In Detroit alone, over 350 people died of heat-related causes, and more than 500 state wide. Her brother, Clarence, worked pouring molten metal at a foundry in Saginaw where the heat and working conditions must have been intolerable.

Jul 12, 1936   Oakley

Dearest Sweetheart – (Sun nite 11:00) End of 5th day of the now commonly called "heat wave." After having morally (or mortally) fortified myself for a good nite's nightmare – with muskmelon, pickled boloney & crackers, banana, cookies & milk – and Doublemint – the budding young schoolmarm decides to take advantage of her absentmindedness and save 3c. For on looking in my box of stationery "what to my wondering eyes should appear" but the letter which flowed from my pen & my heart to you – on nite before last. After 10 o'clock mass without benediction, at which Father G. was merciful & didn't preach at us (much), we spent the day at Dorothy's. We took Jerry a ball & bat – so you know what I've been doing all day. (I was pitcher.) We also produced some masterpieces from Jerry's paintbox. Tom & Nina (Corcoran) were down tonite – looking for a cooler climate, but not finding it, I fear. About Bonnie – the problem child (or stepchild) of the Whalen clan – nobody quite knows what she'll do next. If you see Aunt Stacia, ask her to tell Bonnie that she may come with you (if she hasn't another way). But don't let her inveigle you into anything. She's a chiseler. I'd suggest you leave it up to Aunt Stacia – she's OK. (P.S. Bonnie will probably stay in Owosso Sat nite, but she can stay here. But I don't want her here.) Saw "The Walking Dead" – Boris Karloff horror story, & Walter Huston in "Rhodes" – Cecil J. Rhodes, unifier of South Africa – Saturday night at the Capitol. My contract came

193

Saturday – 9 months beginning Aug 31 @ $116 66/100 – I'm wondering how we'll figure out the fraction. Ellis, I do hope you can get your vacation when you've asked for it – but if not, we can go when you do get it (if you want to). Sleeping in the back yard tonite under the stars – and I'll wish on every star for a dream of you (and I'll wish on the moon for You). Good-nite, Dear. I love you. Daisy xx

Yes, Mom's monthly teaching salary in Remus was $116.66. Doesn't sound like much today, but was probably even a little above average for a starting teacher then. Her friend Helen was getting $100 a month in Mecosta. Also interesting, I thought, was that Owosso had at least three active movie theaters – the Strand, the Capitol and the Minter.

Jul 15, 1936   Oakley

Dearest — (Wed nite) Received your note this morning. I'm so glad we can plan on the week together. Such a relief to have normal weather again. It hasn't rained here yet, but cooled off last nite & is grand again tonite. We're going to Sandusky tomorrow afternoon & coming back Sunday. Margaret is going with us. There are 2 doctors there who offer cures for stomach ulcers. We may go around the edge of the thumb and go swimming in Lake Huron. No news. No inspirations. I still love you. Daisy

---

Jul 20, 1936   Oakley

Dearest Heart — (Sun nite 8:30) Home. It seems two ages since I've seen you & it well seem another age until I see you. But it's always like this. I think that the most important thing that happened to me in college was learning to love you – a painless lesson and quite thorough, I believe. You are a very inspiring teacher, Dearest. We came home this afternoon from Huron County State Park, in the Thumb on Lake Huron, where we spent a very lazy and enjoyable weekend with lots of sun and water and food and sleep. Margaret backed out at the last minute and wouldn't leave home. We listened to Major Bowes tonite. Were you listening? I didn't mind it as much as usual. I think his talent is improving. Dearest, I love you so, but it's getting so close to seeing you again that I'm getting tongue-tied already. If this keeps up, I'll probably be writing you letters for the rest of my life – to tell you – I love you, Ellis. xx See you Saturday. But I don't need letters to send these, do I, Dearest? xx Daisy xx

Major Edward Bowes (1874-1946) hosted the radio show, "Major Bowes' Original Amateur Hour." It was one of the most popular shows on radio, lasting longer than its namesake, running from 1935-1952.

Aug 10, 1936   Oakley

Dearest — (Mon nite 10:00) I saw a shooting star just as I came in tonite and I had to write you. They always make me remember our first evening together. I hope that working again wasn't as hard as you expected today – and that it won't take you too long to recover from your vacation. I'd like to be in Traverse Bay every nite just long enough for a swim, wouldn't you? Helen (Whalen) was sick today and I was there all afternoon – just came back – and may go up again tomorrow. Mama did our washing & Helen's too today. Two days' ironing now. I'm sleeping between words now – must say Good-nite, Sweetheart Dearest. I love you. Daisy xx

And that's it. Mom would not begin her teaching duties at Remus High School for another three weeks, but there are no more letters from this period, her last summer of being single. There are also no surviving letters from her year of teaching the 1936-37 school year at Remus, although I am sure she probably wrote many. In the course of transcribing all of these missives, I noted almost no mention of phone calls. Of course there were telephones, but long-distance calls were something normally reserved for emergencies. Letters were the thing back then. Even years later, in the 1950s, I can still remember Dad calling for everyone to be quiet, saying, "It's long-distance!" – and preparing for bad news.

Of course this was not the end of Mom's story – or Dad's. She finished her year of teaching at Remus in June of 1937. She turned 21 that same month – June 25th. And the following day – June 26, 1937 – Daisy Cecelia Whalen and Ellis Edward Bazzett were joined in matrimony at St Michael's Catholic Church in Oakley. Mom recorded some memories of that event nearly 70 years later.

Journals & Notes

My wedding dress & veil came from Christian's store in Owosso, paid for with nearly the last of my teacher's wages ($1,000 for the year). I had about $6 left in my "pocketbook" (purse) when I was married. There were no invitations sent out except by word of mouth, but I have a hazy memory of walking down the aisle in St. Michael's Catholic Church in Oakley & all the pews were filled. Helen Critchell was my bridesmaid – she wore her yellow organza formal from college proms. Louis Hogan, Ellis's friend from Carson City, was best man ... We walked the short block from church to our back yard, full of tables with a great chicken dinner that my mother & Aunt Daisy had prepared. Pictures under the catalpa tree in blossom were taken of the 2 of us, & of me, & of the 4 of us. Then I changed into the raspberry-colored wool suit I'd bought in Remus from Sally Wernette's little shop, & we took off for our honeymoon cottage at Glen Lake. We did go through Reed City – as we remembered in 1945, when we moved here to live the rest of our lives.

In the same journal Mom goes on to describe the "wee hoose" at Blackburn's Resort on the lake, where they stayed for two weeks. It sported a tiny kitchen with an icebox, and had "pink plaid double blankets" on the bed. "And a back door with a short path to the outhouse." They played golf on a nearby golf course and went rowing on the lake with a boat provided with the cabin. They picked wild strawberries on a couple occasions, then baked biscuits to make strawberry shortcake. There were short trips into Traverse City to shop. Sunday mass was at a church in Empire, but the best part of it all was simply being together.

We were so "wrapped up" in each other we really didn't need to go anywhere. But during that time I had my "period," which, surprisingly, didn't even embarrass me. My husband – all through the 52+ years we had together – was always loving & understanding.

Following that blissful interlude, they made their first home in an apartment (204) at 830 West Euclid in Detroit. Dad was still on the road for General Mills at this time, now working out of the Detroit office at the Stephenson Building. Only a few letters survive from the next several years, some from my dad, and one from Mom. Here are a few of Dad's.

Aug 12, 1937   Hotel Harrington, Port Huron to 830 Euclid West, Apt 204, Detroit

Dearest Mine — (Thurs AM 7:00) Some foxy stationery, eh, Pal? This hotel pen is a pip and the ink looks like it has some of your potent "flour thickening" in it. I have called Herman at his house this morning at 6:45 AM which is pretty early and told his landlady not to wake him but to have him call me when he got up. Am expecting his call any minute now. Just finished shaving and found the hot water bottle and the "eye-opener" note in a very much surprised manner. After saying my prayers last night I finally decided to put the tops of my pajamas on and did. After putting the pajama coat on, I turned out the lights and crawled into bed, but not for long, as the first thing I did was to fold my hands across my chest & discover your loving little note in the pocket. You're pretty sweet, Pal. I arrived here at 11:05 last night. It says 57 miles to Detroit on a sign across the street from the hotel. This hotel is pretty shabby. Am afraid you would get a bad impression of hotels if you were to see this one first. Guess I'll get my bag picked up & packed. Be loving you before long now. Love, Ellis xx

Dad's reference to saying his prayers immediately caught my attention. Because he – and Mom too – never took their relationship with God lightly. Dad was the product of a mixed marriage. His mother, Mary Ellis, was Catholic and a firm believer. But his father, Julius (aka "Juda") was a non-practicing Baptist. In most of my father's years growing up, in Grand Rapids and on a farm outside Wayland, he rarely, if ever, got to attend Mass. It was not until shortly before he met Mom that he began taking instructions, playing catch-up, in sessions with a priest in Carson City, where his good friends, the Churchills, lived. I believe he was baptized and confirmed during that time. And so he began attending Mass and the sacraments with Mom whenever they were together on a Sunday, and also by himself when he was on the road, selling. But the "saying his prayers" part remained constant throughout his life. My five siblings and I all have clear memories of glancing into our folks' open bedroom door at night, at various times of our lives, and seeing Dad on his knees beside the bed in his pajamas, elbows resting on the bed, his head bowed, hands clasped, eyes closed. We knew he was praying. We were taught to do the same, although most of us fell out of the habit once we'd left home. Dad never did. All three of my own children also remember seeing their grandpa in prayer by his bed, and they were suitably impressed. It was a devotion my dad kept up to nearly the end of his life, even when he was sick.

Oct 27, 1937   Hotel Columbia in Kalamazoo to Detroit

Dearest Pal — (Tues eve 11:15 PM) Just a goodnite x before turning in for the nite. We drove Mel's car, arrive in Kalamazoo at 5:30. We are invited to Bright's house for dinner this Sat nite at 6:30. Joe Schuster & wife will also be there. I accepted for the family. Be seeing you, Pal. Love, Ellis xxx

Mel Bright was a friend & colleague of Dad's at General Mills, as was Glen (Lehr?), mentioned in the following letter.

Oct 29, 1937   Whitcomb Sulphur Springs Hotel in St Joseph to Detroit

Dearest — (Thurs eve) Ashamed as can be for not writing to you yesterday but really had a very full day in Kalamazoo. Will try to explain tomorrow nite. Saw Chuck Ide and he is sending you a present. Saw in the paper that Jim's game was on Saturday. Hope so, so that we can go. Glen has a little radio & we just listened to Charlie McCarthy & Rudy Vallee & Major Bowes. Was in Kalamazoo, Bangor & in St Joe. Am going to Battle Creek & to my Sweetheart tomorrow. Love, Ellis xx

There are no other letters to Mom from Dad from those first months of their marriage, but there is one from Mom's Central roommate, Helen Critchell. Judging from Mom's letters, Helen went through several boyfriends during her college years, and when she wrote the following letter to Mom (probably from Mecosta, if she was still teaching there), she was still unmarried and had obviously not changed much. Her letter (typed, with a handwritten postscript) was mostly to let Mom know that she was coming to Detroit for a visit. The letter really speaks for itself.

Sep 25, 1937   (Mecosta?) to Detroit

*Dearest Daisy – (Sunday) I'm glad that you're glad that we are coming
down. But can you leave your mother? I'm not sure just when we will
leave. The whole Funren family have decided now would be a good time
to visit friends in Detroit, I guess. Consequently, "Ma," Ken and Franz are
going. They are visiting friends there somewhere. I don't know where Carl
plans on staying. But I do know where I am planning on staying and can
hardly wait to get there to see you. Carl wants to see the ball game either
Sat or Sunday. I don't care anything about an old ball game but I suppose
I will have to go. I'd much rather go window shopping with you. Maybe
you and I could go downtown in the afternoon and all go to the game on
Sunday. I don't care what we do as long as we are together. I'll tell you
the latest about everyone we know. Went to Mt Pleasant yesterday. My
brother wrecked his car and I went over to see how badly he was hurt. He
got his eye cut rather badly but that is all. I should say above his eye. Poor
kid if he doesn't have the toughest luck. Have had a few dates with Jerry.
Both Carl and Jerry want me to go to the homecoming affairs with them.
So I guess I'll not go at all. I'd like to go and not see either of them. But
they are both going. So I guess I'll go home. Our potato vacation starts
that weekend. Went to Bass Lake last nite. Had fun. Mite go to the show
tonite. We usually do. "The Road Back." Sheldon is rooming with Jean
Lawless. They are very happy. Marvel is rooming with P. Pernert. Peg just
hates teaching. If I tell you all the news in this letter I won't have any left
so I'd better sign off. When I see Carl I'll find out when we plan on going.
I have a lot of papers to look over. Gave tests Friday. I hope your mother
is all rite. It sounds to me as if you still love your husband and after all
this long time. I don't blame you tho – "him is a pretty nice fella." I hope
you don't have any cherry pie while you're there!! I am honored to think
that we are your first weekend guests. 'Til later (over)*

This last part is scribbled in longhand.

*Hi, Pal – (Monday, in school) I sound rather cheerful for a Monday, don't
I? I am – I have only 1 set of papers corrected, but what care I – the kids
can correct their own – they'll remember the mistakes better then! I guess
we'll leave Saturday morning – so will be seeing you about noon. Won't
be long now, keed. Saw Fran & Harry Roberts. Is Fran ever fat! Must start
n' do sumpin' now. Lotsa love, Helen*

It sounds like Mom's fun-loving friend has not changed much since
college, is still stringing along two guys at a time, and doesn't seem
to care much for either one of them. A "potato vacation" was a
common fall break at country schools in farming communities, usually

in October, when all the kids were needed to help with digging and hauling potatoes, an important staple crop throughout the state. And "The Road Back" was a film about post-war (WWI) Germany, based on a novel by Erich Maria Remarque (already famous for his international bestseller, All Quiet on the Western Front).

Although there are no more letters from Central, Mom and Dad's story was, of course, just beginning. And Mom did keep aperiodic diaries and sketchy daily journals off and on for the next forty years or more. And there's that partial memoir she worked at when she was ninety-plus. From that and from the letters she wrote from Central, we know that, as the "baby" of the family, Mom was a rather spoiled girl and young woman, who, it seemed, got pretty much anything she wanted, even in the dark and desperate days of the Great Depression. Indeed, from reading Mom's chatty, enthusiastic letters from Central and Oakley, you would never know there was a Depression. Although her two older brothers were often out of work during her college years, her father, being a US Postal Service employee, never missed a paycheck and seemed to be doing very well, with a new car, a travel trailer to take camping trips with and more. Life was good for the elder Whalens and their youngest child. Mom freely admits that, aside from her jobs at Central, and that one year teaching at Remus, she never had worked outside the home. In fact she never even did any baby-sitting! What kind of sex education Mom had is sketchy or unknown. But she did remember reading "Marjorie May's Twelfth Birthday," an instructional pamphlet that came with a box of Kotex, beginning in the 1920s. I looked it up. In it, menstruation is described as a "purification" process.

But love conquers all, and they obviously must have figured things out, because in early 1938 Mom found herself pregnant for the first time. She tracked the baby's progress in entries from her journal for 1938 –

Feb 25 – Called on Dr. Smith. We're going to have a baby – Oct 27 approximately. Health fine.

Mar 25 – Called on Dr. Smith. Everything OK. Blood pressure up. Wgt. still 134 ½. Baby coming fine at 2 months.

Mom and Dad were still living in the tiny apartment on Euclid during this period, but they were also actively house-shopping, going for evening and weekend drives to look at various houses and conferring with real estate agencies. And they were socially active, going out to dinner and movies, visiting friends and even going dancing, which kinda shocked me, since the only time I ever saw my parents dance was at family weddings. And they attended Sunday mass regularly at two nearby churches – Gesu and Holy Rosary. Dad was still out on the road, selling for Gold Medal and General Mills, sometimes gone for 3 to 4 days at a time. Mom kept house, shopped, read, sewed (making dresses for herself and pajamas for Dad) – and wrote in her journal, sometimes noting how tired she was, or that she had napped for a couple hours, feeling guilty.

May 3 – Washed today. Took a shower & got all ready to visit Dr., he not in office.

May 4 – Paid Dr. a visit & $5 – makes $10 total. Wgt. up a little. Blood pressure lower. Beginning to be noticeable. To Weil's and looked at furniture.

And here's an entry that shocked and delighted me. I mean these are my parents, who never went anywhere! But on this night, after an afternoon of shopping with their friend, Kay Brorby –

May 27 – Had dinner together at Stauffer's. Saw "Vivacious Lady" (Ginger Rogers) at Michigan & stage show – Randall sisters singing songs. At hotel, waiting for fellows. Met Clara Curtis, Joyce Wilson, Nella Lehr. Met Glen Lehr & Herman Z. All to Fischer's Alt Heidelberg for beer & dancing. Grand time had by all. Mrs. Lehr's birthday. Jitter-bugs. Rode home with Mel at 2:00. Asleep by 3:00 with my lover.

I mean, what? Mom and Dad, JITTERBUG-ing?!

Jun 3 – Washed hair & took a shower. Went to see Dr. Smith. Everything OK, wgt. 139, bp 104 – may be normally low. Time to feel life.

Jun 8 – Am almost certain that I felt life this morning for the first time.

So. A new life. And Mom did indeed have normally low blood pressure all of her life. Most of her diary entries are hum-drum housekeeping and shopping things – washing (a communal laundry room in their building, so she had find an open time to use the machines), ironing, cleaning, etc. But there was this from Mom's birthday –

Jun 25 – *Ellis gave me beautiful red roses, timer-clock for roaster, H & V stationery, mother-shawl for baby, pillow cases ... 3 of us took bus downtown, saw "3 Blind Mice" & stage show at the Fox. Met Ellis & out to Oasis for chicken dinner. Drinks on Merry-go-round bar. Floor show. Came home & Ellis made good strawberry ice cream. Bed at 2:00.*

And the next day Mom & Dad drove to her folks' in Oakley, packed up the trailer and tent and went camping up near Traverse City until July 7, where they fished and swam and played golf and enjoyed themselves. Upon their return they learned that their FHA loan had been approved and that construction could begin soon on a new house at their lot on Appoline. At mom's next doctor visit she weighed in at 142 ½, and her bp was 108. She began taking "phos-cal" tablets. Life went on as usual, except now whenever Dad was home, they would drive out to their lot to inspect progress on their new house, and they also began shopping for furniture and appliances for their "dream house come true." Dad was still on the road quite a lot of the time. In mid-August he headed north and visited several small towns and "20 CCC camps," traveling over 1,100 miles that week. (The CCC was, of course, the Civilian Conservation Corps.) And Dad's brother, Ken, stayed with them off-and-on that summer and early fall while he was looking for work in Detroit. On October 11th Mom writes that she "got bassinette, pad & bathinette from Hudson's." The next evening they made another visit to the new house, which was nearing completion. There are no entries for the next three days, and then, finally –

Oct 16 – *(Sunday) Awakened at 7 with first labor pains. Called Dr., took shower and came to hospital at 10:30. Had initial preparation for delivery & spent the day in a lovely room. Ellis with me most of time. Read story & did nails, talked with nurses. Light dinner at 5. Ellis went out to house, couldn't get in. Back at 7 & waited for me on 3rd floor. Richard Ellis, 8 ½ lbs. born at 9:10 P.M. I came downstairs at 9:45 to my Sweet Lover & he had the loveliest flowers here for me – and Dickie. Told me about the house. He looked so sweet to me. He went home & called the folks, wired Bud, & wrote his folks. I went to sleep right away & slept hard all night – so relieved & so happy. I'd seen my baby right away & Honey saw him too.*

The next several days were filled with visitors, flowers, cards, etc. and a few entries about initial difficulties nursing the baby, but then everything got easier, and on October 25 she writes, "Came home to new house. Proud Grandma carried Richard." And her mother stayed to help until the 30th, after which one of Mom's neighbors brought over her housekeeper to help Mom out some. During that week –

Oct 28 – Ellis brings news he may get transferred to Chicago.

And then the boom was lowered for good –

Nov 1 – Now very definite that we go to Chicago ... Talked to Klei & Charles about selling the house.

There are no more entries in Mom's 1938 diary, but she wrote about those days in a journal over sixty years later –

I had 10 "luxury days" in hospital with Richard. He was cared for in the nursery & brought to me for feedings. I spent the whole time in bed, waited on hand & foot & even bed-panned. You'd think giving birth made one an invalid, & it nearly did, as we mothers didn't even touch our feet to the floor. On the 9th day we could sit on the side of the bed and "dangle our feet." On the 10th day those feet went all prickly as we stood briefly to be helped into a wheelchair & baby put in our arms – to be taken home, with all our "loot" – flowers, gifts & magazines, & suitcase with pretty nighties & robe, etc.

Providence was a huge old house converted to a Catholic hospital. The mothers' ward had been an enormous living room, with Mother Seton watching over us from her picture above the fireplace. One of my roommates was from Maple Grove, east of Chesaning & we knew some of the same people. We all were so young & confident & planned to stay in touch, but before December I was in Chicago and never heard from any of them again.

Mom writes a bit more about the scant six weeks she spent in their Detroit dream house, noting that her mother stayed with her & Richard for a week, and then a live-in mother's helper, an older woman whose name she could not recall, came to stay until they moved.

So I & Richard & my mom were the only occupants of that "dream house" for the first week. I was torn between being happy for Ellis's upward climb on "the ladder of success," & being sad for "losing" our home. But not much time to be sad – a new baby I think always makes one glad. Post-partum depression was not yet in our stash of words anyway ... This lady went home weekends when Ellis came back. She was much more knowledgeable about babies than I, since she was a grandmother. When Richard cried & he wasn't hungry & he wasn't wet & would not be comforted by rocking, she said, "Have you got any whiskey in the house?" It happened a wedding present of a bottle of 4 Roses was in the cupboard & had never been opened. A square of white cloth from my sewing basket was made into a "sugar tit" & wetted with the whiskey. Well, with that as a pacifier, Baby soon went to sleep – for quite some time.

I found this anecdote about whiskey as a "baby calmer" very relatable, as thirty-plus years later, when my wife and I were at wit's end about our first baby's endless crying at night, our doctor gave us similar advice – a teaspoon of whiskey in his night bottle. And, of course, it worked. He slept through the night. But he was very wobbly and woeful-looking the next morning, and we never did it again.

The transfer to Chicago was an important promotion for Dad, but the timing was terrible. The news must have been met with mixed feelings. Their "dream house come true" at 17187 Appoline Street would have to be sold, after just six weeks of living there (and Dad was already working in Chicago and only came home on weekends by train), and they would have to pull up whatever shallow roots they'd established and leave the many friends they'd made in Detroit, not to mention moving farther away from their parents and family. On November 12th Dad wrote a letter of farewell to his colleagues in the Detroit office and very soon after that, Mom, Dad, and "Dickie" (who later became Richard, and then just Rich) set off for Chicago. Their next home would be at 7629 Eastlake Terrace, a high-rise apartment building right on Lake Michigan. I found this letter written from there to Dad, back in Detroit on a business trip, her last missive from 1938.

Dec 15   Wed nite, 10:00 –

Darling — Received your two sweet letters today and just had to let you know that Richard and I are loving you much as ever and counting the hours until we see you Friday night. Right now Richard is coo-ing to himself in his basket in the bedroom preparatory to going to sleep. I went shopping down Howard Street today but didn't get nearly all the things I had on my list. Mrs. Lindner stayed with Richard – she's very nice. I've been addressing Christmas cards tonight – writing notes & letters in some of them. Had another nice letter from your mother today.

Thought you'd like to be reminded that Ken's birthday is this week – Wednesday – that's today. Rather tired – so guess I'll be retiring. Good night, Sweetheart. Til Friday. Love you, Daisy & Richard xx

P.S. I looked at baby carriages & beds in the Juvenile shop today. They are open evenings until Christmas. D.

There is an incomplete journal for 1939, but it contains only a few entries, one noting on January 16th that Richard is 3 months old and is 14 lbs and 25 inches. Then on January 19th she has a letter from a realtor who is quite "sure she can sell the house." And the last entry in the journal, on January 20th, says only, "Ellis drove car downtown to sell." And so the "dream house" they only occupied for a matter of weeks will be sold, and so will their car, which Dad apparently decided they wouldn't need during their sojourn in the Windy City. General Mills, in turns out, was most generous in covering all the packing and moving expenses. But that realtor may have been overly optimistic, because things were hard for quite a while in Chicago, and mom remembered that and more in her journal from 2006 –

We were stretched pretty thin for money. For 8 months we paid our Chicago apartment rent plus our Detroit house payments. Our dream house was like an albatross around our necks for 8 months. After the house finally sold, Ellis's boss asked him to figure out how much extra the move had cost him "house-wise," and he was reimbursed for that amount by General Mills. We took some of the money from our car sale and splurged. We bought a movie camera & projector & screen – and supplies to develop our box camera pictures with bathroom as darkroom. We also bought a console radio-record player, which all was a great source of entertainment. Of course Richard was the main subject of our movies and our snapshots ... Our parish church (in Rogers Park?) was St. Jerome's, about a mile or more inland from Eastlake Terrace. One of us would walk to an early Sunday mass, and the other would put Rich in his carriage & walk to meet the one returning from church, give Rich over & go on to the next mass. We did that for a year or more, then all went together.

We found a most friendly group of neighbors in our apartments – nearly all with 1 or 2 young children. A 3-story apt, U-shaped with an inner court & a wide slab back porch 10 or 12 feet up from the water & steps down one side to a sandy beach. It does seem now like we spent all our two summers on that sandy beach & back porch, and the rest of the year walking the babies in their carriages and/or watching them play in that inner court with its gazebo. Moms & little ones were often together at the children's birthday parties. We have movies of them all at Rich's 1st birthday party – the littlest performing by walking straight into the whirring camera.

1939-1940: Chicago - Lake Michigan

Mom goes on to talk about the various young families they socialized with there at Eastlake Terrace – the Rosdells, the McDonalds, the Harbaughs, the Pinkertons, the Stockdales and the Hoffmans (who had a sailboat), as well as the building's superintendent, Gus Van der Voorde, a Belgian immigrant who lived in the basement apartment with his family. But there was a rather frightening period with Rich that she remembers too.

Rich took his first steps when he was 1 year old. He did some walking for a few weeks, then took to creeping again, then to dragging one leg and crying like it hurt him. We took him to our Dr and found he had rheumatic fever. For treatment we were to keep him in the bathtub of warm water as much of the time as we could, plus a Rx of bitter white powders (could it have been sulfa?), each dose in a twist of paper, which we gave him in a teaspoon of applesauce or other strained food. It seems I hung over that bathtub all the time I was not doing absolutely necessary housework. But he did recover with no damage to the heart and was walking again at 16 months ...

But we had 2 wonderful years – Dec '38 – '39 and '40. After two years in the General Mills Loop offices, Ellis was promoted back to the Detroit office as Supervising Salesman. Besides spending time riding with each salesman, he planned & conducted the sales meetings to hype up all those salesmen to sell more Wheaties & Softasilk cake flour & GMKT Gold Medal flour, etc.

Dad was transferred back to the Detroit office sometime early in 1941, and their second child, my brother Bill (William Julius, named for his two grandfathers), was born in Detroit at Mount Carmel Mercy Hospital in March of that year. This time they rented at 17140 Prairie Street, a roomy townhouse (which may have been a duplex).

1941: Detroit – Daisy, Rich and Bill

1941: Detroit – Ellis, Rich and Bill

There is a long "pause" in Mom's diaries, journals and letters following their return to Detroit. The U.S. entered the war at the end of 1941, which would have changed everything for most folks, but there are no notes or journals from the war years at all. I suspect life just became too busy with two small children to care for – and then before long there were three, when my brother Bob (Robert Edward) was born in October of 1942. And, soon after that, the Bazzett circumstances were to change even more. Because, sometime in early 1943, Dad apparently decided he'd had enough of the rat-race of corporate life. I'm sure he talked it all over in detail with Mom, and, in the end, he resigned from General Mills. As Mom explained it to me decades later, Dad had never liked the days on the road selling, and he didn't much like planning and conducting sales meetings or the constant "contests" and competition between the regional offices either. She said he'd been offered another promotion in 1943, but it would have meant another move, this time to the Minneapolis-St. Paul area, and, after living in both Detroit and Chicago, neither of them really had the stomach for yet another big city area. "We were both small-town raised, "Mom explained, "and we wanted to get back to that kind of living." So Dad went back to the kind of work he'd been doing when he and Mom met. He found work at a grain elevator in the small village of Potterville, south of Lansing, and they bought a forty-acre farm nearby, where they kept some chickens and a cow and planted a big garden. There are some pictures, but no diaries from the two years they lived in Potterville, though Mom did seem to have fond memories of that time. And in January of 1944 I was born, son number four, at the Hayes-Green-Beach Hospital in Charlotte. I wonder if Mom, in all her romantic dreams and yearnings during their four-year courtship, ever imagined that in just six short years, she would give birth to four boys. I have no memories of the Potterville place, because in the spring of 1945, they sold the farm and moved north. Dad and his Carson City friend, Mick Churchill, formed a business partnership to buy the Kent Elevator and Seed Company in Reed City, a small town in northwestern Michigan, seventy miles due north of Grand Rapids.

Dad found us an old house on the north end of Reed City, in the Holdenville neighborhood, which they bought using a short-term loan from Mom's parents. Initially there was no indoor plumbing, just an outhouse and a pump out back, but Dad had plumbing and an indoor bathroom installed after the first year we lived there. There was no central heating either, just an oil-burning stove in the living room, and a stove in the kitchen too, of course. There were four bedrooms upstairs, but all were unheated, save the one over the living room, warmed through a ceiling vent. Initially we all slept downstairs, using a large front room as a 'bunkhouse' for the four boys, with Mom and Dad sleeping in a small alcove off that room, separated by a heavy curtain.

1945: Potterville – Tim, Bob, Bill and Rich

I was about one and a half when we moved to Reed City, so my first memories are from that Holdenville house, where we lived until 1952. I wrote about those early memories and more in my own first memoir, Reed City Boy, where more information can be found on those years.

But our family was not yet completed. My sister, Mary Jane, was born in the Reed City Hospital in 1951, and my younger brother, John Christopher, in 1953. But there is a short, incomplete diary from 1946, the only one Mom kept during the Holdenville years. It actually begins with an entry from December 30th of 1945, noting in a matter-of-fact manner –

Ellis went to Mass. My knees very sore from being frozen last Sunday – walked to church at 20 below zero.

She doesn't say why she had to walk to church, but perhaps their vehicle was unreliable. In a January 7th entry she tells us –

Sold Ford for $250. Bought 3 years ago for $150.

Other entries are mostly about her daily tasks of washing, mending, cooking and caring for her four boys. But then, for February 18th, in the final entry of that 1946 diary, tucked between notes about visiting with Mrs. Roggow, the neighbor woman, and the boys all playing outside, she makes the cryptic comment, "Crocheted baby jackets." And then there are no more entries in that diary. I was two at the time.

Decades later, Mom would tell us of a miscarriage she suffered in Holdenville. Dad was at work and she was bleeding heavily, so she called the doctor's office. Our doctors at the time were the Kilmer brothers. Dr Paul Kilmer was the older brother, who helped raise and send his younger brother, David, through college and medical school. It was Dr David who came to the house that day, Mom said. He told her he needed to get her to the hospital, so she staunched the bleeding as best she could with towels. She recalled feeling embarrassed, not because of her own situation, but because Dr David had a new car and she was afraid she might ruin his seat covers. So that was probably her first miscarriage. And then, in 1949, there was a still birth. That pregnancy my siblings and I are all very aware of because there is a stone for that little boy, our brother, Thomas, on the Bazzett cemetery plot. It was an event Mom obviously never forgot, because some fifty years later, she wrote this short paean to Tommy, which I found in her papers after her death, clipped to a photograph of a small black rocker, which had once belonged to her mother.

"Rocking Chair"

I rocked all my babies in this chair – even Tommy, who was "born silent." Our Timmy Jim was five and already in school. I so looked forward to having another baby. When my work was caught up, I would sit in this little black rocker and sing a lullaby to the new little one. I have always been thankful and blessed that little Tommy did get rocked and loved, because on the day after Christmas he arrived only to leave us. I had got a book on natural childbirth and was doing very well, with nothing to put me to sleep, when suddenly an ether cone was clamped on my face. Doctor Kilmer knew the baby could never breathe. When I awoke in the hospital bed, the nurse very gently told me my baby boy was dead. I wanted to see him and hold him. They tried to tell me it was best I not see him at all. But finally, in a dim light, he was brought to me, wrapped in a soft blanket with only his sleeping face showing. And I held him in my arms.

I wept when I read this. I still do. Because we all know how much my mom loved children, and especially babies. So, after this terrible disappointment, the subsequent births of my sister and brother were indeed joyful occasions. And in 1958, the year I attended St Joseph Seminary, a boarding school in Grand Rapids, Mom was pregnant again. I remember her maternity dress, and her excitement, when they came to visit me on parents' day. But she must have miscarried, as there was no baby, and I don't remember much ever being said about it again. Mom was 42 then.

In 1962 I left home for the Army. In 1964, when I was stationed in northern Turkey, Mom's letters informed me that she and Dad had filed paperwork to adopt a ten year-old girl named Cathy, who had spent some time with them at their still new house on West Church. She was quite excited about the prospect, her mothering instincts in high gear. However, much to her disappointment, the adoption process fell through.

And finally, in another journal from 1966, an entry from February 8, , a Tuesday, she notes, "I felt rotten – cramps, headaches, etc." Then, after more comments about doing the ironing, fixing supper, and other housework, says, "Went to bed at 7:30 – 2 aspirin." The next day she notes, "I had bad time & stayed in bed all day." Then she seemed to return to her regular grueling routine of cooking, baking, cleaning and more. On February 16th she notes, again, very matter-of-factly, "I went to Dr Kilmer – confirmed miscarriage – first time he had seen it in woman my age." Mom was four months shy of 50.

I was home from the Army by this time, a full-time student at Ferris State College, where I worked part-time 5-9 every night and all day on Saturdays. So I was usually gone from roughly 7 in the morning until 9:30 at night. So I was pretty much oblivious to what was happening to Mom. In full-on menopause by this time, she continued to suffer from heavy, irregular periods. I only know this now, through her journals. At the time I had no idea. In her journal entry July 12th of 1966, she writes –

Had a D&C surgery Tuesday morning & slept off & on all day. Was very sick each time I lifted my head. Finally Lillian Wood gave me a shot about 8pm that stopped sickness. Then I had toast & milk & juice. Dr Kilmer tells me, "You are Dr Lincoln's patient as I'm not doing any surgery at the hospital now, since I had a 'row' with the scrub room crew." Dr Lincoln tells me, "I'm doing this surgery as a favor to Dr Kilmer – you're really his patient." So I feel like nobody's child, tho they both come in & visit with me. it's really so good to be with all the people you know – nurses, Drs & friends – Laura Couture, Dorothy Stanton, Ann Erbes, Mrs Chess, Lillian Wood, Mrs Sager, such a pretty Faye Atkinson from Baldwin, etc.

Comments like these were just "so Mom," always self-deprecating, and putting the best face on a difficult and awkward situation. Mom was over fifty by this time and was coming through a very stressful and difficult time, physically and emotionally, coping for months with Dad's mother, my Grandma Bazzett, who had been living with them since Grandpa's death in September of 1965. Grandma began a rather rapid descent into dementia during that time and soon became unable to care for herself. But Mom tried valiantly to keep her comfortable, at a high price to her own health. Finally, on the recommendation of Dr Paul Kilmer, Grandma was placed at Lakeview Manor, a nursing home in Cadillac, where she lived until her death in 1967.

Mom's child-bearing years were now behind her, but she never lost her love for children and babies, and always loved visiting and visits from her many grandchildren and great-grandchildren. She could have been so many things, my mom, but she chose to be a wife and a mother.

Not so many years ago, after my wife and I retired back here to Reed City, I asked Mom if she ever regretted not staying in teaching, or doing other things. She smiled and said, "Why, no, never. I always thought I was doing the most important job there was, raising you kids. And I tried to teach you all that I could too." And she meant it.

But Mom did yearn to travel – and she did. She and Dad made three trips to Europe. In 1965 when Rich and I were both living in Germany, they visited us there, bought a Volkswagen and drove all over Europe for nearly six weeks. They came again in 1978, when I was again stationed in Germany with the Army, to meet our latest addition to the family, Susan Elizabeth. And again they toured Europe, with a week in Ireland.

Mom could have been a fine writer too. I found a few attempts among her papers. This was an unfinished poem fragment –

"A Mother's Dreams"

Her first-born son's a wanderer
No ties can hold him down
And she recalls how once she dreamed
Of distant roads and towns.

Her love of music echoes now
When Bill strums his guitar ...

Bronzed runners on their pedestals
Attest to Bobby's speed
Her dreams once ran with Mercury
Her feet were winged indeed.

Her gifted fourth son now employs
The pen she laid aside
To raise a brood of noisy boys
Now scattered far and wide.

The headstone of small Tommy Gene
Gleams with a somber hue
Once she dreamed of Heaven
Did all her dreams come true?

Or –

Tom sleeps now in a soldier's grave
Oh, God, why was he killed?
Once you dreamed of Heaven
Now all your dreams are filled.

Years later, Mom obviously still thought about her stillborn son, Tommy, and realized that he would have been prime cannon fodder for the Vietnam war. The other verses my brothers – and I – could easily understand. Richard, Mom's "first-born" was indeed a wanderer. Discharged from the Army overseas in 1965, he never really came home again, working most of his life in Europe and Asia. Sadly he died in 2001, at just 62, a cancer victim.

Mom's faith remained important to her, albeit somewhat modified from what it was when she was young. Here is a short essay she wrote which reflects that –

"Reflections at Christmas 1999"

Happy Birthday, dear little Jesus! And you did have some happy ones, when you were very young – and all you needed was the loving security given by two devoted parents. But each year, as you grew in body and mind – did the inborn knowledge that you were born to die, gradually sadden your birthday celebrations? Did you feel the enormous responsibility that would be yours – to redeem all mankind? Was your sacred heart so bursting with love for all people that your life became a bittersweet gift from you Father? – the sweetness of experiencing the beauty and the joy and the satisfaction of humankind – and the bitterness of knowing that you must relinquish it all in one last great sacrifice? Thank you, dear Jesus, for living and dying for me.

Daisy

Here is another shorter reflection –

Life is risky.
Life is fragile.
Life is precious.
We live it day by day.
Life is not forever.
It is a preparation for the wondrous life to come –
with all our loved ones together again.

216

Mom was a prolific writer her whole life. Her writing took the form of newsy letters to her friends and relatives, and finally to her children and grandchildren. She preferred getting a letter to a phone call, explaining, "When a phone call's over, it's over. A letter you can read over and over again." I regret now that I did not save her many letters. She did save almost all of mine over the years, which I have collected in a private book, *Love, Tim*, which I will leave for my children. I am so grateful that my dad saved her letters from their long courtship. Besides letters, she also tried to keep a family record in the form of diaries and journals. I have found complete or partial diaries and journals for the years 1933-36 (a 5-year Diary), 1938, 1939, 1946, 1958, 1960, 1963, 1964, 1965, 1966, and 1978 (a European diary). And she also worked sporadically on her memoirs after turning 90 in 2006, which resulted in her "Notes from my Nineties," which I will add here as an Appendix.

APPENDIX:
Notes from My Nineties
Daisy Cecelia (Whalen) Bazzett

July 1, 2005 – I am seven days into my 90th year. Never did I "plan" to live this long. But when did life ever go according to plan? I assured my son, Tim, when he gave me these two composition books for my birthday that I would at least begin to write my "memoirs." He suggested that I begin with when I entered college – the fall of 1932. (I may digress, going backwards and forwards – so this may be mostly digressions.)

CSTC – Central State Teachers College in Mt. Pleasant, Michigan.

When I walked into 203 Ronan Hall to meet Helen Critchell, who would share a room with me, she looked me over and figured I was a spoiled rich girl. Why? Because I was carrying a life-size white stuffed toy dog named Fluffy that I set on the floor by my bed, where he was to stay all that year. My other treasured possession was a portable Olivetti typewriter with elite type in its carrying case. Besides typing my assignments it earned me money typing term-papers for girls in the dorm – at 10 cents a page.

Helen Critchell was from Williamsburg, up near Traverse City – eighteen years old, a black-haired, world-wise (in my estimation), sparkling-eyed beauty. No doubt the exact opposite of Daisy Whalen in those attributes. But we must have complemented each other in many ways, as we lived together four years in that dorm in harmony. I can't remember us ever having a serious argument.

Helen's mother, Nellie, was a widow, whose husband, an engineer, had died when they lived in Spokane, Washington, after some years in Sand Point, Idaho. After her husband's death, Nellie had moved with her children – Helen and her brother, Donald – back to her old home, the Boyd family farm near Williamsburg to live with Helen's two maiden aunts. Helen's Aunt Leah Boyd spent her whole working life caring for patients at the Traverse City State Hospital. Aunt Mary Boyd spent her life keeping house on the family farm. Helen's mother, Nellie Boyd Critchell, also worked in Traverse City, at the Globe department store, in ready-to-wear. So, with her mom's employee discount and sewing expertise, Helen was always very well-dressed. Brother Donald had already earned his teaching certificate, and he and his wife, Elsie, were both teachers.

Even lacking a father, Helen's life sounded idyllic to me. The Boyd farm had its own lake down the lane where she swam all summer. She had a boy-friend at home, Earl Ridgeway, and a cousin at Central, Tommy Boyd, who was her first of a succession of beaus "at school."

Helen, who had a nickname of "Billie," had been very popular in high school, as the new kid on the block, and enjoyed a great deal of freedom as only Aunt Mary was home to supervise her activities most of the time.

I had just turned sixteen on June 25th of that year, after I graduated from Chesaning High School, class of 1932. Looking back, I know now that I'd lived a very sheltered life in the small town of Oakley, and some years on the Whalen farms, a mile west of Oakley. My father, William Whalen, had been a rural mail carrier out of Oakley since I was five years old. I had two older brothers: Harold, six years older, and Clarence, two and a half years older than I.

I knew how to dust (my very first job – and I still hate to dust), wash dishes, do plain cooking, sweep and vacuum, make beds and help with all the housework. But I was never over-worked. I did what my mother asked and then would spend my time reading. "Daisy always has her nose stuck in a book" was one of my mother's frequent descriptions of me – very apt, which was probably why it soon became known, in my early freshman days at Central, that I had the highest IQ of anyone who had ever entered the school. No doubt it all came from the extensive reading I'd done – as the test was based on "book-learning." Which you may have guessed left me woefully ignorant in other ways – especially of the social graces – and in practical knowledge. Not only had I read all the books in our high school library, but I had discovered when I was still in grade school that I could request (I thought) any book title (in the world?) and have it mailed to me from the State Library in Lansing. And all it cost me was the return postage, which was pennies. So I had books coming and going constantly. Besides that we had newspapers – the Saginaw Daily News and the Chesaning Argus weekly – and magazines: Peoples Popular Monthly, Colliers, Saturday Evening Post, Literary Digest, Reader's Digest, and Ladies' Home Journal. I read everything I could get my hands on, including the little folders that came in Jell-0, and the tiny stories of Nikki Norge the Princess, that came in some other grocery product.

So it was no wonder I scored high on the IQ test, which I now realize didn't really make me as smart as or smarter than any other of the 700-plus students at Central. I just luckily (?) had more book-learning. (I find, in consulting my 1933 Chippewa year book, that the whole class of 230 freshmen "had the enviable record of having the highest intelligence rating of any class ever to enter Central." Maybe I helped bring up the class average (?) Unfortunately all those records were destroyed when the CSTC training school burned.)

In any case, my "reputation" set me apart to a certain extent – the entire faculty recognized me by name, and I was looked on with a bit of awe by some of the students. I lived up to my rep and earned all A's in my first year. So – on the strength of that rep, Helen and I were both "rushed" by all four of the women's Literary Societies (forerunners of sororities): Warriner Lit, Rachel Tate, Lucy A. Sloan, and Ronan Round Table. At the rushing parties the girls looked us over. I'm sure Helen would have made it, but we were already a package deal – and we were not invited to join any of the elite groups. But we must have improved our image some – or maybe I did acquire some social graces – because the next year we were invited and joined Ronan Round Table. And, wonder of wonders, the year after that I was elected president, which I'm sure was not due to any executive ability, but simply to the fact that I got along with everyone and had no enemies.

Helen and I also joined other campus clubs, like Mercier (now the Newman Club), which was open to all Catholic students. We also joined the Cliophiles, for History students (majors and minors), and the French Club when we took French. And the Appleblossom Club, which was mainly for rural teachers, but their activities were usually fun, and we were looking for fun. Groups of Appleblossom "entertainers" went by bus to give programs at rural one-room schools, with department head, Dr. M.L. Smith giving a talk, "Better Schools for Country Children," along with one or two plays, and some music. We were in the girls' chorus. I was a second soprano, which I think meant I couldn't go very high or very low, but was willing. "Baby's Boat's the Silver Moon" and "O Sole Mio" were two songs in our repertoire. The bus rides were fun and there were always great refreshments to end the evening. This happening every week or so may have been one reason why my 5' 9" frame filled out that first year from 115 to 135 pounds.

The other reason was the excellent food at the dorm. We had ample breakfasts and lunches cafeteria style – and delicious formal dinners each night.

We had to "dress" for dinner, and we gathered in the two parlors on the first floor until the dining room doors opened at 6 PM. It was really part of our social training. Usually we visited while waiting, and someone played *the piano and we'd gather round and sing too, maybe for a half-hour or so. There was no mad rush when the doors opened.*

Each week we sat at a different table, with the girl at the head acting as hostess. At first we were assigned to tables. Later there was a sign-up sheet posted and we could choose our own groups at tables.

One special table always had Mrs. ("Gracie") Frear, our social director and business manager, who had her own apartment and office in the dorm, and Miss Lois Trefethen, the dietitian (later Mildred Omlor) who lived there too, and the resident doctor, a very meek retiring little woman (which is probably why I can't remember her name), and three girls who rotated each week. It was a somewhat questionable honor to be seated at this table.

We filed in and stood behind our chairs until all were in place, then sang one verse of "Praise God from Whom All Blessings Flow," and then were seated. There were six plates in front of the table hostess. (All had turns at being hostess.) A white-uniformed waitress (a dorm girl working for her board) brought in the main dish of meat, along with side dishes of potatoes and vegetable. The hostess put a serving of meat on a plate, passed it to the next girl, who served the potatoes, to the next one, who served the vegetable, and passed them on until everyone was served. Only then did we pick up our silver and begin to eat. We had white tablecloths and white cloth napkins – all very formal. Our waitresses (Dorothy Cox and Esther Haksluoto) removed the dishes when we were finished to the tray on a folding stand and carried them to the rear of the dining room where they went onto the dumb-waiter down to the basement kitchen whence the food had come. Then after a brief pause dessert was brought in and served. We had milk or water for a beverage.

There would be some time for talk after the meal. One thing we did once in a while was to "lift the table." We found that the heavy wooden table came up easily when each of us put our two forefingers under the table edge, breathed together – "1-2-3, LIFT" – and up it came, light as a feather. (Try it. It works!) Only when the social director had stood and said an after-meal prayer did we finally rise and exit the dining room.

Sadly, at the end of my freshman year, the dining room closed, and we dorm girls bought our meals at the college cafeteria, 3rd Floor west in the Administration Building.

That first year Helen was one of the lucky ones to have a job in the dorm dining room – at breakfast or lunch, which was cafeteria style. We took a tray and went through the line and could take whatever we wanted – a great temptation to overeat.

I was assigned a job "secretary-ing" for Coach Lodewyk and Coach Parker during my first year, which I really liked doing, using my high school skills of shorthand and typing.

The next year Helen and I both had jobs in the college cafeteria, working for the Newtons, Fred and "Mrs." I never knew her first name. It's signed in my yearbook, but I can't decipher it. Helen worked serving hot dishes at the steam table on the line. I went in early and made salads and put them on small plates in the "cold" section of the line – and then kept replacing them as they were picked up. I made big bowls of "tossed" vegetable salad and fruit salad, and some "fancy" little salads of prunes stuffed with cream cheese and walnuts, and others I can't now recall. There was tuna salad too, and tomatoes, egg salad in a lettuce cup, etc.

Mrs. Newton always put onions in her vegetable salads. Some fussy people going through the line would ask, "Are there onions in this?" I was instructed to answer, "I'll go and find out" – and not come back until they'd picked up their salad and moved on.

"What they don't know won't hurt them," Mrs. Newton would say. The boys and girls who worked together in the big kitchen – boys mostly washing dishes – got to be friends. One big football player, Bill Diekman, liked me, I know (the way one knows these things), and I liked him, but nothing ever came of it, mainly because back then none of us ever had any extra money – or time. A girl named Catherine was the cashier, which consisted mostly of punching meal tickets. She lived with the Newtons and babysat their children some in return for her room and board.

Sometimes there were banquets or dinners for different organizations that the Newtons catered in the after-hours in the dining room or adjoining women's commons. And five or six of the girls who worked the cafeteria would serve in our white uniforms. It was always a job we looked forward to, as we got real money for that, doled out to us by Mrs. Newton – sometimes as much as $3 for an evening! There were Helen and I, Doris Sheldon, Vonnie Wilcox and Dorothy Cox.

I never had to pay tuition, as I had a scholarship for my first year – which was renewed each year. As I recall, it was only $100 per term – or per year, I'm not sure. It doesn't sound like much now, but in the 30's $100 was not easy to come by. None of us ever had much money. We paid our room rent at the dorm business office at the start of each term. My mother would sometimes send me an extra dollar or two in a letter, which was always a treat.

One time Helen and I walked downtown on a Saturday and shopped at Penney's. We must have both been flush, as we bought matching dresses, dark *red knit with long sleeves and a "bow" neckline. They were quite clingy and form-fitting. We enjoyed being twins when we wore them. Cost us each $2.*

I learned a great deal about personal hygiene from my roommates and observations in our communal bathroom. I'd never shaved under my arms (or needed to), or used an underarm deodorant, or washed my hair in a shower – or used a shower at all. On 2nd Floor North that first year, the bathroom was right across the hall from our room. Among the upper class girls who lived in the west end of the hall were roommates Marge Scheper, Phyllis King (P.K.), and Ruthie Feinberg (who each owned a fur coat to wear to football games); Nedra Walcutt, a lovely dreamy-eyed Grace Kelly type; a short-haired blonde whirlwind of energy, Marian Horton; and Rosalie Cunningham, a dark-eyed Mata Hari-looking brunette. And our freshman suite-mates were Margaret Hahn and Margaret Benson, from Owosso and Flint – who quickly became simply Hahn and Benny.

The suite doorway from the hall opened into a small entry with two rooms opening from it. Each room was furnished with two single beds with simple metal rods at head and foot and link springs, a double desk with a chair on each side, two desk lamps, center drawers and end shelves for books – plenty of room for two to study. Plus one larger wooden chair to share. We also shared a large closet, each side of which had a large shelf and a clothing rod, and there were two towel bars on the inside of the closet door. And there was a mirror and dresser in which we each had a small top drawer and two full-size drawers. Plenty of room for all I had – very neatly stored.

The bathroom had six sinks with mirrors, one bathtub in a cubicle, one shower stall, and four toilets with doors and dividers. It will no doubt horrify present-day young readers to know that no one then took daily showers, and we only washed our hair once a week. Showers were usually Saturdays or evenings, and tub-baths were only luxuriated in before serious dates.

I was an early riser, and was usually one of the first in the bathroom mornings, quite often with Nedra Walcutt. Helen preferred to sleep as long as possible, squeezing in a hurried last-minute bathroom trip. While Helen had shining black hair (we brushed our hair then every day), mine was sort of a dishwater blonde. I'd had golden curls as a little girl that darkened as I got older. I spent time and money on Blondex shampoo that had to be left on for a time during a shower, but I can't say that it ever did much good. I was pleased when my hair became "light brown" in later years.

I learned to paint pink Odor-O-No on my underarms with a sponge applicator, to use nail polish, and a bit of lipstick, rouge and face powder. I could do my hair in waves and pin curls – and even did Helen's for her, and sometimes did other girls' hair for 10 cents, especially before parties.

Some girls sent their laundry home in the mail and had it returned the same way. But we had a laundry in the dorm basement with built-in cement washtubs and hot and cold water. I had a small washboard that I used for scrubbing anything really dirty, and my own bag of clothespins for hanging things to dry on the lines that criss-crossed the half the large basement room. Our bed linens were furnished for us, dropped off at our doors once a week, and our "dirty" sheets and pillowcases were picked up at the same time. We only had to remember to strip our beds on that morning. If we didn't, the linens would not be exchanged. We made up our own beds.

There were also three sewing machines and a large "cutting table" available. I took three sewing classes at Central, and bought material at 10-to-20 cents a yard, and made some dresses for myself in my second and third years there. My mother had always sewed for me, but never let me use her sewing machine. (I can't remember that I ever really wanted to!) She'd say, "You wash the dishes and sweep. I'll sew this afternoon." She made my pajamas and dresses and skirts and blouses. I found out at Central that I really enjoyed sewing my own clothes. One of my first major purchases when I had a teaching job was a Singer sewing machine in its own maple cabinet, for $80, which I still use. Just five years ago my Singer had some things not working right – making sparks, etc. We took it to Julie Ann Fabrics in Cadillac and had it "overhauled." It came back in "like-new" condition, and cost me $88.82, or 10% more than its original cost – but worth it!

A bonus from having friends in the dorm was access to a more varied wardrobe. We traded clothes – not too easy for someone as tall as I. But June Shelander (from LeRoy) and I were the same size. I can't remember that I had much to offer, but June had a great selection of clothes and was very generous with me. I learned that a seamstress came to their home for an extended stay – once a year, I think – and sewed for the whole family, for June and her little sister, Alice, and for their brothers too. One dress I remember with affection I borrowed a lot – a fine brown wool crepe two-piece. It had a side-zipper skirt and a top with long sleeves and a front neck opening that laced with brown ribbon. I wore it one fall Sunday when Margaret (Peg) Emery (from Belding) had her steady boyfriend, Judd Vanderlip (from Gowen) up for the day. Judd had brought a friend along, and Peg invited me to double-date with them. My date was the son of the owner of the Greenville refrigerator plant. I can't remember his name anymore, but do recall that he was very good-looking, with curly dark hair.

We had fun that day. One thing we did was to drive over to Oil City where *we ran up and down the metal stairs that spiraled up and around the huge cylindrical oil tanks there. That's all I can remember about that date – that and wearing June's brown dress. My mother later made me one that looked nearly the same. She also made me a dark red one-piece long-sleeved dress with a belt and a round neck. I wore several different fancy white collars with that one. Those collars made one or two basic dresses do double- and triple-duty and were very popular. A look through any of my four yearbooks proves this, as many of the girls in group pictures arrayed in these varied-pattern multi-use white collars.*

I was not allowed to date in high school. According to my father, I was too young (and really was), and had practically no opportunities anyway. Mostly, if there was a school party of any kind, my brother Clarence drove, and we went together.

My first year at Chesaning High School (1928-29) I walked to a gas station on the north end of Oakley by the railroad. There, at the corner of Ridge Road and M47, for one dollar a week, I would be picked up by Calvin Criner in his Ford coupe. He lived on the Roy Cole farm a mile and a half west of town. There were no school buses, and I should probably mention too that not everyone went to high school back then. It was almost like going to college is now. Out-of-town kids paid tuition and walked, or found their own ways to school.

I always got to the corner early; I didn't want to miss my ride. I didn't expect he'd wait for me, but I was never late. I waited inside the station and its little store to keep warm in the winter, where "Doc" Jones and his wife Mary were very nice to me. One thing I remember there was a punch-board. For a nickel you could punch out a tiny rolled-up paper that told your prize – usually a stick of gum or a penny candy, but always the chance of the "big prize" – a kewpie doll.

There were two other girls who also frequently rode with us, but didn't pay – Virginia Hill and Lena Belle Clymer. They would just "happen" to be standing by the road in front of their houses when we passed, and Calvin never ignored them, maybe partly because Virginia was so pert and pretty, and so was Lena Belle, with her dark curls and freckles. But with four people in that little coupe it was pretty crowded.

The next year my brother Clarence started high school and my dad bought a second car – a dark green '29 Pontiac for Clarence to drive to school and take paying passengers. (This was in addition to Dad's mail car that he traded each year for a new one – always a Ford or Chevrolet.) Clarence was fourteen and a very good, careful driver. I don't remember if he had (or needed) a driver's license. When the car salesman, Larry Schultz, brought the new car to our house in Oakley, he volunteered to give me a driving lesson. After that my dad took me driving until I was quite proficient, but I never drove that car again, as either my brother or my dad was always there to drive. That car lasted for four years.

James Hillis walked to our house from the west side of town and rode with Clarence and me. And we picked up Mary Gassman a block north, Helen Jones another block north, and Una Hart a half mile east, on that four-mile route to Chesaning. Each paid a dollar a week, which paid for car expenses.

Clarence dropped the five of us off at school, then took the car to Walser's garage, where it was parked inside until he picked it up after school. Then he walked back to school. Dad had made these arrangements so there would be no "ramming around town" – or any temptation to – during the noon hour. I don't think Clarence would ever have don that anyway, as he was always the perfect example of the "good son" – maybe from observing what happened to our older brother, Harold, who was many times the transgressor. But that's another story.

How did Clarence feel about having his little sister – two and a half years younger – a year ahead of him in school? I've wondered about that in recent years, but never had the chance to ask him (and he died in 2006). We didn't talk about feelings then. And maybe he just accepted that that's the way things were. We accepted many things then as children without questioning.

I said I had no dates in high school, but I had one "almost" date. Neil Hoover was a football player, a good-looking boy, with an outthrust jaw a bit like Jay Leno's. He asked me if I could go to the movies with him. We called it "the show." He had his own car and drove it to school, which very few kids did then. He would pick me up at my house in Oakley and we'd go to Owosso (ten miles south) to one of the three theaters there. I told him I'd like to, but I didn't think my father would let me go. He came anyway – knocked on our door early on Friday evening. I greeted him at the door and invited him in. He sat down with the family and talked a while, then asked my father if I could go with him to the show. My father said, "No." We talked a little bit longer, then he said good-night and left. That was that. I wasn't too disappointed since I knew to start with that I couldn't go.

Besides not wanting to see me go out with some hulking football player – no matter how polite – I'm sure my dad figured he took us all to the show on a regular basis. From the time I was six or seven we went once or twice a week. So I wasn't really missing anything by not going with

Neil. There were three theaters in Owosso: the Lincoln (the oldest), the Strand, and, later, the Capital. The Strand always had a cliff-hanger serial on Wednesday nights, besides the features and the comedy. And we never wanted to miss a chapter of that. One I remember vividly was The Indians Are Coming. Sometimes we even got hamburgers after at the Swallow, around the corner east of the Strand. The hamburgers were not in patties. The cook (who was the only one there, probably the owner) stirred the meat loosely around on the griddle with chopped-up onions. Then he held a big bun in a large square of oiled paper and "shoveled" the meat-and-onion mix into it with a big spatula. In my memory, it is still the most delicious "hamburger" I ever tasted, and it cost just ten cents. Part of the joy, I think, was the mouth-watering aroma that filled that tiny room while we were waiting.

Later on there was an unexpected bonus from that "almost date" with Neil Hoover. He worked for a couple years after high school graduation, so, like me, he entered Central as a freshman in 1932. He and Ed Cote, another Chesaning grad, were roommates. So we had a few real dates there, going together to the "lecture" courses, etc. But I think he dropped out after a year when his money was used up.

I also had two or three such dates too with a Chesaning boy named Miller, whose folks had a store, but I can't remember his first name anymore.

And though we never dated, there were two other fellows, roommates from Reed City, I could always count on for dances at the college "mixers" and dorm dances that everyone attended in groups of boys or girls. They were Norman Lincoln and Loren Kilmer. Luckily, both were taller than I, which was quite important to me. Norman became a teacher, and joined the service during the war, then went on to university to become a doctor. He first practiced at Lake Odessa, and then came home to Reed City where he was our family doctor for many years until he retired. Loren came back to Reed City and was a teacher to all my children here at Reed City High School. Sadly, both of them are gone now.

In all honesty I should tell about my very first date at Central, which embarrassed and humiliated me, and that I would rather forget. I still don't like to remember it. But Tim told me to be honest, so here it is.

During orientation week, before classes even began, Helen's cousin, Tommy Boyd, came to the dorm to take Helen to the movies. He brought along his house-mate, Wilbur Boyden, an upperclassman and a football player. As Helen's roommate, I was drafted as Wilbur's blind date. It was a mile walk to the theater downtown, but everyone walked everywhere, so that was no problem. Helen didn't really know any other girls yet. And she didn't really know me very well yet either or she never would have asked me, because I was just about as green as they come – and definitely not good at "small talk."

But the boys bought our tickets and we climbed to our balcony seats. Shortly after the lights went out and the movie started, my "date" left his seat, I assumed to go to the bathroom. But as time went on and the movie progressed I realized to my utter shame that he was not coming back at all. And he didn't. I don't now – and didn't even then – blame him a bit. He had been stuck with a "nothing" date. Needless to say, it was a long walk home to the campus and the dorm for the three of us. I can't recall that Helen ever asked me to "double-date" again. But the next year when I met my future husband and he came to Mount Pleasant every three or four weeks in his Ford roadster with its rumble seat, then we'd take Helen and her date with us.

Helen never lacked for boyfriends. Her first one at Central was Dwight Gover, a local boy whose folks ran Gover's store in town. Then there was Ralph Rawson, from somewhere up in Michigan's thumb, followed at various times by John Coady, Harry Layman and Gerry Rideout. (Some years later, this same Gerry Rideout, who ended up working for Buick in Flint, married one of my best friends from Chesaning High School, Marjorie Devereaux.) One thing I learned from Helen was to never let go of one boyfriend until you had another one lined up for sure.

But that was never a problem for me, as I met Ellis Bazzett in 1933, the summer I turned seventeen, and we "kept company" until our marriage in 1937. After that first summer in Oakley, however, it became a long-distance "affair," when Ellis took a job with General Mills, working out of Grand Rapids, Kalamazoo and Detroit.

He drove a panel truck loaded with General Mills products – GMKT (Gold Medal Kitchen-Tested) flour, Wheaties, and Softasilk cake flour. He called on grocers and took orders for and delivered GM products. One grocer he called on in Greenville was Hendrik Meijer, whose wife, Ellis figured, was the "brains" of the operation, and whose son Fred "was not very smart and would never amount to much."

Ellis told me years later that he didn't really like the job of being a salesman, and dreaded going to work every morning. (He could never understand how our son, Bob, wanted to be and even seemed to enjoy being a salesman.) But he said that once he'd made that first call on a grocer, he was okay for the rest of the day.

His uncle, J.B. Ellis, got him that job. J.B. was a flour salesman for General Mills and called on bakeries all over Michigan's Lower Peninsula. He worked out of the GM office in Detroit, where he lived with his wife, Ella, and six children: Jim, Ed, John, Bob, Mary Ellen, and Tom. Later, our own family paralleled theirs, with Rich, Bill, Bob, Tim, Mary Jane and Chris.

Ellis boarded with J.B.'s family in Detroit for a time before we got married. Not too long after we married and were living in a Murphy bed studio apartment at 830 West Euclid, J.B. prevailed on us to spend a week at their house with the children so he could take Ella with him on a sales trip to northern Michigan up around Traverse City and Petoskey. I can't even imagine now trusting me – the baby of the Whalen family, who'd never even baby-sat any kids – to cook for and look after all their children. Of course, Jim was already going to the University of Detroit, Ed and John were in high school and Bob was in grade school. But Mary Ellen was only three – an adorable doll with golden curls and big blue eyes – and Tom just a tiny two year-old toddler, a sweet baby with brown eyes and dark curls. Of course both were toilet-trained already, as children were then, as soon as they were walking. But Ella showed me how to make an oven-ful of breakfast toast and how to make creamed tuna in large amounts, and then went confidently off on a carefree trip with her husband. Surprisingly – at least to me – all worked out fine, as the older boys followed their routines, and they and Ellis helped with the little ones in the evenings. If I had been more experienced and known all the things that could go wrong in such a busy household, I might not have been so confident in my role as substitute Mom. But I did learn things in that week that stood me in good stead many years later – like how large families could keep things running smoothly by each one doing his share of the work and helping each other when needed.

It was a wonderful time, that summer of 1933, when Ellis and I met and began dating. He had worked in Lansing for Ed Maloney at a Christian Breisch elevator, and, when an elevator in Carson City owned by the same company needed a manager, Ellis was sent, first to Middleton, then to Carson City to do the job. Then when the manager position at the Oakley elevator needed filling, he came to Oakley. He was 23 that summer and I was 17, with a year of college already "under my belt."

I'd seen Ellis in church, sitting a few seats ahead of me. He had the most clean-looking back-of-the-head ever. My mother bought butter and cream from Belle Gower, who lived in a lovely big square red brick house (with indoor plumbing) on the south edge of Oakley and had a big garden with berries, and a Jersey cow. It was like a very small farm. Ellis roomed and boarded there. Belle took pride in "setting a good table," and the food was good enough that Ellis even went "home" there for lunch each day, as it was only two blocks from the big tall red elevator. On Fridays Belle made homemade ice cream for a treat, as her Catholic boarder couldn't eat meat on Friday in those days. She thought Ellis was pretty special, and kept telling him what a nice girl Daisy Whalen, the mail-carrier's daughter, was. He had gone out with Anna Ruzeka a few times, and even with my cousin, Miriam Mickles, when she was staying a few weeks with our Grandma Mickles, who lived right on the main street in Oakley.

I did take some walks straight west from our house – across Main Street, past the row of cement block houses, on past the red elevator (there was also a "black elevator" a block north), and down a two-track trail to the Oakley cemetery, where I picked roses growing in the empty part of the graveyard – always hoping to see (or be seen by) the young elevator manager. And I was, as I learned later. The lone employee, Joe Stasek, teased Ellis about it.

Then one weekend my mother and dad went to a relative's funeral in Grand Rapids and stayed overnight there. Before leaving, however, Mom told Clarence and me we could have some young people over Saturday evening. So Clarence cranked out some homemade ice cream and I made a cake, and we invited Sayde Yarabek and Ellis and a few others and had a party. I think we played cards, and spent some time outside too. I don't remember who else was there really, as "I only had eyes for" Ellis – and vice-versa. The next day he took me and Clarence and his date in his roadster with a rumble seat to a Chesaning park where we went swimming in the Shiawassee River where there was a springboard over the river. I had taken a term of swimming at Central and had learned to swim – and to dive off the edge of the pool, head down and thumbs hooked together. So I was very confident when I dived off the board, but not prepared at all for the bounce. I hit the water in a belly-flopper – not very graceful, I'm sure. It felt like my head and heels almost touched and something broke in the middle of my back. But do you think I let on that it hurt? Of course not! So we did go on swimming – but with no more diving on my part.

After that weekend, Ellis and I went somewhere once or twice a week for the rest of the summer, sometimes with another couple in the rumble seat. The most fun we had was at dances at Kimmel's Grove, somewhere east of Chesaning. There was a lane off the road that led to a pasture on the Kimmel farm with a grove of trees in one corner where a large wooden dance floor had been built, and there was an "orchestra" with an accordion, drums, banjo, etc. There was always a big crowd there on Friday and Saturday nights. I remember one night giving Steve Potucek a ride home. He rode along with us, and all the way, out of deference for a smooching couple, hung his head out the window, singing "Somebody Loves You."

Somebody loves you,
I want you to know
Longs to be near you wherever you go
Somebody loves you, Sweetheart, can't you see?
And that some-body is me-ee.

Steve lived next door to Una Hart, with his sisters Anna and Mary, and they all went to Oakley school with me.

If you're wondering about all the foreign names, let it be known that the farms in the Oakley area were first settled mainly by the Irish, with names like Whalen, Ryan, Brennan, Welch, Carmody, Coyne, McPhillips, Keyes, McCartney, etc. The old back part of St. Michael's Catholic cemetery is filled with stones bearing those names. The newer front part of the cemetery has more names like Stasek, Yarabek, Vitous, Agnetta, Kuchar, Sivak, Galbavi, Bila, Basoski, etc. While the first and some of the second generation Irish settled the land and worked the farms, the third generation pretty much moved to the cities and took factory jobs, and the farms were sold to the Slovaks, Hungarians, Bohemians, and Polish – all immigrants who came over from the "old country," and were willing to work hard to own land. Many of the Irish, I must admit, were not that ambitious. Meaning no disrespect, we often called these newer arrivals Hunkies, Polocks, Bohunks, and so on.

It was a lovely summer – that summer of my first and only lifelong love. Ellis, with a background of growing up on a farm, enjoyed doing business with the farmers. One morning he came to work to find the office had been broken into and the safe cracked open. But the robber had found only the account books, as every night the young manager took all the cash home with him in a bag, where Mrs. Gower slept with it under her pillow!

Ellis's uncle, J.B. Ellis, was ambitious for his young nephew, and found him a job opening with his own employer, General Mills, as a grocery product salesman. This opened up more opportunity for advancement, as well as more money. Ellis applied for the job and was accepted, but he would be moving to Grand Rapids. When he broke the news to me, we were in the back seat of "Clarence's" green Pontiac, and I thought it was the end of the world. I cried and hung around his neck and felt that my whole world was collapsing. But he assured me that he would still come to see me on weekends, in Oakley or Mt. Pleasant. Which he did, and this continued for my last three years of college and through my one year of teaching at Remus High School. Ellis commuted faithfully back to me nearly every weekend, first from Grand Rapids, then from Kalamazoo, and, later, Detroit.

So it was a long-distance courtship, but a solid one. I went home often on weekends. My dad and mom enjoyed driving to Mt. Pleasant on Friday afternoons to pick me up, and very often Ellis would come on Saturday to Oakley, where the Gowers were very happy to have him as an overnight guest. And on Sunday afternoon he would drive me back to the dorm. Some weekends he came directly to Central on Saturday, especially if there was a big dance or football game, or something going on that we could both take in. On those weekends sometimes he would stay at a small downtown hotel, but more often he would just stay at the house of whomever Helen was dating at the time.

It was always a sad good-bye on Sunday night, parked in front of the dorm at closing time – 9PM on Sunday nights, waiting for the porch lights to blink, the signal to go in, as the doors were locked after the second blink, a few minutes after the first. Then I would go in and study for whatever Monday classes I had, and think of my Ellis, alone on the long drive back to Grand Rapids or Kalamazoo.

We hadn't really talked about marriage, as we both knew I had to finish college. But then one afternoon in my senior year, as we were lying on a blanket in Cathedral Woods near campus (a regular destination for many courting couples, all carrying blankets), Ellis asked, "Will you cook my beans for me?"

By that time, I was more than willing. And he had a good job and could afford a wife. So the next time I went home I told my mother we were ready to get married after I graduated in June.

She looked at me and said, "Oh, Daisy, you will have your teaching certificate. Don't you think you should teach at least a year, so if you ever need to get a job you'll have the experience?"

That was all it took. I knew we'd have to wait another year. I think Ellis was more disappointed than I was. Because I did look forward to this new experience of teaching. And that year in Remus turned out to be one of the best of my young life.

Ellis and I were not formally engaged until December of 1936, when for Christmas he gave me a diamond ring. He had already gifted me with a cedar chest, which I hoped to fill with traditional household linens. As it turned out, by the time we were married I had in that chest: two bedspreads, a dresser scarf and a three-piece vanity set I cross-stitched myself, two double bed sheets, and two pairs of pillow cases my mother had embroidered with crocheted edgings. A little later Ellis's mother gave us a pair of pillows. I helped her fill the ticking material with feathers from an old feather tick, which was a kind of bed-size pillow that used to be used next to the mattress for extra padding, and made a bed all puffy-looking – until you lay down on it! She had sewed the ticking for four pillows, and one windless day we took it all outside, and, with dishtowels tied around our hair, we ripped open the feather tick and filled the two pairs of pillows and then basted them shut until they could be properly stitched on the sewing machine. As I said, it was a windless day, but we still lost a good deal of the downy feathers that either stuck to us or flew away in the air. But we salvaged enough down so there was enough for a pair of pillows for us, and a pair for Don and Isabel, Ellis's brother and sister-in-law, who already had a little girl, Donna Jean. And there was enough down left over to later make another pair of pillows for Ellis's other brother, Ken, and his wife, Clarice.

But getting back to my dating situation, I never had a "steady" in college, as I was "Ellis's girl" during and after that summer of '33. But it was understood between us that I could go places with boys at school, as that was never anything serious.

My college major was English, with a minor in History, and I could have taught Home Economics too, as I had six terms of courses in that department.

Dr. E.C. Beck, from Nebraska, was head of the English Department, with Harry Miller and Fred Bush as professors, and two women instructors – Karolena Fox and Florence McClinchy. But I only had classes from the three men.

All incoming freshmen were required to take penmanship class from Professor Robinson, the head of the Commerce Department – unless they passed a test in the Palmer method of handwriting, which I did. In fact most did pass this test, because in grade schools back then everyone took penmanship through all eight grades at least once a week. Two of Professor Robinson's sons – Paul and Charles – were students at Central the same time I was. And I think there is a men's dorm, Robinson Hall, still there at CMU. Most of the buildings there now are named after faculty members who taught in the 1930s, when I was there.

The campus then was quite compact, and easily walked between classes or to and from the dorms. There was the "Ad" (administration) Building, which held classrooms, the library, offices, the cafeteria, and music rooms in its tower. It is now called Warriner Hall, named after E.C. Warriner, who was the college president, or "Prexy," when I was there. He lived in a large white house about halfway downtown. We always passed it when we walked down Franklin into town. I was inside it once, at some kind of reception-open house for honor students.

Then there was the Science Building, where I had psychology and geography classes.

The gymnasium had a pool and basketball courts. All freshmen were required to take at least three terms of phys ed. I took a class in phys ed every term through my senior year. Some courses I can remember are: swimming, folk dancing, tap dancing, natural dancing and tennis. Some of the instructors were Georgia Hood, Mary Ruth Wolf, and Josephine Rogers, and the department was chaired by the gracious and aptly named Grace Ryan. I took all the phys ed course I could fit in, because I felt I not only needed the exercise, but also whatever physical skills I might gain to overcome feeling so awkward and clumsy, which always seemed my lot growing up, when I was always taller than most kids in my class. Whether all these classes did me any good is questionable, but at least I became more comfortable inside my own body, which I probably didn't analyze then, but can feel it now, looking back.

There was also the Training School, directly in front of the dorm – a most impressive three-story brick building that housed a kindergarten and nine grades (for practice teaching), the Manual Arts Department, and the appointment office and student records. It burned to the ground in January 1933. Nothing was saved. Everything was destroyed, including those IQ records of our freshman class. We watched the early morning fire from the front windows of our dorm. I have pictures of Helen and me, along with Ellen Graham, Muriel Krieg, and Betty Darger, standing in the blackened rubble later.

And there was a log cabin in a corner of the campus near the dorm and ad building which had no electricity, but was furnished and used occasionally for small group meetings.

That pretty much constituted the campus of 1932-1933. To the west was a lovely forest with paths and a creek that we called Cathedral Woods. The land belonged to the college and was used unofficially by groups and couples for picnics, courting and carousing.

I'm sure that I, and most college students then, were serious about wanting to learn everything we could in our years at college. To go to college then was a privilege accorded to few high school grads. Even high school in those years was not for everyone. The law was that you were to attend school through the eighth grade, or until age sixteen. So, many, especially boys who were needed for farm work, did only the minimum. Besides that, most students worked part-time and summers to pay for their education. Whey you pay for yourself, you don't fool around, and you study hard so you don't flunk out. All the men, and all the women too, who did not live in the dorms (which was by far the majority), lived in groups in apartments or houses and did their own housekeeping and cooking, many of them bringing most of their food from home (farms).

We did have chances to socialize in whatever spare time we had. There was a faculty reception at the start of the year. And there were club meetings, as well as afternoon teas in the Women's Commons, sponsored by literary societies (forerunners of sororities). There were also lecture courses and dances held in the dorm basement or recreation room. But everyone knew he or she was there to get an education.

If you kept a high enough grade point average (GPA) you were allowed to take five classes instead of the usual four, which I did each term, plus phys ed. Besides English, History, Speech Psychology, Latin, and French, I took classes in Agriculture, Home Ec, Geography, Astronomy, and Health Ed – and during one six-week summer school I took Bookkeeping, along with Tennis.

Early one morning Helen and I were playing tennis on the dorm court, which was asphalt, with rather crumbling edges. I slipped and fell flat on a crumbly spot and tore open the skin on my right hip (and still have the scar), but it was more fun than hurt.

In Home Ec I had two courses in sewing, two in cooking, one in child care and home nursing, and one "general" – all of which served me in good stead way beyond my teaching year. We learned to make a bed with mitered "hospital" corners, and I still have the textbook, filled with much good information on child care and common diseases, etc. Plus I learned about balanced meals, and, until only recently, always served a dinner of vegetable, fruit and salad, besides meat and potatoes and dessert. And I learned about budgeting – how to adjust monthly expenditures to income: one-fourth for rent or house payment, and a certain percentage for food, for clothing, for entertainment, etc.

I kept budget books for our first six years of marriage, when Ellis had the General Mills job and a regular income, keeping track of every penny. We didn't feel limited by it. It was more like a game. The first 10% always went into a savings account, and the next 10% "tithe" was evenly divided between church and charities.

When we were living in Chicago, Ellis was budgeted 25 cents a day to buy his lunch, but he even economized on that, and saved part of it each day towards buying his mom a refrigerator. His brothers contributed too on this project, and she was just overjoyed with the gift, and even learned to make homemade ice cream in the ice cube trays for her "men-folks'" dinner.

But then in 1943 we bought a forty-acre farm a mile and a half outside of Potterville, and Ellis took a job at Otis "Ote" Donley's elevator at $40 a week. One week's salary paid the monthly mortgage, but otherwise we pretty much tossed the budget out the window. We only bought what we had to and got most of our food from the farm. The hens gave us eggs; our cow gave us milk, butter and cottage cheese. For meat we raised pigs and a beef steer. Our garden gave us vegetables, and we had apple and cherry trees for fruit.

We never did go into debt for anything, except for that farm mortgage, and, later, in 1945, a bank loan to buy a half interest in the Kent Elevator in Reed City (where Ellis was initially partners with Clarence "Mick" Churchill). We also took a loan from my folks to buy our house in Holdenville that same year, but both debts were paid off in two years. This was accomplished by our taking a very minimum amount from the business for salary, and by the fact that we never bought anything until we had the money in hand to pay for it.

I'd had two years of high school Latin, and took two more years from Anna Barnard. I'd also had a taste of French in a "French Club" in high school, and took two years of French at Central from Rachael Loachridge, a young red-headed teacher. Many years later, on a motor trip in France, I found my French was not much good at all. Signs were very confusing and everyone talked too fast.

I did my practice teaching at the public high school downtown in Mt. Pleasant. Sometimes when I was hurrying back to campus, a mile down Fancher, Father Mulvey, our sweet old white-haired Irish priest (who was also our Mercier Club advisor) would drive by with a cheery smile and a wave. I could have used a ride and was a bit put out at this, especially when it was raining or snowing. But he later explained to me that he was carrying the Sacred Host with him to take Communion to the home-bound, and was not allowed to have anyone ride with him. Evidently that was the rule then, but now even I have carried the Host in a small gold pyx to a friend who couldn't get to Mass anymore.

Ethel LaMore was my critic teacher for ninth grade English, and Constance Stegenza for ninth grade Latin I – or was it vice-versa? In any case, I much enjoyed the teaching. I took methods classes, but never figured they helped much, or were even at all practical. I never had discipline problems in a classroom. When I taught English at Remus High for all four grades, the children were from rural and small-town homes and one-room schools, and many from St. Michael's grade school, and all were well-behaved and attentive.

Occasionally even now, in my ninetieth year, I wake up sweating from a nightmare where I'm walking down the hall of the Ad Building, kids coming and going all around me, clutching my notebook, with no idea of where my next class is, and knowing I'm not prepared for whatever it is, wherever it is. It's such a relief to wake up and know I don't have to worry about anything like that anymore. I never did have that happen, so I don't know where that dream comes from.

It was always satisfying to have a schedule with every hour of the day mapped out on a grid in my notebook, showing what class at what hour. If there was one free period between classes, I could study at the library or in an empty classroom. Two free periods in a row [I started to say "two consecutive free periods," but Doc Beck emphasized never using a big word when a small one would do] meant I could return to the dorm to study.

Weekday evenings were pretty much free, but for maybe a club meeting or two. Saturdays meant housekeeping, like doing laundry, cleaning the room, etc. Once that was taken care of there might be a whole afternoon to enjoy – often spent lying on my bed reading a book and eating peanuts! A cozy feeling, especially in the winter. Gover's store sometimes put a coupon in the Centralite for a nine-cent pound of salted peanuts, a bargain which we always took advantage of.

Sunday mornings Helen and I always went to Mass downtown, a mile walk each way. But if we timed it right we might get a ride with the Bambers, who lived just kitty-corner across the street from the dorm. Their daughter, Eleanor, was in our class, a really sweet dark-haired beauty.

When there was a week-long mission Helen and I went to early morning mass every day and to the evening service too, when we didn't mind walking. The daily walking we did on campus too may have been one of the reasons my weight stayed steady at 135 pounds for three years.

After my first year I didn't go home weekends very often. Part of the college experience was weekend events – lecture courses, football and basketball games, dances, etc. There was a large rec room in the dorm basement where dances or parties were held, usually on Friday nights, no charge.

Proms were held in the gym – maybe one a term. I still have a black satin dress I wore to several proms with low-heeled black sandals. The dress is long and belted, with a bias cut skirt and a neckline made in such a way that it could also be worn backwards. It had a hip-length jacket that could be worn backwards too – so one dress could have at least four different looks. Hey, prom dresses were high-priced! You sometimes traded with a friend, but unless your folks were rich, you didn't get a new dress for every formal dance.

There was a kitchenette in the dorm basement we could sign up for for a set time and get the key to it, and we would go in and make popcorn or fudge for snacking on later in our rooms.

Helen and I did some independent exploring in the dorm. Sometimes we went into the warm and friendly kitchen and visited with the cooks, two motherly ladies who might be tending huge dripping-pans of Swiss steak or pork chops or meatloaf in the ovens. In the corner of the rec room we discovered a square door that we pried open and found a tunnel with lights on in it, and pipes and cables. Of course we knew we shouldn't, but we went in and followed it for maybe a block, and it came out in the heating plant, which was mostly underground at the center of campus. It was the source of heat and power for all of the campus buildings. Luckily there was no one around, so we didn't get in trouble; we just "broadened our education."

I have a picture of five of us up on the flat roof of the dorm, wind blowing in our hair. I suppose we shouldn't have been up there either, and I can't remember just how we got up there. But another picture shows us next to a ladder that arches over the roof parapet from below. How we got to that ladder I don't recall, unless it was through a third-floor hall window, as none of us lived on the third floor.

Helen and I lived our first year in room 203, on the second floor northwest. Then we moved to room 221, right above the office and apartment of the dorm Social Director, Helen Porterfield.

Mrs. Porterfield was a welcome change, like a breath of fresh air after Grace Freer. "Gracie" was a maiden lady of uncertain age, not known to smile much, who kept a tight rein on the girls under her care. Her replacement was a widow with grown children, very understanding and gracious. Helen and I had pooled our money and bought a little radio, which we kept on a small table between our end-to-end beds where we could both reach it. After we finished studying and got into bed, we'd turn on some nice music and sometimes we both went to sleep with the radio still on. In those days radios had a tendency to get louder later in the night. Mrs. P's bedroom was right under ours, and quite often she came up in the night, tiptoed in and turned off our radio. As if she needed to tiptoe! If the blaring music didn't wake us up, what would? She'd tell us of it later. It still happened, but rarely.

Late one night near the beginning of our senior year we wend down to one of the parlors on the first floor and "borrowed" a rocking chair – polished hardwood one that we made a bit more by placing a pillow on the seat. It became the seat of honor for any guest – whenever one of us was not sitting in it, rocking. We'd not have been surprised if it had been returned to the parlor during our absence, but it stayed with us until we graduated.

"Pa" Pitts was the janitor who swept the halls with his push broom, grey-haired head down and rarely looking up, usually around only during the day when most of us were at classes. It was a lady who cleaned the bathrooms and delivered our clean bed linens each Friday. We stripped our beds Friday morning and left the sheets and pillowcases out for her. She also vacuumed our room. But there was a vacuum cleaner in a hall closet we could use other times.

There was also a telephone room in each wing of each floor. Whoever was nearest answered the ring and called out who it was for. For a long-distance call "out" we had to go to the entry office. Whoever effected the call was usually right there to answer it, and could close the door for privacy. The only furniture in the room was a shelf for the phone, so there was no comfort for long conversations – which were not encouraged anyway.

June Shelander and Shirley Allen were right across the hall from our room (221), with Margaret "Peg" Emery and Marvel Vanderlip as their suite-mates. One winter Saturday one of them obtained a pack of cigarettes, and we used our room for the big "smoke-out" (or smoke-in?). We put rugs and blankets against the crack under the door and opened the window wide. Each of us had a cigarette. I'm not sure if any of us finished her smoke – or tried inhaling – but it took only a few puffs for me to be "satisfied" - for life. This episode didn't last very long, as it got mighty cold in that room quickly. Need I say it was against the rules?

Shirley Allen lived on a farm near Clare, not far from Mt. Pleasant. Once in a while her folks would let her bring their car back with her on Sunday afternoons. Helen and June and I went home with her one weekend. Another time we took an afternoon picnic and went just a few miles from town on a country road, spread blankets on the roadside grass and studied a while in the sunshine – as evidenced by a picture of June with a typewriter on her knees – and then had our lunch and went back to the dorm much refreshed.

Rarely did a student marry before graduation. Some married couples came back for their degrees after teaching for a few years on a limited certificate. But I remember only two full-time students who married during "school days" while I was at Central.

One was Richard "Dick" Houseman, a good-looking football player with close-cropped curly red hair. He married his high school sweetheart from Greenville during his senior year. They lived in a tiny house just off campus. One our group, Doris Sheldon, from Greenville, was a friend of the new bride, and we once visited her with Doris in their little "doll-house" that had a story-book quality to it. They were very poor, and it was a struggle for them, but they were obviously very much in love. And no – there was no baby, not until much later. It was not a "have-to" marriage.

The other "bride" was Hilda Hulbert, who lived in one of the two-person dorm rooms with its own bath on first floor south, with her roommate, Mary Elizabeth Bradley. Her dad had a hardware store in St. John's, where Hilda had worked during high school. Rumor had it she needed someone to show her how to make up her bed her first day in the dorm, and it was common knowledge she knew nothing about cooking. But she was pretty and good-natured and well-liked. During her junior year she married Harry Millette, who drove a convertible and looked like the movie star, George Raft. I didn't think he was a student, but, looking in my yearbook, I found Harry's picture. His family must have had money, as they seemed to lack for nothing after they married. They had a very nice little house, and Hilda did go on to graduate. (No baby there either!)

A group of us talked about vacationing together the summer after my freshman year (1933). Besides Helen and I, the girls involved were: Ellen Graham, a junior from St. Charles; Betty Darger, a senior from Saginaw; Marguerite Ehrhardt, from North Bradley; Marvel and Beverly Milner; and Muriel Krieg. After a couple of false starts, our plans finally gelled and we called and reserved a site at the Bay City State Park. My dad came up and pitched our old tent in the park for us. We had two tents close to the beach and were within walking distance of Paraleon, an amusement park with dancing every night. Of course the first thing we did was go swimming and then lay in the sun all afternoon. The other girls may have had a tan already or were more sensible, but I got horrendous sunburn on my back and shoulders, and pretty much stayed in the shade the rest of the week. In spite of that we had a wonderful time though – lazy days at camp and evenings spent dancing. And there were always a few boys hanging around our camp. I remember one named Bob Gransey.

The following week I went "home" with Helen – to Kingsley, where her brother Don and his wife, Elsie (both teachers), were living, and their mom was keeping house for them. Helen's mom was quite worried that my deep sunburn might get infected, but it didn't. In fact I even endured hands on my back at a dance at Fife Lake where Don and Elsie took us one night. Helen and I were very popular, as there was a soldiers' camp nearby, and all the "boys" were there. A tall officer claimed me for most of the dances, but "big brother" Don took us home to Kingsley at the end of the evening.

Most of the girls in our group that first year were Early El students. Winnie the Pooh, by A.A. Milne, must have been popular with them then, as they all talked a lot about Pooh. "Says Pooh, says he" was sprinkled throughout their conversations. Much later I heard references to Christopher Robin, Piglet, Roo and Eeyore, but I never actually read the book until about two years ago, and I enjoyed it immensely. My son, Chris, and I took turns reading it aloud to each other one winter.

That summer of '33 passed like a dream. It was like the song, "When I fall in love, it will be forever." And it was true; I came back home to Oakley – and met Ellis.

When I was growing up I was never very fond of my name – Daisy. And, looking back, I think I spy the reason. When I was four or five and lived in town in Oakley, I was allowed to go from our house one block east of the main street to my Grandma Mickles' house, just north of the Methodist church. Sometimes on my walk to Grandma's I would meet our old priest (well, I thought he was old), Father Lehnzen, whose rectory was just a block south.

"What's your name?" he'd ask me.

"Daisy," I'd answer.

"Daisy? That's not a saint's name," he'd say. "What's your middle name?"

"Cecelia," I'd reply, quaking inwardly and bottom lip trembling.

"Oh. That's all right then. That's a saint's name," he'd reply.

This came to be kind of a game, and I'd know what to expect whenever we met. I was probably in my thirties before I finally got to like my name.

I'm going to go back further in my life now – far back into the mists of memory, before I lose myself, as my mother did start to at age 95 (when she lived part of the time with Ellis and me). She had a tremendous store of information on friends and family. Mornings at breakfast she'd say, "This would have been Dolly Brennan's birthday. She'd be 92, but she died young."

Or Jenny Merrill, or someone else from her past. Or maybe one of her seven brothers or two sisters, or her aunts or grandparents.

But after she'd turned 95 I would ask her about one of her family or someone from Oakley, and she would put her head on her hand and think for a moment, and then she would say, "You know, Daisy, I should know that, but I can't remember." And then she would cry.

So I learned to stop asking direct questions, but would lead up to my question by telling her what I remembered about so-and-so. Then we'd talk about it for a while, and usually then she would start to remember. My mother – Lettie Jane Mickles Whalen – lived two more years. She was in a nursing home in Chesaning for a little over a year when she stopped eating, because she wanted "to be with Will" – my dad. Two weeks later she didn't wake up one morning. She was "with Will."

My religious education. St. Michael's Catholic Church in Oakley was still a mission of Our Lady of Perpetual Help (not Garrison Keillor's "Our Lady of Perpetual Responsibility") Church in Chesaning when I was baptized there in July of 1916, with my grandparents, William and Christina Whalen, as godparents. It was a Father Studer who baptized me, but I remember only Father Godfrey T. Lehnzen, who was, I think, St. Michael's first resident pastor.

His housekeeper was a pretty, rosy-cheeked, buxom young woman with short dark curls – Mary Rehman. She lived in the rectory, a two-story white square house on Main Street, a block and a half from the church.

Catechism for the children was held on Saturday mornings in the summer (school vacation time) at the church. But in my memory those Saturday mornings were always warm and sunny, and our classes were outdoors, in back of the church by the cemetery, along the riverbank – a most pleasant place where we sat in the grass. Mary Rehman was the teacher for the girls and the little ones. She quite often had her little niece, Marie Hager, with her. Marie had had some kind of hip problems as a baby, and had been in various casts for most of her short life. So, besides being so pretty, she was quite fragile and precious, and I loved helping to care for her during the class. (At least I thought I was helping.)

A very small booklet called The Baltimore Catechism was our text, and each week (and each year) we progressed through the lessons, starting with:

> *Q: Who made the world?*
>
> *A: God made the world.*
>
> *Q: Who made you?*
>
> *A: God made me.*
>
> *Q: Why did God make you?*
>
> *A: God made me to know Him, to love Him and to serve Him in this world and be happy with Him forever in the next.*

And right there is the essence of Catholicism. But we went on to more intricate ideas – all based on the Ten Commandments and the Seven Commandments of the Church. There was a core of prayers to memorize – The Lord's Prayer, the Hail Mary, the Apostles Creed, the Confiteor, the Act of Contrition, Act of Faith, Act of Hope, Act of Charity, etc. My favorite back then was a morning prayer to my Guardian Angel.

> *Angel of God, my guardian dear*
> *To whom His love commits me here*
> *Ever this day be at my side*
> *To light and guard, to rule and guide.*

Each week we had one or two chapters assigned to memorize the answers – a study session for which was usually crammed into a Friday afternoon and evening. And that would be our lesson for the Saturday morning, plus reviewing the prayers we'd learned.

I remember that the Slovak and Polish and Hungarian girls always knew their lessons perfectly, and could rattle off all the prayers, even the more obscure ones in the back of the catechism. Where were the boys? I think they were inside the church, being taught by the priest himself. Some of the parents from the aforementioned "old country" spoke little or no English, especially the mothers who ventured from home only to go to Mass on Sundays. But they saw to it that their children learned their catechism, and they probably were stricter about this than our English-speaking parents were. We "had to go" to catechism class through the eighth grade.

I still think that little book contained everything we needed to know about our religion. It seems almost ridiculous to now have a catechism that needs another book to explain it. I have both of those books, but must confess I've yet to "wade through" them. I wish I still had a copy of that original Baltimore Catechism. I do have one, copyright 1941, with the name Billy Bazzett (my second son) printed on the protective paper cover. It was his from the time he began second grade at St. Philip's school around 1950. Even that edition is much bigger than the original, and has all sorts of explanations, some in charts and pictures, of the original contents, making it a bigger and thicker book.

I have, too, a smaller catechism (still c. 1941) with Dick Bazzett's name in it, which was given to my first son by a chaplain when he joined the army in 1961. This book too contains all the most basic Catholic beliefs.

Several years ago I went through a year of RCIA (Rite of Christian Initiation of Adults), training as a godmother, or sponsor, to a friend who was "joining the Church." I was absolutely amazed at how "watered down" our beliefs have become. The person I was sponsoring didn't even have to memorize the Catechism or know all the answers – and no mention was ever made of the Seven Commandments of the Church. She did, however, get a copy of the Ten Commandments, which – if believed and followed – should get her to Heaven – everyone's goal (?).

No doubt all of my children have a deeper understanding of their faith than I or their dad. Ellis was the product of a "mixed marriage." His mother was an Irish Catholic who married a Baptist, and had no way to get to Mass, so four of their five sons did not go to church until they left home. Three of them became practicing Catholics. Ellis, the oldest, was instructed by Father O'Toole in Carson City, and was baptized and confirmed at St. Mary's Church there at age 21.

But as parishioners here in Reed City, Ellis and I helped to build St. Philip's Catholic School, and all six of our children graduated from eighth grade there. Shortly after our youngest graduated, however, the school was reduced to six grades. And sadly, not long after that, financial difficulties forced the school to close its doors. The School Sisters of Notre Dame could no longer supply us with enough teachers, even at their very low wages. And hiring lay teachers took more money than we could possibly raise. The diocese now subsidizes its schools, but that policy began after our school had already closed.

When I was teaching a weekly class in ninth grade religion (the year my own ninth-grader, Bob, was at the seminary in Grand Rapids), I tried to simplify the lessons to make them more interesting and easier to remember. The parts of the Mass were reduced to: (1) Adoration = I love You; (2) Penitence = I'm sorry; (3) Thanksgiving or the Eucharist = Thank You; and (4) Petition = Please.

My own morning prayers, which reflect those four things, are still:

> *Dear God, I love you. I'm sorry for all the times I've hurt you.*
> *Please forgive me and help me not to do it again. Thank you for all*
> *your blessings, especially .... Please take care of all my dear ones,*
> *especially ... (naming all my family and friends and neighbors and*
> *everyone I said I would pray for). Please help me to be what you*
> *want me to be and to do what you want me to do, and give me the*
> *health and strength and courage to do it. And please keep me going,*
> *God, until no one needs me anymore. Then grant me the grace of a*
> *peaceful death.*

But somehow – though I think one should feel closer to God near the
end of one's earthly life – I can never quite get back the feeling I had as
a child, until the end of my fifteenth year – of closeness to God. Could it
be because I had no sisters, and, having a bed and room all to myself,
I was "alone with God" every night? It seemed I could feel Him hovering
just below the ceiling, and hearing all my thoughts and prayers – a lovely
warm and safe feeling.

There was a "Thirty Days' Prayer to the Blessed Virgin Mary" in my tiny
First Communion prayer book that took up seven pages. I knew it by heart,
as I would hardly finish one thirty-day session before I would start another,
asking for some favor. And it worked! Of course I worked very hard too for
whatever I asked for, but the actual prayer seemed the most important part
of the "deal."

But then, somewhere – maybe it was when I went away to college and a new
life – I lost that precious closeness to God. Could He have been crowded out
of my life by so many new people and so much always going on? I did pray
every morning and night, and went faithfully to church all my life – but it
hasn't been the same since I was sixteen.

I pray, Please come back to me, God. Please be real again. It's not He who
is lacking, I know. It's me. Maybe sometime ... ?

* * *

***April 2, 2006** – I have a small yellow tattered clipping taped to a shelf here*
on my desk. It says: "Old age is a gentle slope, but even at the bottom of a
very gentle slope, the pebbles suddenly begin to roll terribly fast." I may be
nearly to the bottom. I realize it when I discover my "children" are talking
to each other about me, and wondering, What can we do about Mom?

Here I thought I was still pretty much in charge – in control – of myself and my life. But they're saying to each other, Mom shouldn't be going up and down stairs anymore [to do laundry, and to put things in and take things out of the freezer, etc.] She shouldn't be pushing a vacuum cleaner ...

Well, I solved that last one for them. When I bought a new vacuum cleaner last year I let Chris choose it, and gave it to him and said, "That's yours, and you can use it." Since then I've only used it a few times, when Chris was out of the house, working.

But I tell myself, that's what keeps me going. I can still keep house. I don't dust very often any more. I never did like to do that anyway. And I haven't baked bread in quite a long time. I do still bake cookies, although it takes me all day. Like this: Get ingredients together and measure them out. [Sit down a while and knit or crochet.] Stir up the cookie dough. (Sit down, etc.) Make the cookies and put them in the oven. [Sit, etc.] Take cookies out of oven and leave them on counter to cool. [Sit.] Wash bowls and utensils and cookie sheets. [Sit.] Fill cookie jar and package rest for freezer. Because it's just not worthwhile to bake just one batch. Double or triple batches are time-savers.

I should explain here that all the sit-downs are needed because my back starts to hurt if I'm on my feet too long. When it gets to hurting real bad, I have to sit down. Then, after a half hour or less of resting, I can get back up and do some more.

Hey this does begin to sound like I'm slipping into old age, doesn't it? I have to laugh when I think of it, because otherwise I might cry. And feeling sorry for myself serves no useful purpose. I can still "keep house" – I think. I make meals, though I'm down to two a day most of the time. I do the dishes, clean the bathrooms on laundry days, make my bed, and keep everything "reasonably" neat.

Tim gave me this notebook last summer on my birthday – actually two notebooks – and asked me to write my memoirs.

"Mom," he said, "if you just write one page a day, on both sides, by your next birthday, you'll have a book written."

Well, it seems my tidy self must have everything else done before I sit down to write, so it hasn't happened at all lately. But here I go again, Tim. That was my "one page on both sides" for today.

April 3, 2006 *– Could hardly believe my eyes when our April rain turned to snow today about 11:00, and we had more than an inch ...*

* * *

I remember when the Superintendent of the School for the Deaf in Flint addressed the whole student body at Central one Friday. He was hoping to recruit some teachers for his school. His talk had been announced beforehand, so Helen and I had tentative plans made for it. We talked to the man after the assembly, expressing much interest in his school, and asked if we could come and visit it. He was very pleased and offered to take us back to Flint with him. This was exactly what we had hoped for. He picked us up, with our small overnight bags, right at the dorm. During the trip we learned much more about the school. Our very good RRT friend, Ida May Clapper, who'd graduated the year before, was teaching in Flint; she had a small apartment there, and wanted us to come for a weekend. Upon our arrival in Flint, we were given a most interesting tour of the School for the Deaf. Then, gentleman that he was, the superintendent even gave us a ride to Ida May's apartment. We had a great weekend with Ida May.

But what I remember most vividly was a double date Helen and I had Saturday night with one of Helen's Williamsburg boyfriends. His friend was my blind date. I don't remember now what we did on that date, except walking in a park at the end of the evening. We had gotten along very well, and then the next thing I knew I was lying prone beside him on a backless park bench. How could I have been so naïve as to not know how to say, "No"? But he was much more knowledgeable than I, and – luckily for me – very kind.

He said, "You've never done this before, have you?"

Then out came my NO! and he said he'd never "take advantage" of a girl. So I still had my virtue intact.

The next day, after going to Mass with Ida May, Helen and I set out, each with our little bag, to hitch-hike back to Mt. Pleasant. It was not at all difficult for two young girls to get rides, and we were back in our dorm room by early afternoon. Although, when we were let off from one ride in Owosso and were waiting for another, I wanted to hide, as we were only about ten miles from my folks in Oakley. I knew they would not look kindly on what we were doing. But back then hitch-hiking, or "thumbing a ride," was an accepted method for young people to get around, since hardly anyone in school had cars as they do now. Only those gainfully employed had cars, and not even all of those. So nearly everyone with an empty back seat happily picked up hitch-hikers, as they all knew it could very well sometime be one from their own family with a thumb raised along the road. (This was, of course, in an era long before hitch-hiking adventures could end in grisly murders, as, sadly, they often do today.)

Oakley folks ...

Ella Keyes lived just a couple of houses up the street from us. Oakley back streets were more like two-tracks, some with gravel, some not. Ella had lived alone in her attractive house since her folks died. They had been a farm family some three miles west of town. The parents and Ella moved to town when the son and his wife, Bill and Julia, took over the operation of the farm. When I was still in grade school, Ella would come and knock on our door and ask my mother to do some sewing for her, bringing a skirt to be shortened, a dress to be taken in at the seams, or something. She would invariably come just as we had finished a meal, and say, "Lettie if you fix this for me, I'll wash your dishes and whatever else you've got for me to do."

Then, while Mother was at her sewing machine in the bedroom, Ella would "clear" the table, which always included eating whatever was left – a couple cold boiled potatoes, a wiener, or maybe even a whole side dish of beet pickles. The poor thing was so always hungry, and Mother knew it, so she never begrudged it to her.

But once in a while, after Ella got to be a nuisance, my mother would see her Ella coming and say, "I'm just not going to let her in. I'll lock the doors."

Ella would go away from the door and walk around the house wringing her hands and saying, "Oh, Lettie, please let me in. Let me in, Lettie. I know you're in there. Please, Lettie, let me in!"

I can still see exactly how she looked – so pitiful – an old lady with snow-white hair, skin nearly as white (she may have been anemic), tall and gaunt in an old-fashioned long skirt, walking and wringing her hands, moaning and begging. Of course, Lettie always did relent and let her in.

The way Ella lived was very sad. She'd take her little wagon and walk three blocks west to the red elevator and bring back a bag of cull beans and a wagonload of corn cobs. I think the culls were a penny a pound – usually sold to farmers, who cooked them in a big outdoor kettle over a fire to feed to their hogs. The corn cobs were in a big pile by the elevator free for the taking.

Ella never used the front door of her house, though it always looked welcoming enough, flanked by two lace-curtained windows. Her back door led from a good-sized back porch into a big country kitchen. Here she cooked her castoff beans on a small cast-iron laundry stove fueled by the corn cobs. And she slept on a cot in the kitchen. We only saw all

249

this after she died there. One winter day she was found frozen to death in her cot with no fire in the stove. She had spread a layer of newspapers between the two blankets covering her cot, probably for extra warmth.

Poor Ella. Why didn't her brother look after her? He and his wife had tried. They even took her to live with them once. But after she tried to climb the stovepipe in their house, and brought it tumbling down with all the soot, they cleaned her up and brought her back "home," where she wanted to be. After her death her brother had an estate sale, and we finally saw the inside of her house. The kitchen was pitifully bare, but the rest of the house was beautifully furnished, including beds with blankets and quilts that she never used. It turned out she also had a bank account that she'd never drawn on, perhaps because she was afraid she'd use it up and be destitute. Or maybe she had no idea she had it – or how to use it. A few years ago I looked at her stone in the cemetery and learned she was only 58 when she died – now considered the prime of life for an active healthy woman.

Our little town had an assortment of people who, like Ella, we just accepted as living their lives the way they wanted to. Now, looking back, I cannot figure out what they lived on. Where did they get their cash money? There was no old-age pension then, no Social Security. Where did they get what money they needed for groceries, or to pay property taxes, etc.?

I think now of my own Grandma Mickles, who lived alone for about ten years after Grandpa died, in the little hotel they'd run for many years, and where the youngest of her ten children had grown up – and where her many grandchildren came from the Detroit area to spend summers with her. She and Grandpa must have had money saved, and she did still own the little family farm just outside of town and must have rented out the fields. She always had lots of beds for the kids in the little upstairs hotel rooms, and lots of food in the pantry. That pantry was a long narrow room in back of the kitchen. Across the end by the door was a pump over a sink, always with a bar of Jap Rose in the soap dish, a golden translucent hand soap that disappeared when Japan became an enemy. There were cupboards on each long wall, with tip-out wooden bins underneath the counters holding flour and white sugar, etc. For a special treat, we children were sometimes allowed to open up the brown sugar bin and take out a lump or two to suck on – dee-LISH-us! And there were some big crocks on the floor that held fried cakes, cookies and pickles. This had been a hotel pantry, of course, but it remained well-stocked this way for years after the place had closed as a business.

Sometimes my mother would give Harold a quarter in the morning, when she didn't pack lunches for the three of us. It seemed strangely free those mornings to be walking to school without swinging a dinner pail! This was when we still lived a mile west of Oakley on the Whalen farm and walked to the Oakley eight-grade school.

Handing Harold the coin, she'd say, "Harold you go to Jim Rundle's [store] and buy a can of salmon and take it to Ma's, and you ask her if you can all come there for dinner [at noon]."

And sure enough, Harold, Clarence and I would race over Grandma's on our noon hour, knowing we'd have a hearty dinner of salmon balls and creamed potatoes, and, of course, pickles and cookies or pudding, or whatever else Grandma had garnered from her pantry.

Grandma was a very good cook. She knew how to "fix" any kind of vegetable or meat there was. But after feeding a family of twelve and keeping up a hotel and doing for boarders for years, in her old age she liked to sit in her rocking chair between the range and the kitchen window and watch Oakley's little world go by. In the summertime she'd sit in one of the rockers out on the porch on the other side of that kitchen window. Lush trumpet vines formed a "wall" that shaded one end of the porch, and the other rocker was usually occupied by someone who was passing by and stopped to "set a spell" and visit. By that time in her life she was quite content to let family fend for themselves in the kitchen and pantry.

If we'd stop by and ask her to go for a ride with us, she'd always say, "Just wait 'til I get my hat and coat. The work will still be here when I'm gone, and there'll be somebody here to do it."

It was always a treat to just "go for a ride" on the country roads around Oakley and look at the crops and the houses. Whenever we'd pass an old house no longer lived in, Grandma would invariably say, "Oh, look at that poor old house. It would make such a nice home for some family."

And now I feel the same way whenever I see an abandoned house, and am reminded of some lines from an old poem by Joyce Kilmer,

> "The House with Nobody in It" –
> ... If I had a lot of money and all my debts were paid
> I'd put a gang of men to work with brush and saw and spade
> I'd buy that place and fix it up the way it used to be
> And I'd find some people who wanted a home
> And give it to them free ...
> But a house that has done what a house should do,
> A house that has sheltered life,
> That has put its loving wooden arms around a man and his wife

A house that has echoed a baby's laugh
And held up his stumbling feet
Is the saddest sight, when it's left alone,
That ever your eyes could meet ...

I remember my Grandma Mickles as always being old. Her hair was white and a bit curly, always done in a round bun on top of her head – like Mrs. Butterworth. And she still wore long skirts in the late 1920s and into the thirties. My mother said Grandma's one vanity was her legs, which were indeed still very smooth and white, even after bearing eleven children. (Her first son, Andrew, died at just two years of age.) She always had some round white peppermint candies in her apron pocket, and I don't remember ever seeing her without an apron. She doled these sweets out to grandchildren and local neighbor children alike.Whenever her pocket came up empty, she'd say, "Daisy, go in my bedroom and bring me more peppermints."

On her dresser in her handkerchief box there was always a bottomless (I thought) brown paper bag of the white candy.

Grandma did have one bad knee, and sometimes walked with a limp. She'd explain it by saying her "rheumatism" was "acting up." In cold weather, when she had a fire going in the big cook stove (range) in the kitchen, she'd leave the oven door open and lay a long strip of grey flannel on it. When it had gotten very warm, she'd remove it and wrap it around the knee, and it gave her comfort.

My grandma – Sarah Alice Overpack Mickles – died in August of 1935, at the age of 77. I was 19. So, if she was 58 when I was born, no wonder she was always "old" to me. Back then 60 was old!

My college roommate, Helen, and I were on a two-week trip to Yellowstone Park with my folks in their travel trailer when Grandma had a heart attack, and died in her own bed a few days later. The State Police in several states were looking for us, but never located us. When we came home the funeral was over and Grandma was already buried. What a terrible shock it was to my mother. She seemed to go around in a daze for weeks, and cried for a long time, but Grandma was gone. Her house was empty.

And I do mean empty. The relatives from Detroit had come to the funeral with their trucks and trailers and completely emptied the house of all its furniture and pictures and keepsakes. Even the piano was gone.

For years after, my mother would think of something of Grandma's and would say, "I wonder who got that. I'll bet Henry did" – her oldest brother – and I'd think to myself, "Greedy Henry."

My Aunt Daisy Clark – Grandma's youngest child – lived just down a path through two back yards on the other side of the block, on Parshall Street, with her husband, Ed, and her children, Margaret and Byron. In fact, I am named for my aunt Daisy, who was very tiny. But she was always "Big Daisy" and I was "Little Daisy," when I was growing up, even though I grew tall, and, by the time I was fifteen, she could stand under my arm.

Aunt Daisy and my mom, Lettie, had both been "looking after" Grandma in her last years. But Daisy had stayed away from the house after the funeral, while the other relatives were "divvy-ing up the loot." So she didn't know who got what either. I myself still wonder sometimes what happened to that big heavy bible with all the family records in its center pages. It had always lain on that marble-top table in the big living room that had once been the hotel lounge. It had always been too heavy for me to lift until after I was grown, but I was allowed to open it and look at all the family names as soon as I could read.

There were seven Mickles sons – Henry, Harry, Bert, George, Ray, Milo and Ernie – but only Ernie had sons who may lived to maturity, Clare and Gilbert ("Gig"). But our family lost touch with those Detroit-area Mickles over the years, and we have no records of Clare and Gig beyond their childhood. If there are any Mickles descendants though, they would probably be Clare and Gilbert's children.

My uncle Milo never married, but later in his life he did move in with a "lady-friend." There were two children who bore her last name, but always called him "Dad." Whether they were Milo's children, we never knew. The fragility of family ties – now broken and perhaps lost forever.

* * *

Florence Martin was a most kind and understanding teacher who taught in the "little room" – the first four grades – of the Oakley school. When I was four years old and my two brothers were in the second and fifth grades, I often followed them to school which was only two blocks north of us. I can remember Miss Martin letting me "recite" with the first-graders in reading and spelling – until my mother came and found me and took me home. So, when I did begin school, I went quickly through the Primer ("primmer"), and the 1st and 2nd Readers, and started third grade when I was six. Each Friday afternoon we took turns reciting poems we'd memorized (which I still remember), beginning with little ones like this:

Politeness is to do and say
The kindest thing in the kindest way.

and

Hearts like doors will ope with ease
To very, very little keys
And don't forget that two of these
Are Thank you sir, and If you please.

and

If you have to do a thing
And mean to do it really
Never let it be by halves
Do it fully freely.

These quickly escalated to such longer poems as the following, from Robert Louis Stevenson.

The friendly cow all red and white
I love with all my heart
She gives me cream with all her might
To eat with apple tart
She wanders lowing here and there
And yet she cannot stray
All in the friendly open air
All in the light of day
And cooled by all the winds that pass
And wet with all the showers
She walks among the meadow grass
And eats the meadow flowers

or

How do you like to go up in a swing
Up in the air so blue
Oh I do think it the pleasantest thing
Ever a child can do
Up in the air and over the wall
Til I can see so wide
Rivers and trees and cattle and all
Over the country side
Til I look down on the garden green
Down on the roof so brown

Up in the air I go flying again
Up in the air and down

or

I have a little shadow
That goes in and out with me
And what can be the use of him
Is more than I can see
He is very very like me
From the heels up to the head
And I see him jump before me
When I jump into my bed

These are all, I think, from Stevenson's A Child's Garden of Verses. It's been over eighty years since I learned them, but I still remember them, more or less. And there was Emily Huntington Miller's verse –

I know the song that the bluebird is singing
Up in the apple tree where he is swinging
Brave little fellow the skies may be dreary
Nothing cares he while his heart is so cheery ...

I loved the rhythm of such real rhyming poetry that made it very easy to memorize. And children then could easily relate to the subjects of cows and bluebirds and swings and such. Now many city children, I suppose, would not know what those old poems mean and could not relate to them. Raised on TV cartoons and Sesame Street, their world seems so artificial.

In the seventh grade and eighth grade we went to a central school at the end of the school year and spent a whole school day writing exams for each subject. We'd not know if we'd passed until a letter came tin the mail from County School Commissioner, Miss Otillia M. Frisch – signed in a perfect Spencerian hand.

In the seventh grade our English Lit exam was based on "The Vision of Sir Launfal," by James Russell Lowell. I memorized the whole thing, and can still remember long stretches of it. The beginning –

Over his keys the musing organist
Beginning doubtfully and far away
First lets his fingers wander as they list
Then builds a bridge from dreamland for his lay ...

And when Sir Launfal returns from his adventures and again meets the beggar at the gate, and then recognizes Him as the Christ –

255

> Who gives himself with his alms feeds three:
> Himself, his hungering neighbor, and Me ...
> And gives Him water –
> Only water from a wooden bowl
> But 'twas red wine he drank with his thirsty soul ...

How that stash of poetry enriches the soul. I often find myself recalling snatches of verse when faced with a picture or a situation – like the bluebird in the apple tree.

I always found – made – time to read bedtime stories to my children, and it was often poetry – from A Child's Garden of Verses or Silver Pennies. One of Chris and Mary's (my two youngest) favorites was Alfred Noyes' "The Highwayman." (Yes, the very same poem recited by the title character of Anne of Green Gables.) The poem is really filled with violence and bloodshed – and, of course, romance. It starts with the highwayman coming riding up to the old inn door, and Bess, the landlord's daughter was waiting for him, "plaiting a dark red love knot into her long black hair."

He asks for "one kiss, my bonny sweetheart. I'm after a prize tonight ..." and promises her, "I'll come to thee by moonlight ... though hell should bar the way."

The redcoats come and bind poor Bess, "with a musket beneath her breast." She struggles 'til "the tip of one finger touches" the trigger, then waits until she hears his horse – "tlot-tlot, tlot-tlot" – and "warns him with her death." What gore! Then, when the highwayman learns of her sacrifice, he turns and spurs his horse back to the inn and is shot down "like a dog on the highway" ... with the bunch of lace at his throat. The conclusion even contains haunting images of the lovers' ghosts.

But Mary and Chris loved the story, and the rollicking rhythm of it, as they did other pieces of verse such as John Masefield's "I must go down to the sea again ..." etc.

How dull would be a life without poetry. I still treasure my tattered copy of All the Silver Pennies, as well as various volumes of verse by Robert Frost, Sara Teasdale, Robert Service, Edna St. Vincent Millay, and others. They really worked at their craft, and produced and timeless and unforgettable images and ideas and stories – far superior to the weak blank verse today's so-called poets churn out.

* * *

Grandma Mickles always had two cats – Bridget and Buster. Always the same names, although I'm not sure anymore if they were always the same two cats. Bridget – from her little "nest" in the back room – regularly produced batches of kittens, which were eagerly visited by all the neighborhood children. After being weaned, the kittens were doled out for adoption, each to a child who promised to take the best care of it. One day where there was a new batch of kittens I was out on the little porch with Grandma when old Mrs. Miller stopped by, a neighbor from the next block. She let it be known that she'd be willing to take a kitten, but "it had to be a male."

Grandma didn't promise her anything, but after she'd left, Grandma got this very disgusted look on her face and said indignantly, "If she thinks I'm going to go around turning up kittens to see if they're male or female, she's got another think coming!"

Once I heard Grandma call my great-aunt Florry "an old chippie." No one explained to my satisfaction what a chippie was. Not until after Aunt Flora died, at age 93, did my mother tell me her story. Flora was the mistress of a well-to-do storekeeper in Owosso, where he "kept" her in an apartment. It seems she announced to her "Lothario" that she was pregnant. The story was that he paid Uncle Phil $600 to marry her, which Phil did. There was never a baby. Whether she lost it, or had lied about being pregnant, no one ever knew. But she lived a life of luxury by the standards of the times, waited on hand and foot by Uncle Phil, who adored her.

I remember her as always sitting in a rocker by the bay window of their big house by the Catholic Church, just a block down the street from us in Oakley. I was permitted to push my doll carriage with its "baby" over to their house to visit them. Aunt Florry would always be busy making something – what we now call arts-and-crafts. She made quilts; she made all kinds of dolls. She gave me a sock-doll with a dark green suit and a painted face that I named Jack – and eventually wore out. She made intricately woven necklaces and bracelets of tiny beads in all sorts of designs. I still have a quilt she made me with postage stamp-sized pieces called "A Trip Around the World," as well as the remains of a beaded necklace.

Uncle Phil did all the housework and cooking, and even carried the commode bucket she used to the outhouse every day, so she never needed to go outside to use the toilet. Uncle Phil died first, and we found out then that she could walk fine, and even wait on herself. She sold their big house to the church for a rectory, and bought a smaller house downtown. There she waited on herself, continued with her "crafts," did her own

257

cooking, and walked to the post office and the store every day. She even bought our player-piano, though she found out she couldn't reach the pedals to pump it, so she only heard it when a visitor played it for her.

Years later, when we visited my folks in Oakley, I took my four little boys – Rich, Bill, Bob and Tim – over to see Aunt Florry in her little cement-block house. She'd look the boys over and say, "No girls, Daisy? All boys?" Then she'd pat my hand and say, "That's all right, Daisy. When the boys grow up, they'll bring you the girls."

Which turned out to be true. Although we did eventually have a girl, Mary, as well as another boy, Chris.

Earlier in their marriage, Uncle Phil and Aunt Florry owned a hotel in Oakley. He "manned" the office, and she did the cooking, quite reluctantly, as my mother told it. Phil tried to keep her happy by complimenting her on her cooking.

He'd say, "That's a wonderful pie, Florry."

To which she'd snap back, "I know it. I made it!" – which became a byword in our family.

And, as another byword, or much-used phrase in our family – Not long After Ellis and I were married, we discovered that his dad, Juda Bazzett, knew my great-uncle Jim Whalen. Juda was policeman in Grand Rapids around 1915 or so. He and his family – "Mayme" and three little boys: Ellis, Don & Ken – lived in a little house with a big garden on Carrier Street. One hot summer day when Juda was walking his beat, he left the top button of the tunic of his wool uniform unbuttoned. And whom should he meet but city police Sergeant Jim Whalen, a large imposing man who stood nearly six and a half feet tall.

"Bazzett, button your coat!" Whalen roared.

"But Sergeant," Bazzett protested, "It's a hundred degrees in the shade today!"

Whereupon Sergeant Whalen thundered back, "You don't have to stand in the shade!"

Needless to say, Juda had no love at all for my great-uncle Jim (who, incidentally, actually spelled his name "Whelan"). In any case, another family phrase was born: "You don't have to stand in the shade!"

* * *

September 5, 2006 – *Starting over? ... I am finally getting back to this writing job I began so many months ago, so hopefully – then neglected shamefully later, when so many good books to read took so much of my time ... Now, back to "my life" ...*

An almost sad feeling comes over me as I begin again to think back on things – a feeling akin to Emily Dickinson's "That it will never come again/ Is what makes life so sweet ..." So I put on three CDs – Dottie West, Floyd Cramer and Johnny Mathis – to listen to while I knitted and reflected – interrupted only briefly by Terry Holmes stopping by to pick up a bag of jig-saw puzzles for his Delores to do while recovering from knee surgery.

The street is empty – except for the Bowmans, who walk by nearly every day; and later Harold Anderson and his lady-friend, probably twenty years younger. Harold appears to struggle valiantly to walk effortlessly and keep up with her, leaning slightly and almost limping with each painful-looking step. How much longer can he do that? And the Bowmans just had their golden wedding anniversary recently, shortly after burying a daughter, Sheila, who lived on in a coma for more that twenty years after an auto accident at age eighteen, when she was engaged to be married. They still have a son – who is spending life in prison – but also a happily married daughter and grandchildren in a neighboring state – Illinois or Indiana, I think.

And now, while leaning on my cane and looking out the front door (the mailman hasn't come yet), coming slowly down the hill I see a motor scooter(?) with a square bright-red canopy and two yellow plastic bags (from Vic's) hanging on the back. I don't know the slightly portly man driving it, but he waves to me and I wave back. I've never seen him or his strange vehicle before, so I suppose he's taking the "scenic route" home from the store.

How fragile all these people seem, and will they come again?

Why am I leaning on a cane? The calf of my left leg has been sore for a week – feels like it's beginning to cramp whenever my knee bends to take a step. I've been able to cover it up by walking slow. It happened when Chris parked his truck by the post office this morning. In walking fast to cross the street to go to the Nestle Inn, that muscle in my calf felt like it snapped and broke – hurt terribly. I grabbed Chris's arm and did get the rest of the way across – slowly. I think I convinced him it was like a charley-horse and would soon go away. But it hurts more now if I try to walk naturally, so I find if I take a long step ahead on my left foot with the knee stiff, I can "catch up" with the right. But I got out my mom's grandfather's (Philip Mickles) cane for extra support and safety.

September 6, 2006 – And used it all day. But found today I don't really need it. I'm not in danger of falling. I even got in and out of the tub for my shower okay, and down and back up the stairs.

My mother, Lettie Mickles Whalen – her grandfather, in his last years lived alone and had gone blind. He'd walk to town from his little house a quarter mile south of town. The house was built into a hillside above a spring, and on the bank of a creek. When he was ready to go home, he'd give some child a penny or two to "guide" him home – downhill along the gravel road, and across the creek and up the hill to his house, always using his cane to "feel" the way. He probably could have actually gotten home alone, but he enjoyed having the company of a child.

That all would have been well over a hundred years ago. And now that same cane Great-Grandfather Mickles used is my cane...

"Life is not forever."

My dad, Ellis Bazzett, died of cancer in 1989. Mom lived on for a long time. A few months before she died, I asked her if she was afraid of dying. She shrugged her shoulders, sighed, and said, "No. I just hope it doesn't hurt too much."

Daisy Cecelia Whalen-Bazzett died of natural causes April 8, 2013.

She was 96.

She was my mother.

Acknowledgements

On behalf of my mother, I would like to thank Frank Boles and Bryan Whitledge and their staff at CMU's Clarke Historical Library for their willing cooperation and help in "the Daisy project." And a very special thanks to my collaborator in this whole "books thing" for the last seventeen years – my son, Scott Bazzett, graphic artist extraordinaire. His grandmother would be so very grateful, pleased and proud.

About the Author

Daisy Cecelia Whalen Bazzett was born in Oakley, Michigan in 1916. She graduated from Chesaning High School in 1932. After earning her BA from Central State Teachers College (now CMU), she taught for a year at Remus High School. In 1937 she married Ellis Bazzett After living in Detroit, Chicago and Potterville, in 1945 the Bazzetts moved to Reed City where they settled and raised their six children. She died in 2013 at the age of 96.

About the Editor

Born in 1944, Timothy James Bazzett earned a BA and MA at CMU and taught English at Monroe County Community College for five years. He later enjoyed a thirty year career with the Department of Defense, including eight years with the US Army. Since his retirement he has written five books. He lives in Reed City with his wife and two dogs.

Made in the USA
Monee, IL
09 October 2021

79687155R00163